the
everyday gourmet

cover design and illustrations by j. elizabeth parkinson

the junior league of northern westchester, inc.
bedford hills, new york
1980

The purpose of the Junior League is exclusively educational and charitable and is to promote voluntarism; to develop the potential of its members for voluntary participation in community affairs; and to demonstrate the effectiveness of trained volunteers.

The proceeds realized from the sale of THE EVERYDAY GOURMET will be returned to the community through projects of The Junior League of Northern Westchester, Inc.

First printing November 1980 7,500
Second printing June 1981 15,000

Additional copies may be obtained by addressing:

THE EVERYDAY GOURMET
P.O. Box 214
Chappaqua, NY 10514

For your convenience, order blanks are included in the back of the book.

ISBN 0-9604314-0-3

Printed in the United States of America

CONTENTS

The Original Cookbook Committee

Chairman: Nancy Hoggson
Cover and Illustrations: J. Elizabeth Parkinson
Copy Editor: Anne Seltzer
Copywriter: Ann Costello

Testing Chairmen:

Karin Carlson
Madeleine Egan
Susan Lubin
Leslie Marra

Peggy Smith
Barbara Suval
Mary Watson

Committee:

Frances Bartlett
Lucie Campbell
Judith Hubbard
Christie Jenkins
Kathryn Mack
Mary Markoff

Margo Muccia
Victoria Ohlandt
Keene Rees
Marcia Sandner
Alice Sessa

Typist: Carolyn Creavy

Introduction

Cooking is an art. It is exacting, yet open to inspiration. The more you cook and learn about cooking, the more adventurous and proficient you become. No matter how skillful you are, this book presents a wide selection of recipes to interest and excite you. If you sharpen your cooking skills while preparing them, so much the better.

Naturally some recipes are more complicated than others to prepare. This we have indicated by a rating of chef's hats.

Easy =

Average =

Complicated =

We have not estimated the time it takes to prepare each recipe, since some people take half an hour to slice a pound of mushrooms, while others take five or ten minutes.

In preparing these or any recipes, observe the following guidelines for best results:

- Buy and use only the best cooking equipment and the best and freshest ingredients.
- Read through a recipe before going to the market.
- Assemble all equipment and ingredients beforehand.
- Pay close attention to what you are doing while you work. Precision in small details can make the difference between passable cooking and great cooking.
- Allow yourself plenty of time. Many recipes can be assembled in advance, at least in part.
- To avoid confusion, clean up as you go.

Above all, have a good time with this book. We enjoyed putting it together. We hope the feeling is contagious.

The Cookbook Committee

appetizers

New Beginnings

Unwind and fluff an Armenian string cheese. Arrange on a platter surrounded by a variety of Greek olives.

Place camembert or brie on pumpernickel slices. Broil briefly, then top with a sliver of pear or apple.

Spread a little Jalapeño Jelly (see Index) and a little brie on crackers.

Use boiled ham as a wrap for quartered artichoke hearts. Secure with a toothpick, then broil.

Wrap thinly sliced smoked ham around celery stalks, raw green beans, asparagus, or fennel. Dip in mayonnaise mixed with curry powder and Dijon mustard.

Roll your own Carpaccio "cigarettes" and arrange them on a platter.

Place cherry tomatoes, vodka, and curry powder in three separate bowls. Dip tomatoes in vodka then in curry powder.

Chop feta cheese into small cubes. Offer with a variety of the best imported olives.

Serve prosciutto-wrapped slices of fresh pear or Kiwi fruit.

Top thin slices of Italian bread with mozzarella cheese and prosciutto. Broil until lightly browned.

Little Dippers

Your own melba toast: Preheat oven to 300°. Remove crusts from thinly sliced white or whole wheat bread. Cut into squares, triangles, rectangles, or circles. Put bread shapes on a cookie sheet. Toast in oven for about 20 minutes until lightly browned. Remove from oven. Cool and store in an air-tight container. These will keep for weeks and may be frozen.

Melba toast with a twist: Before baking, spread bread shapes with melted butter and a sprinkle of parmesan cheese. Or use a little olive oil topped with a dash of Pesto Sauce (see Index).

Sesame-pita dippers: Split pita rounds. Spread with melted butter. Sprinkle with sesame seeds and bake in a 300° oven for 20 minutes until lightly browned. Cool and break into various sizes.

Appetizers

Arugula-Watercress Canapés

2 dozen

Homemade melba toast
½ bunch fresh arugula (if
  unavailable, use all watercress)
½ bunch fresh watercress
½ small white onion, grated
Dash tabasco sauce
Salt to taste
1 tablespoon lemon juice, to taste
4 ounces cream cheese
1-2 tablespoons mayonnaise

• Cut bread in circles with a biscuit cutter or juice glass. Bake at 275° for 20 minutes to make melba toast.
• Remove stems from arugula and cress. Rinse in cold water and squeeze out all excess moisture. Chop finely. Add grated onion, tabasco, salt, lemon juice, cream cheese, and mayonnaise. Adjust seasoning to taste.
• Before serving, spread mixture on toast rounds or put mixture into serving dish. Garnish with sprigs of cress and arugula.

Mary Vance Watson

Baba Ghanoush

1½ cups

1 eggplant, about ¾ pound
3 tablespoons freshly squeezed
  lemon juice
3 tablespoons tahini (sesame seed
  paste—available in specialty food
  stores)
2 garlic cloves
½-1 teaspoon salt
Chopped parsley
Toasted pita bread

• Preheat oven to 400°. Wash and dry eggplant Slash lengthwise 3 or 4 times and place in lightly greased shallow baking dish. Bake 30-40 minutes. Remove from oven and cool.
• Peel eggplant and cut into chunks. Put in blender or food processor. Add lemon juice, tahini, garlic, and ½ teaspoon salt. Purée. Add more salt if desired. Spoon into a serving dish and sprinkle with parsley. Split pita bread and spread with melted butter and sesame seeds. Toast in a 300° oven for 20-25 minutes until crisp. Serve with Baba Ghanoush.

Walter Parkinson

3

Appetizers

Caviar-Stuffed Pumpernickel

Serves 6-8

1 round loaf unsliced pumpernickel
3 tablespoons chopped green onions
1 pint sour cream
1 jar (4 ounces) red or black caviar
1-2 drops tabasco sauce

• Cut a round hole in top of bread. Remove bread to make a well in loaf. Tear bread in large bite-sized pieces. Store with the scooped-out loaf in a plastic bag until serving time.
• Rinse caviar gently in a strainer and drain. Mix with remaining ingredients. Chill.
• To serve, spoon caviar and sour cream mixture into the bread. Place bite-sized pieces of pumpernickel around loaf on a tray.

Mary Vance Watson

Cheese-Stuffed Bread

Serves 20-30

1½ pounds sharp cheddar cheese, grated
¼ pound roquefort or blue cheese, crumbled
1 teaspoon dry mustard
2 tablespoons butter
1 teaspoon worcestershire sauce
2 teaspoons grated onions or chopped chives
1 can (12 ounces) beer
1 loaf (2-2½ pounds) unsliced rye bread, round or oval
1 loaf party rye
Paprika
Parsley

• Put all ingredients except beer, breads, paprika, and parsley in a bowl to soften for 30 minutes or longer.
• Hollow out the round or oval loaf of rye bread. Reserve as much as possible to slice for spreading.
• Cream cheeses and butter. Add beer slowly. Beat until smooth and fluffy. Fill the bread with this mixture. Garnish with paprika and parsley. Refrigerate until serving time. Serve with party rye.

Victoria Eastman Ohlandt

4

Appetizers

Broccoli Bunches

1 bunch fresh broccoli
⅓ cup cider vinegar
⅓ cup vegetable or corn oil
3 tablespoons olive oil
1 teaspoon dill weed or dill seed
1 teaspoon monosodium glutamate
½ teaspoon salt
¼ teaspoon freshly ground pepper

Serves 4-6
● Wash broccoli. Cut flowerets from stems. Drain and dry.
● Combine remaining ingredients. Marinate and refrigerate broccoli flowerets in this dressing for 24 hours. Drain to serve.

Alice VanNuys Sessa

Camembert Mousse

½ cup cold water
1 envelope unflavored gelatin
3 ounces camembert cheese
4-5 ounces roquefort or blue cheese, to taste
1 teaspoon worcestershire sauce
1 egg, separated
½ cup heavy cream, whipped

Serves 6-8
● A day ahead: Sprinkle gelatin over ½ cup cold water in a glass measuring cup. Set cup in a pan of hot water until gelatin dissolves.
● Blend cheeses together until smooth. Beat in worcestershire sauce and egg yolk, then gelatin.
● Beat egg white until stiff. Fold into cheese mixture with whipped cream. Pour into a lightly greased 3-cup mold and chill.
● To serve, unmold and garnish with parsley or watercress. May be served with fresh fruit as a dessert.

Georgia Moseley Adams

5

Appetizers

Caviar Mousse

5 hard-cooked eggs, finely chopped
2-3 tablespoons grated onion
1 cup mayonnaise
1½ teaspoons worcestershire sauce
2 tablespoons lemon juice
⅛-¼ teaspoon cayenne pepper, to
    taste
½ cup sour cream
1 jar (4 ounces) black lumpfish
    caviar
1 envelope unflavored gelatin

Serves 8

● Lightly oil a 4-cup mold.
● Mix *all but* 2 tablespoons chopped hard-cooked eggs with onion, mayonnaise, worcestershire, lemon juice, cayenne, and sour cream. Fold in all *but* 2 teaspoons caviar. Save extra chopped hard-cooked egg and caviar for garnish.
● Sprinkle gelatin over ¼ cup cold water in a glass measuring cup. Set cup in a pan of hot water until gelatin dissolves. Cool and fold into caviar mixture.
● Spoon mixture into lightly greased 4-cup mold. Cover with plastic wrap. Chill 3 hours or overnight.
● Unmold to serve. Decorate with reserved chopped egg and caviar. Serve with toast rounds.

Barbara Clucas Aulebach

Blue Cheese-Olive Spread

1 small garlic clove, minced
1½ tablespoons chopped chives
¾ cup chopped parsley
½ cup chopped stuffed green olives
4 ounces blue cheese, softened
½ cup butter, softened
8 ounces cream cheese, softened
1 tablespoon brandy

2 cups

● Combine all ingredients. Mix well. Chill several hours before serving on toast rounds.

Margaret Williams Young

Appetizers

Herbed Cream Cheese

8 ounces cream cheese, at
    room temperature
4 tablespoons butter, at room
    temperature
½ teaspoon minced garlic
¼ teaspoon salt
¼ teaspoon freshly ground pepper
1 teaspoon chopped fresh dill
1 teaspoon chopped fresh parsley

2 cups
• Blend cream cheese and butter until fluffy. Beat in remaining ingredients.
• Chill 2 hours in a small mold. Turn out to serve. Freezes well.

Stephanie Fay Arpajian

Chicken-Almond Drums

¼ pound cooked chicken
1 celery rib, minced
1 tablespoon minced green onions
¼ teaspoon curry powder
Salt and freshly ground pepper
2-4 tablespoons mayonnaise
12 very thin slices whole wheat
    bread
¾ cup sliced almonds, toasted and
    chopped
Additional mayonnaise

2 dozen
• Mince chicken. Combine in small bowl with celery, onion, curry powder, salt, pepper, and enough mayonnaise to bind. Correct all seasonings.
• With a biscuit cutter or a juice glass, cut bread in 48 rounds, each about 1½". Spread half the bread rounds with chicken filling. Top with remaining bread.
• Stack 4 to 5 sandwiches together. Spread sides evenly and lightly with mayonnaise. Roll sides of stack in chopped almonds. Separate into individual sandwiches and arrange on a platter. Serve chilled.

Nancy Beck Hoggson

Appetizers

Cold Crabmeat Dip

1 can (6½ ounces) king crabmeat
⅔ cup sour cream
2 teaspoons horseradish
½ teaspoon freshly ground pepper
2 tablespoons bottled Italian dressing
Party pumpernickel or sliced
    cucumber rounds

2 cups
● Drain crabmeat. Combine with sour cream, horseradish, pepper, and dressing.
● Refrigerate for several hours or overnight. Serve on cucumber slices.

Susan Don Lubin

Crabmeat Mold

1 envelope unflavored gelatin
1 can (10½ ounces) cream of
    chicken or cream of celery soup
8 ounces cream cheese
1 can (7½ ounces) crabmeat
1 cup chopped celery
2-3 small green onions, chopped
    with stems
1 tablespoon worcestershire sauce
1 cup mayonnaise

4 cups
● Sprinkle gelatin over 3 tablespoons cold water in a glass measuring cup. Set cup in a pan of hot water until gelatin dissolves.
● Heat soup. Add cream cheese and stir until smooth. Add remaining ingredients including dissolved gelatin. Mix well.
● Pour into lightly greased 4-5 cup fish mold. Chill until firm.

Barbara Smith Suval

Curry Dip

2 cups mayonnaise
3 tablespoons catsup
3 tablespoons honey
3 tablespoons chopped onion
1 tablespoon curry powder
1 tablespoon lemon juice
2-3 drops tabasco sauce
Salt

2 cups
● Mix all ingredients. Season to taste. Chill overnight.
● Serve with fresh raw vegetables.

Margo Dineen Muccia

Appetizers

Dill Dip

1 cup mayonnaise
¼ cup sour cream
2 tablespoons chopped fresh dill, or
    1 tablespoon dried
1 tablespoon chopped green onions
1 tablespoon chopped parsley
1 tablespoon Dijon mustard
1 teaspoon lemon juice
1 teaspoon seasoned salt

1 cup
● Combine all ingredients. Chill several hours. Serve with fresh vegetables.

Anne Ruthrauff Seltzer

Double Cheese Dip

⅓ cup crumbled roquefort or blue
    cheese
6 ounces cream cheese
1 tablespoon chopped fresh parsley
2 tablespoons chopped green onions
Dash cayenne pepper
Dash worcestershire sauce
2 heaping tablespoons mayonnaise
4 tablespoons sour cream
1 tablespoon vodka (optional)
¼ teaspoon horseradish
Salt to taste

2 cups
● Cream cheeses. Add remaining ingredients.
● Chill to set flavor. Serve with fresh raw vegetables.

Nancy Miller Wright

9

Appetizers

Guacamole

3 ripe medium-sized avocados
1 small onion, finely chopped
2-4 tablespoons diced green chile peppers
2-3 tablespoons hot jalapeño relish or tabasco
2 small tomatoes, finely chopped
2 tablespoons lemon juice
1 tablespoon salad oil
1 teaspoon garlic salt

3 cups

● 1-1½ hours before serving, peel and pit avocados. Save pits. Process 2½ avocados in food processor or blender. Mix with onions in a small bowl. Chop remaining avocado half coarsely and stir into mixture. Add remaining ingredients.
● Set pits in the guacamole to keep it green. Cover and refrigerate. At serving time, remove pits. Serve with tortilla chips as appetizer. Spoon into lettuce cup to serve as salad.

Victoria Eastman Ohlandt

Hummus

2 cups drained chick peas
¾ cup tahini (sesame seed paste—available in specialty food stores)
¾ cup freshly squeezed lemon juice
1 teaspoon chopped fresh garlic
1 teaspoon salt
Pinch sharp paprika
2 teaspoons water, optional
Chopped parsley
Pita bread

2 cups

● Rinse and drain chick peas.
● Stir tahini paste with its own oil until well blended. Blend lemon juice and chopped garlic. Add chick peas a little at a time. Gradually add tahini paste, salt, and paprika. Adjust seasonings with more salt, garlic, or lemon juice. Add water to thin. Garnish with parsley.
● Serve with pita bread which has been split crosswise. Spread with melted butter and sesame seeds. Toast in a 300° oven for 20-25 minutes until crisp. May also be served with raw vegetables.

Joan Cooley May

Appetizers

Green Mayonnaise Dip

2 tablespoons chopped Italian
   parsley
1 tablespoon chopped chives
1 tablespoon chopped tarragon
1 teaspoon chopped chervil
1 teaspoon chopped dill
2 cups mayonnaise, preferably
   homemade (see Index)

2 cups

• Mix all herbs with mayonnaise. Chill. Let stand at least 4 hours before serving, to set flavor. Good with raw vegetables or as a sauce for salmon.

   Note: When fresh herbs are not available, substitute chopped fresh watercress or spinach (about ¼-½ cup each), increase parsley, and use dried dill weed.

Betsy Gimpel Mena

California Spinach Dip

1 package (10 ounces) frozen
   chopped spinach, thawed
1 cup mayonnaise
1 teaspoon seasoned salt
½ cup chopped green onions
1 tablespoon snipped fresh dill weed,
   or 1-2 teaspoons dried
½ teaspoon dried Italian seasoning
½ lemon, squeezed for juice
1 cup sour cream

2 cups

• Drain thawed spinach well. Mix in blender or food processor until smooth. Add remaining ingredients and mix thoroughly. Refrigerate 24 hours to blend flavors.
• Serve with raw vegetables.

Susan Sample Marx

11

Appetizers

Carpaccio

Serves 8

1-1½ pounds filet or prime round of
  beef, sliced paper-thin in 3″ to 5″
  pieces
½ cup olive oil
¼ cup wine vinegar
¼ cup soy sauce
¼ cup cognac
1½ teaspoons salt
1 teaspoon freshly ground pepper
1 teaspoon thyme
1 large onion, finely chopped
2 garlic cloves, minced

● Pound beef slices until paper-thin. Combine remaining ingredients and pour marinade over beef slices. Let stand, turning beef several times, for 4-6 hours or overnight in refrigerator.
● To serve, garnish Carpaccio with thin lemon slices, chopped parsley, and cornichons or capers.

Note: Good with French bread and a sauce made by mixing Dijon mustard and mayonnaise.

Ann Evans Gum

Dolmadas

3 dozen

4 medium onions, finely chopped
1 teaspoon salt
⅔ cup uncooked rice
¾ cup olive oil
1 teaspoon chopped fresh mint
1 teaspoon chopped fresh dill
½ cup chopped parsley (save stalks)
3 large bunches green onions,
  chopped with stems
Salt and freshly ground pepper
Juice of 1 lemon
1 jar (12 ounces) grapevine leaves
1 cup boiling water
Additional lemon juice

● Steam onions 5-10 minutes over very low heat with 1 teaspoon salt, stirring occasionally. Remove from heat. Stir in rice and ½ cup olive oil. Add herbs and vegetables, salt, pepper, and juice of half the lemon. Stir well.
● Wash grapevine leaves thoroughly to remove all brine. Separate leaves carefully, removing thick stem portions. Cut large leaves in half. Place 1 tablespoon filling on underside of leaf. Starting at base, fold over. Fold in sides and roll tightly toward point.
● Interlace parsley stalks on bottom of saucepan. Arrange dolmadas in layers. Add remaining oil and lemon juice. Weight dolmadas with a heavy plate. Cover saucepan and simmer 20 minutes over low heat. Add boiling water and simmer 25 minutes longer.
● Cool or chill to serve. sprinkled with fresh lemon juice.

Susan Willett Castellano

Appetizers

Calvados Pâté

1 cup butter
½ cup finely chopped onion
2 tablespoons finely chopped
   shallots
¼ cup chopped, peeled tart apple
1 pound chicken livers
¼ cup Calvados, applejack, or
   cognac
2 tablespoons heavy cream
1 teaspoon lemon juice
1½ teaspoons salt
¼ teaspoon freshly ground black
   pepper

3 cups

● Set aside ½ cup butter to soften.
● In a heavy skillet, melt *4 tablespoons* of remaining butter. Add onions, shallots, and apples. Cook until lightly colored, about 5 minutes. Remove from pan.
● In the same skillet, melt the other 4 tablespoons butter over medium-high heat. Add chicken livers when butter is melted and bubbling. Cook 3-4 minutes, stirring, until they are brown on the outside and still light pink inside. Remove pan from heat. Flame livers with ¼ cup warmed Calvados.
● Place chicken livers and all their juices in blender or food processor with onion-apple mixture and heavy cream. Purée until quite smooth, and cool.
● Meanwhile, cream the softened ½ cup butter. As soon as the liver paste is cool, beat it into the butter 1 tablespoon at a time. Stir in lemon juice, salt, and pepper. Pack into pottery crocks or terrines. Smooth tops with a spatula. Seal tops well with plastic wrap or clarified butter.
● Refrigerate until chilled (3-4 hours). Serve with crackers or thin bread slices.

Betsy Gimpel Mena

13

Appetizers

Pâté Maison

1 medium onion
1 garlic clove
½ cup butter
½ pound chicken livers
½ bay leaf
2 sprigs parsley
Pinch thyme
Salt and freshly ground pepper
1 tablespoon brandy or Calvados

1½ cups
● Chop onion and garlic finely. Cook to soften in *2 tablespoons* butter, about 5 minutes. Add chicken livers, herbs, and seasonings. Sauté together 3-5 minutes. Cooked livers should be pink when cut. Cool.
● Place in blender or food processor with remaining butter and brandy. Purée mixture until smooth and taste for seasonings. Fill a terrine with paté. Smooth the top with a spatula. Cover and refrigerate until serving time.

Donna Chisholm Clark

Pickled Mushrooms

⅓ cup red wine vinegar
⅓ cup salad oil
1 small onion, thinly sliced
1 teaspoon salt
2 tablespoons chopped fresh parsley
1 teaspoon Dijon mustard
1 tablespoon brown sugar
1 pound mushrooms

2 cups
● Bring to a boil all ingredients except mushrooms. Add mushrooms and simmer 5 minutes.
● Chill overnight. Drain and serve.

Anne Ruthrauff Seltzer

Smoked Salmon Rolls

8 ounces cream cheese, at room temperature
1-2 tablespoons sour cream
½ pound sliced smoked salmon (not too thin)
1 jar (2 ounces) red caviar

Serves 6
● Blend cream cheese with sour cream and gently fold in caviar.
● Place salmon slices on wax paper. Spread with cream cheese mixture.
● Roll each slice and chill. Cut into 1½" lengths.

Leslie May Marra

Appetizers

Radish Sandwiches

20 canapés

8 large radishes, trimmed
6-8 ounces cream cheese
2 tablespoons butter
1 tablespoon chopped parsley
1 teaspoon snipped chives, fresh or
   freeze-dried
Fresh lemon juice
Salt and freshly ground pepper
10 thin slices firm pumpernickel, cut
   in 1½" rounds
4-6 thin-sliced radishes and coarse
   salt for garnish

• Grate radishes in food processor or by hand. Place in a colander and squeeze out all liquid.
• Cream the cheese and butter until light and fluffy. Add grated radishes, parsley, chives, lemon juice, salt, and pepper to taste.
• Just before serving, spread on pumpernickel rounds. Slice remaining radishes paper-thin and arrange on canapés, overlapping slightly. Sprinkle with coarse salt.

Nancy Beck Hoggson

Salmon and Shrimp Mousse

3½ cups

1 package (6 ounces) frozen tiny
   shrimp
½ cup boiling water
1 envelope unflavored gelatin
¼ cup chopped green onions and
   stems
2 tablespoons lemon juice
½ cup mayonnaise
1 can (15½ ounces) salmon,
   drained, with skin and large
   bones removed
1 cup sour cream or plain yogurt
¼ teaspoon salt
⅛ teaspoon cayenne pepper
¼ teaspoon paprika
¼ cup snipped fresh dill, tightly
   packed to measure

• Thaw, drain, and coarsely chop shrimp. Set aside.
• Pour boiling water into blender or food processor. Sprinkle with gelatin. Blend until gelatin is dissolved. Add chopped green onions, lemon juice, and mayonnaise. Blend until mixed. Add salmon, sour cream, salt, cayenne, and paprika. Purée mixture. Place in a large bowl and stir in dill weed.
• Cover and refrigerate about 1 hour. Mixture should thicken and mound on a spoon. Stir in coarsely chopped shrimp. Pour into lightly greased 4-cup mold. Refrigerate overnight.
• Before serving, turn mold out onto a plate and garnish with thin lemon slices and sprigs of fresh dill.

Virginia Lawrence Evans

15

Appetizers

Miniature Seafood Medallions

60 pieces

8 slices bread
12 ounces (1½ cups) fresh raw
  seafood (shrimp, scallops,
  flounder, sole, or halibut, in any
  combination)
2 teaspoons salt
¼ teaspoon cayenne pepper
¼ teaspoon nutmeg
1 cup heavy cream
1 tablespoon butter
1 lemon, cut in wedges

● Remove crusts from bread. Crumble to make 2 cups fine breadcrumbs.
● Mix seafood and seasonings in blender or food processor. Add cream and purée until smooth. Add *1½ cups* breadcrumbs. Process until smooth. Refrigerate 3 hours for ease in hanling.
● Form into balls the size of a teaspoon. Roll in ½ cup of the remaining breadcrumbs, to coat well. In a small skillet, melt butter until it sizzles. Add miniature medallions. Flatten to ¼". Sauté 2 minutes on each side until firm. Drain and serve with toothpicks. Garnish with lemon wedges.
    Variation: May be served in larger patties for a main course.

Georgia Jones Hennig

Seviche

Serves 4-6

1½ pounds sole or flounder fillets cut
  into ½" strips
1 cup freshly squeezed lime juice
½ cup olive oil
2 tablespoons finely chopped canned
  or bottled green peppers, with
  seeds and stems removed
¼ cup finely chopped green onion
¼ cup finely chopped parsley
1 garlic clove, finely minced
1 teaspoon salt
¾ teaspoon freshly ground black
  pepper
Dash tabasco sauce
1 tablespoon chopped fresh
  coriander leaves (oikantro or
  Chinese parsley)

● Arrange fish strips in a glass baking dish. Pour lime juice over them. Turn each piece to coat. Cover with plastic wrap and refrigerate 4 hours. The citric acid will "cook" the fish. Flesh will be opaque and firm to the touch.
● Drain lime juice. Combine remaining ingredients except fresh coriander. Cover fish with this mixture. Turn carefully. Cover and chill 45 minutes. To serve, sprinkle with chopped coriander.

Ann Dodds Costello

16

Appetizers

Shrimp-Artichoke Marinade

½ cup olive oil
¼ cup peanut oil
¼ cup wine vinegar
1 beaten egg yolk
2 tablespoons Dusseldorf mustard
2 tablespoons chopped chives
2 tablespoons chopped parsley
2 tablespoons chopped shallots
    (optional)
24 large cooked shrimp (about ¾
    pound fresh)
1 can (14 ounces) artichoke hearts,
    halved if large

2 dozen
● A day before serving, combine olive oil, peanut oil, and vinegar. Add beaten egg yolk and mustard. Mix well. Add remaining ingredients. Chill 8 hours, stirring occasionally.
● Serve with toothpicks as an appetizer or on lettuce as a first course.

Susan Don Lubin

Shrimp Butter

8 ounces cream cheese, at room
    temperature
12 tablespoons butter
Juice of 1 lemon
2 tablespoons minced onion
4 tablespoons mayonnaise
3 cans (4½ ounces each) shrimp,
    drained
Salt to taste

2 cups
● Combine first five ingredients. Add shrimp and mix well. Salt to taste.
● Serve on thinly sliced French bread. Garnish with watercress.

Dorothy Mead Fossel

Appetizers

Sole en Escabeche

3 tablespoons butter
¾ cup olive oil
Flour
6 small sole fillets
Salt and freshly ground pepper
1 onion, sliced thinly and separated
  into rings
1 green pepper, cut in thin rings
1 garlic clove, minced
½ cup orange juice
Juice of 2 limes
¼-½ teaspoon tabasco sauce
Orange slices
Lime slices
1 tablespoon grated orange rind
Watercress or lettuce (optional)

Serves 6

● Heat butter and ¼ cup oil in a skillet. Flour fish fillets lightly. Sauté until delicately browned on both sides. Season to taste with salt and pepper.

● Arrange fillets in a flat serving dish and top with onion rings, pepper rings, and garlic. Combine remaining ½ cup oil, orange juice, lime juice, tabasco, salt, and pepper to taste. Blend well and pour over fish while it is still warm. Refrigerate 12 to 24 hours.

● Garnish with orange slices, lime slices, and grated orange rind. Nice with a sprig of watercress or on lettuce.

Adrienne Wheeler Rudge

Steak Tartare Balls

½ pound very fresh sirloin steak,
  trimmed of all fat
Freshly ground pepper to taste
2 teaspoons cognac or brandy
2 teaspoons worcestershire sauce
2 teaspoons Dijon mustard
¼ cup capers, drained and chopped
1 egg yolk
1 green onion, chopped, top included
¼ cup finely chopped parsley
2 tablespoons snipped chives
24 thin pretzel sticks

24 balls

● The day of serving: Grind trimmed meat in food processor or meat grinder or have the butcher do it. Mix meat lightly with pepper, cognac, worcestershire, mustard, capers, egg yolk, and green onions. Taste and correct seasoning. Roll into 1" balls.

● Combine parsley and chives. Roll meat in chopped herbs, shaking off excess. Arrange on a chilled platter. Refrigerate until serving time.

● Before serving, insert a pretzel stick into each ball.

Nancy Beck Hoggson

18

Appetizers

Tapenade

1 can (6½ ounces) tuna in olive oil
8 ounces pitted oil or salt-packed
    Italian black olives (a must for
    this dip—don't use ordinary black
    olives)
1 can (2 ounces) anchovies in olive
    oil
½ cup capers, washed and drained
2 garlic cloves, chopped
6 hard-cooked eggs, peeled
2 tablespoons olive oil
1 tablespoon fresh lemon juice
Freshly ground pepper

3-4 cups

- In a blender or food processor, mix tuna, olives, anchovies, capers, and garlic to make a coarse purée. Empty into mixing bowl.
- Chop eggs. Combine with purée. Add olive oil, lemon juice, and pepper. Adjust seasonings and chill.
- Fill fresh mushroom caps or cherry tomatoes. This also makes a nice spread.

Nancy Beck Hoggson

Crab-Stuffed Cherry Tomatoes

30 cherry tomatoes
Salt to taste
½ cup mayonnaise
2 tablespoons finely chopped
    shallots or green onions
1 tablespoon chopped fresh chives
1 teaspoon tarragon
½ tablespoon basil
½ tablespoon finely minced garlic
1 hard-cooked egg, finely sieved
½ pound lump crabmeat or 1 can (6
    ounces) crabmeat
Freshly ground pepper to taste
Fresh chopped parsley

30 tomatoes

- Core cherry tomatoes and salt the insides. Place cut-side-down to drain on paper towels.
- Combine remaining ingredients except parsley. Fill tomatoes and refrigerate until serving time. Garnish with chopped parsley.

Susan Sample Marx

19

Appetizers

Artichoke Squares

Serves 8-10

2 jars (6 ounces each) marinated
  artichokes, finely chopped
1 small onion, finely chopped
1 garlic clove, minced
4 eggs
¼ cup dry breadcrumbs or cracker
  crumbs
2 tablespoons chopped parsley
¼ teaspoon salt
¼ teaspoon freshly ground pepper
¼ teaspoon oregano
¼ teaspoon tabasco sauce
½ pound sharp cheddar cheese,
  grated

● Drain artichokes, reserving marinade. Sauté onion and garlic in marinade until transparent. Place a double thickness of paper towels on skillet to soak up excess oil, leaving onions in place.
● Preheat oven to 350°.
● Beat eggs. Add crumbs and seasonings. Stir cheese and artichokes into mixture in pan. Pour into a buttered 7" x 11" pan.
● Bake 30 minutes. Cool in pan. Cut into squares. Serve warm or cold.

Karen Rudge Richards

Angels on Horseback

Serves 6-8

12-18 slices bacon
12-18 fresh oysters
Freshly ground pepper
1 lemon, thinly sliced
Garnish: parsley

● Cook bacon slices about 5 minutes in a skillet, then drain. Don't let them become crisp. They must be limp to wrap around the oysters.
● If you are shucking your own oysters, use only those with tightly closed shells; discard the others. Season each oyster with pepper and wrap with a slice of bacon. Secure with a wooden toothpick or skewer. Arrange in a shallow baking pan.
● Bake at 425° until bacon is crisp.

Madeleine Galanek Egan

Appetizers

Hot Artichoke or Crabmeat Dip

1 can (14 ounces) water-pack
   artichoke hearts, or 1 can (6
   ounces) crabmeat, drained
1 cup grated parmesan cheese
1 cup mayonnaise
1 garlic clove, minced

1½ cups
● Chop artichokes or flake crabmeat to remove any shells. Mix cheese and mayonnaise. Add to artichokes or crabmeat. Mix well.
● Bake at 350° for 30 minutes. Serve on pumpernickel rounds or with taco chips.

Nancy Miller Wright

Hot Cheese-on-Rye Canapés

½ cup grated parmesan cheese
½ cup mayonnaise
1-2 dashes worcestershire sauce
1 onion, finely chopped
Oregano to taste
Party rye bread slices

32 canapés
● Combine cheese with mayonnaise, worcestershire, chopped onion, and oregano.
● Spread on bread slices and bake at 350° for 10 minutes. Broil 1-2 minutes to brown.

Barbara Jordan Holmén

Ricotta Cheese Rounds

½ cup soft butter
6 ounces cheddar cheese, at room
   temperature
1 pound ricotta cheese, drained
⅔ cup flour
1 teaspoon salt
2 tablespoons chopped parsley
1 egg
¼ teaspoon freshly ground pepper
Pinch cayenne

50 puffs
● Blend butter and cheddar cheese. Add remaining ingredients and combine thoroughly. Place by teaspoonfuls on a baking sheet and freeze. When frozen, remove from baking sheet and place in a plastic bag to store.
● To serve, preheat oven to 450°. Arrange frozen puffs on baking sheet and bake 10 minutes until brown.

Ann Keyser Griffin

Appetizers

Cheese Straws

2 cups flour
2 teaspoons salt
Freshly ground pepper
Dash cayenne pepper
½-1 teaspoon dry mustard
1 cup butter, softened
2 firmly packed cups very sharp
    cheddar cheese, grated

80-100 straws

● Mix flour, salt, pepper, a good pinch of cayenne, and mustard. Add butter and cheese. Blend until dough is smooth. Taste for seasonings.

● Form dough into rolls about 1 inch in diameter. Refrigerate or freeze until ready to use.

● When ready to bake, preheat oven to 375°.
Cut dough rolls into thin slices; *or*
Roll dough, cut it into "straws" and twist gently several times; *or*
Put dough in a pastry bag and pipe onto baking sheets.

● Bake 12-15 minutes on ungreased baking sheets, until lightly browned. Cool before removing from baking sheets.

Nancy Beck Hoggson

Sesame Chicken Wings

12 large chicken wings (about 2½
    pounds)
1 egg, beaten
2 tablespoons milk
1 cup flour
½ cup toasted sesame seeds
¼ cup finely chopped nuts (optional)
2 teaspoons salt
2 teaspoons paprika
1 teaspoon baking powder
½ teaspoon ground ginger
¼ teaspoon freshly ground pepper
½ cup butter

Serves 8

● Remove wing tips. Halve wings at the joints. Mix beaten egg and milk. Pat chicken dry and dip in egg mixture.

● Combine all dry ingredients in a paper bag. Shake chicken pieces to coat thoroughly.

● Melt butter in a 400° oven in a shallow baking pan. Roll coated chicken in melted butter. Bake in a single layer for 20 minutes. Turn and bake until tender, 20 minutes more.

Margaret Velde Uyeki

22

Appetizers

Chiles Rellenos Squares

2 cans (4 ounces each) chopped
   green chiles, drained
3 cups grated monterey jack cheese
   (about 12 ounces)
4 eggs, beaten

15 squares

● Preheat oven to 300°. Sprinkle green chiles and cheese evenly in bottom of a greased 8" square baking pan. Pour eggs over cheese mixture and bake 1 hour, until firm in center.

● Remove from oven. Place pan on a wire rack to cool for 5 minutes. Cut in 2" squares. Serve or cover and refrigerate up to 3 days. Reheat by baking 15 minutes at 300°. Makes 15 hors d'oeuvres.

   Variation: Bake in a 9" pie plate for a brunch or luncheon entrée to serve 6.

Nancy Beck Hoggson

Savory Clams

48 fresh cherrystone or littleneck
   clams
Water
6 slices bacon, diced
1 pound mushrooms, finely minced
3 tablespoons finely chopped shallots
¼ pound gruyère or swiss cheese
4 tablespoons finely chopped parsley
2 garlic cloves, minced
1½ cups fine fresh breadcrumbs
1 cup finely minced celery
6 tablespoons dry white wine
2 egg yolks
Salt
Freshly ground pepper
1 cup grated parmesan cheese
Lemon wedges

4 dozen clams

● Wash clams well and place in a kettle. Add 3" water, cover, and steam until clams open. Remove clams from shells, keeping shells. Chop clams.

● Cook bacon until crisp. Remove and set aside. Drain off all but 4 tablespoons bacon fat. Add mushrooms and shallots. Cook, stirring, until mushrooms are soft. Cool.

● Dice cheese. Add to mushroom mixture with parsley, garlic, breadcrumbs, celery, wine, egg yolks, and chopped clams. Season with salt and pepper.

● Fill clam shells with this mixture. Sprinkle with grated parmesan. Bake 10 minutes at 400° until bubbly and brown. Serve with hot lemon wedges.

Sonia Collum Oram

23

Appetizers

Clam and Beer Canapés

½ cup butter, melted
½ cup breadcrumbs
¼ cup beer
1 small onion, minced
4 garlic cloves, minced
2 tablespoons minced fresh parsley
1½ teaspoons Italian seasoning
½ teaspoon oregano
Salt and freshly ground pepper
4 cans (6½ ounces each) minced
    clams
36 toast rounds or clam shells

3 dozen

● Combine first 9 ingredients. Blend well. Drain clams, reserving juice. Stir clams into breadcrumb-herb mixture. Moisten with reserved clam juice if needed. Refrigerate.

● Preheat oven to 375°. Spread clam mixture on toast rounds or spoon into clam shells. Bake for 10 minutes. Broil until brown. Serve immediately.

Nancy Reese Corbett

Hot Crabmeat Spread

8 ounces cream cheese
1 tablespoon milk
1 can (6½ ounces) flaked crabmeat
2 tablespoons finely chopped onion
½ teaspoon cream-style horseradish
¼ teaspoon salt
Dash freshly ground pepper
⅓ cup toasted sliced almonds

Serves 6-8

● Soften cream cheese with milk. Blend with next 5 ingredients.

● Spoon into greased oven-proof dish. Sprinkle with almonds. Bake at 375° for 15 minutes.

JoAnn Hixon Mills

Appetizers

Duxelles Strudels

2 cups well seasoned Duxelles (see Index)
6 sheets phyllo pastry
½ cup butter, melted (more, if necessary)

75 pieces

● Dampen a tea towel slightly. Wring it out well and spread it on work surface. See Index for tips on working with phyllo dough. Place 1 sheet of pastry on dampened towel. Set aside the other sheets, as directed (page 311).

● Brush pastry lightly with melted butter. Spread 4-6 tablespoons duxelles along the long edge of the pastry. Roll up carefully using the towel to guide the roll. Put roll on a baking sheet. Brush with melted butter.

● Repeat with remaining sheets of pastry and duxelles. Refrigerate all the rolls on the baking sheet.

● When rolls are well chilled, trim ends. Cut on the diagonal in 1¼" pieces. Freeze, if desired, until ready to serve.

● Bake at 375° for 10-12 minutes until well browned.

Penelope Johnson Wartels

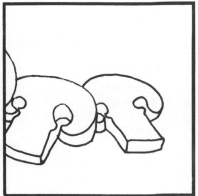

Appetizers

Empanaditas

1 recipe Cream Cheese Pastry (see Index)
3 tablespoons olive oil
¾ cup chopped onions
½ cup chopped green pepper
½ cup chopped tomato
½ pound ground beef
2 teaspoons A-1 Sauce
1 teaspoon salt
⅛ teaspoon cayenne pepper
½ cup chopped stuffed green olives
2 hard-cooked eggs, chopped
1 egg yolk
1-2 teaspoons water

2 dozen
● Prepare cream cheese pastry. Chill several hours or overnight.
● Heat oil in skillet. Add onions and sauté 5 minutes. Add green pepper and tomatoes. Cook 5 minutes more. Add meat, A-1 Sauce, salt, and cayenne. Cook over low heat 10 minutes, stirring frequently. Mix in olives and eggs. Taste for seasoning. Cool.
● Roll chilled dough thinly. Cut in 3"-4" circles. Place a generous spoonful of filling on pastry. Fold into a half-moon. Press edges together. Seal with cold water and crimp with a fork. Repeat until pastry and filling are used up. Freeze, or bake now.
● Preheat oven to 400°. Mix egg yolk and water. Brush glaze on top of each empanadita, pricking each one with a fork. Bake 15 minutes until pastry browns.

Betsy Gimpel Mena

Norwegian Flatbread

Norwegian flatbread
Whipped butter, at room temperature
Freshly grated parmesan cheese
Beau Monde Seasoning

30 pieces
● Break flatbread in half and spread each piece with butter.
● Sprinkle with grated parmesan. Shake Beau Monde Seasoning over top. Bake at 250° about 7 minutes. Serve warm or at room temperature.

Suzanne Rich Beatty

Appetizers

Jalapeño Bean Dip

1 can (7½ ounces) mild Jalapeño
    relish
2 tablespoons chili powder
1 garlic clove, minced
¼ cup minced onion
1 can (15 ounces) refried beans
⅔ cup beer
4 ounces cubed provolone cheese

2 cups
● Combine all ingredients. Heat in a chafing dish until cheese has melted. Serve with tortilla chips.

Susan Don Lubin

Cocktail Meatballs

1½ pounds ground meat
1 cup breadcrumbs
¼ cup milk
1 egg
½ cup finely chopped onion
1 teaspoon salt
¼ teaspoon nutmeg
¼ teaspoon thyme

Sauce
1 cup brown sugar
1 cup vinegar
½ cup water
2 teaspoons dry mustard
1 tablespoon cornstarch
Generous dash nutmeg

4 dozen
● Combine ingredients for meatballs. Form into balls and bake 20-30 minutes at 350°.
● Combine ingredients for sauce. Simmer several minutes. Mix cornstarch with a little cold water and stir into sauce to thicken.
● Pour sauce over meatballs and serve.

Katharine Knapp Sherwood

Appetizers

Mushroom Toasts

½ pound mushrooms
3 tablespoons chopped green onions
4 tablespoons butter
2 tablespoons flour
¾ cup heavy cream
1 teaspoon salt
Dash cayenne pepper
1 tablespoon chopped parsley
½ teaspoon lemon juice
¼ teaspoon oregano
Thinly sliced bread
Melted butter

3 dozen

● Chop mushrooms and green onions separately in blender or food processor.
● Melt butter in a skillet and add onions. Cook until soft. Add mushrooms. Stir over high heat until moisture has evaporated. Lower heat. Add flour and stir well. Add cream. Bring to a boil, stirring constantly. Simmer for 5 minutes. Add remaining ingredients, except bread and melted butter. Refrigerate or freeze.
● To make canapés, cut crusts from bread. Halve each slice, and flatten with a rolling pin.
● Spread cooled mushroom mixture on bread. Roll like a miniature jelly roll. Place on a baking sheet. Freeze now, if desired.
● Preheat oven to 350°. Brush rolls with melted butter. Bake 15 minutes, until brown.

> Variation: Cut bread in circles to fit tartlet tins. Brush pan with melted butter and press bread circles into pan. Add mushroom mixture and bake as above.

Pamela Sullivan Livingston

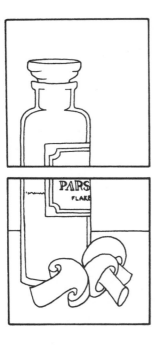

28

Appetizers

Hot Olive Cheese Puffs

1 cup grated sharp cheddar cheese
3 tablespoons butter, at room
   temperature
½ cup sifted flour
½ teaspoon paprika
¼ teaspoon salt
30 stuffed green olives

30 puffs

● Blend grated cheese and butter. Stir in flour, paprika, and salt and mix well. Wrap 1 teaspoon dough around each olive, completely covering olive. Wrap and freeze before baking if desired.
● Preheat oven to 400°. Arrange puffs on ungreased baking sheet and bake 10-15 minutes.

JoAnn Hixon Mills

Gala Pecan Spread

8 ounces cream cheese, at room
   temperature
1 tablespoon milk
1 jar (2½ ounces) dried beef
¼ cup finely chopped green pepper
2 tablespoons minced onion
½ teaspoon garlic salt
¼ teaspoon freshly ground pepper
½ cup sour cream
½ cup chopped pecans
2 tablespoons butter
½ teaspoon salt

Serves 6-8

● Combine cream cheese and milk. Mix to blend well. Stir in beef, green pepper, onion, garlic salt, and pepper. Mix well. Fold in sour cream. Spoon into greased 8″ pie plate.
● Preheat oven to 350°. Toast pecans in butter and salt. Sprinkle over mixture in baking dish. Bake 20 minutes. Serve warm with crackers.

Lucie Ling Campbell

Pizza Hors D'oeuvres

1 medium onion, finely chopped
1 jar (4 ounces) roasted red peppers,
   minced
½ pound grated cheese (sharp
   cheddar or mozzarella)
Tabasco sauce
1 tablespoon dried basil or oregano
1 loaf party rye bread

40 pieces

● Thoroughly mix onion, peppers, cheese, seasonings. Spread on bread. Bake at 325° for 10 minutes, then broil until cheese bubbles. Serve hot.

Judith Huggard Hubbard

29

Appetizers

Sausage-Spinach Tarts

Pastry for 2-crust pie (see Index)
1 pound sweet Italian sausage
¼ pound mushrooms, finely chopped
1 small onion, finely chopped
1 garlic clove, minced
1 package (10 ounces) frozen
    chopped spinach, thawed
¼ teaspoon oregano
⅛ teaspoon freshly ground pepper
2 eggs
½ cup milk
1½ cups grated swiss cheese (about
    ¼ pound)
1 tablespoon grated parmesan
    cheese

18 tarts

● Preheat oven to 400°. Prepare pastry. Roll and cut to fit 18 tartlet tins. Prick and bake shells 3-5 minutes. Do not brown.
● Remove casing from sausages. Sauté 5 minutes. Drain fat. Add chopped mushrooms, onion, and garlic. Cook, stirring for 3 minutes. Drain thawed spinach. Add to skillet with oregano and pepper. Reduce excess liquid and cool.
● Preheat oven to 350°. Beat eggs and milk together. Stir in sausage mixture and grated swiss cheese. Put in the tartlet shells. Sprinkle with grated parmesan. Bake 30 minutes until set.
● Serve hot or cold. Freezes well.

Barbara Isaac O'Donnell

Nantucket Seafood Turnovers

Dough
8 ounces cream cheese, at room
    temperature
½ cup butter, at room temperature
1½ cups flour

Filling
3 tablespoons butter
1 large onion, finely chopped
½ pound mushrooms, finely chopped
¼ teaspoon thyme
1 teaspoon salt
Freshly ground pepper
2 tablespoons flour
¼ cup sour cream
6 ounces shrimp, cooked and
    chopped
1 can (6½ ounces) minced clams,
    drained

5 dozen

● To make dough: Mix cream cheese and butter thoroughly. Add flour. Work until smooth. Chill well for 30 minutes. Roll dough and cut into 3" rounds. Preheat oven to 450°
● Heat butter in a skillet. Add onions and brown lightly. Add mushrooms. Cook 3 minutes. Add seasonings. Sprinkle with flour. Stir in sour cream and cook until thick. Add shrimp and clams.
● Place 1 teaspoon filling on each round. Fold in half and press edges with a fork to seal. Brush with egg to glaze. Bake 10-15 minutes.

Pamela Schott Turner

Appetizers

Chinese Fried Shrimp Balls

2 dozen

1 pound fresh shrimp, shelled, washed, and minced
½ cup chopped water chestnuts or bamboo shoots
1 egg white
1 teaspoon salt
1 teaspoon cornstarch
1 teaspoon sherry
½ teaspoon minced fresh ginger root
¼ teaspoon sugar
Dash freshly ground pepper
Oil for deep frying

• Combine all ingredients except oil. Shape mixture into balls with a teaspoon.
• Heat oil and deep-fry shrimp balls until golden. Drain and serve immediately or keep warm in oven. Good with hot mustard or plum sauce.

Lucie Ling Campbell

Shrimp Taiwan

2 dozen

24 raw shrimp, cleaned and deveined
12 water chestnuts
12 slices bacon
½ cup soy sauce
½ cup honey
2 tablespoons sherry
2 garlic cloves, minced

• Two days before serving: Halve water chestnuts and bacon slices. Place water chestnut inside curve of each shrimp. Wrap with bacon. Secure with toothpick.
• Combine soy sauce, honey, sherry, and garlic. Pour over shrimp. Refrigerate 2 days.
• Preheat oven to 400°. Bake shrimp on a baking sheet with sides for 20 minutes until crisp and brown.

Barbara Smith Suval

31

Appetizers

Spinach Balls

2 packages (10 ounces) frozen
    chopped spinach
2 cups herb-seasoned stuffing mix
2 cups chopped onion
6 eggs, beaten
¾ cup melted butter
½ cup grated parmesan cheese
1 garlic clove, minced
½ teaspoon thyme
½ teaspoon freshly ground pepper

60-70 balls
- Cook spinach and drain well. Mix with other ingredients. Refrigerate at least an hour.
- Form into 1" balls. May be frozen.
- Bake at 350° for 15-20 minutes, or 25 minutes if frozen.

Gail Murray Arkin

Spinach Quiche

1-2 cups chopped fresh spinach, or
    1 package (10 ounces) frozen
    chopped spinach, thawed and
    drained
2 eggs, well beaten
1 cup flour
1 cup milk
½ cup butter, melted
1 pound mild or sharp cheddar
    cheese, grated

30 squares
- Preheat oven to 375°.
- Combine all ingredients in a large bowl. Mix. Place in buttered pan (9" x 9" or 7" x 11"). Bake 35 minutes until set.
- Cool and cut into squares. May be refrigerated or frozen.

Ann Keyser Griffin

Appetizers

Tiropitakia-Spanakopita

8-9 dozen

½-¾ pound phyllo pastry sheets, defrosted (see Index)
3 tablespoons butter
4 tablespoons flour
1 cup milk
½ pound crumbled feta cheese
3 ounces grated gruyère cheese
2 eggs, beaten
1 tablespoon finely chopped parsley
¼ teaspoon nutmeg
⅛ teaspoon freshly ground pepper
1 package (10 ounces) frozen chopped spinach, thawed
¾ cup melted butter

● Melt butter. Add flour to form a paste. Add milk. Cook over medium heat, stirring until sauce thickens. Stir in cheeses, eggs, and seasonings. Spoon half of sauce into a small mixing bowl. Reserve other half for basic cheese filling for tiropitakia.

● Drain defrosted spinach, squeezing out excess moisture. Stir into cheese sauce in small bowl to make spinach filling for spanakopita.

● Dampen a tea towel and keep phyllo wrapped in it when not handling. Peel off a sheet of phyllo and cut in 2" strips. Brush each strip with melted butter. Put ½ teaspoon of the cheese or spinach mixture on the end of a strip and fold the entire strip into a triangle. Repeat until all fillings are used. Arrange tiropitakia on baking sheets. Brush with additional melted butter. Freeze until ready to serve, or bake as follows.

● Preheat oven to 425°. Bake 15-20 minutes until brown.

Anne Ruthrauff Seltzer

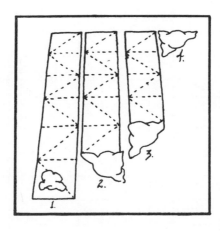

33

soups
and breads

Seven Easy Steps To Yeast Bread

1. Dissolve yeast in lukewarm water (110°-115°). "Proof" for 5-10 minutes until it bubbles or foams. If it does not foam, begin again.

2. Combine liquids and half the flour. Stir 200-300 strokes. Stir in rest of flour.

3. Knead dough until it is smooth and satiny, about 10-15 minutes, adding more flour to eliminate stickiness. It is impossible to over knead.

4. Put dough in a greased bowl. Rotate in bowl so greased side of dough faces up. Cover with a damp cloth. Set in a warm spot until doubled in bulk, about 1-2 hours. No warm spots in your house? Set a heating pad on low and put the bowl on top of it. Pilot lights on gas ovens assure good rising spots too.

5. Punch down dough with fist. Knead briefly. Return to bowl. Cover and let rise again until doubled.

6. Punch down dough. Knead briefly and shape in greased baking pan. Cover and let rise until double. Bake in preheated oven.

7. Do not cut hot, fresh bread right after baking. Wait at least an hour. If you must slice it sooner, heat knife under hot water and dry before using. This will keep bread from crumbling or tearing.

Soups and Breads

Cream of Artichoke Soup

2 cups chicken broth
1 can (15 ounces) artichoke hearts
2 teaspoons salt
Freshly ground white pepper to taste
1 teaspoon fresh lemon juice
½ cup heavy cream
Finely snipped chives or thinly sliced
    scallion greens for garnish

Serves 4

● Bring chicken broth to a boil. Drain artichoke hearts. Rinse well and drain again. Add artichoke hearts to boiling broth. Simmer, partly covered, until tender, 10-15 minutes.
● Drain artichokes, saving broth. Purée in blender or food processor with a little broth. Return purée and all the broth to cooking pan. Season with salt and white pepper to taste. Add lemon juice. Stir in cream.
● Reheat gently to boiling point. Serve hot, or chill and serve cold. Garnish with chives or scallions.

Nancy Beck Hoggson

Soupa Avgolemono

4 cups chicken stock
¼ cup uncooked rice
2 eggs
¼ cup fresh lemon juice
Salt and freshly ground white pepper

Serves 6

● Bring chicken stock to boil. Add rice. Partially cover pan. Simmer 15 minutes. Rice should not be cooked through.
● Beat eggs well until thickened. Beat in lemon juice. Gradually add 1 cup hot chicken broth to egg mixture. Beat well after each addition. Slowly stir mixture into remaining soup. Cook below simmering point. Beat constantly until thick and smooth. Do not let soup boil. Add salt and white pepper to taste.
● Serve hot or chill several hours. Add a tablespoon of sour cream and fresh mint to each bowl of chilled soup.

Susan Don Lubin

Soups and Breads

Swiss Beer Soup

1 cup French bread cubes (no crust)
3 tablespoons olive oil
1 large onion, chopped
1 garlic clove, minced
12 ounces beer
3 cups chicken broth
Freshly ground pepper
2 tablespoons minced parsley
1½ cups grated gruyère cheese
1 teaspoon paprika

Serves 4-6

• Arrange bread cubes on a baking sheet. Toast in 400° oven until golden brown. Turn occasionally.
• Sauté onion and garlic in oil until golden. Stir in toasted bread cubes. Add beer and broth. Bring to boil. Add pepper and parsley. Blend well.
• Ladle soup into individual ovenproof bowls. Sprinkle cheese over tops. Dust with paprika. Broil until golden brown.

Nancy Reese Corbett

Black Bean Soup

1 pound black beans
½ cup olive oil
½ pound bacon, diced
3 carrots, diced
6 onions, chopped
1 green pepper, chopped
3 celery ribs with stalks, chopped
2-4 garlic cloves, minced
2 quarts beef stock
2 cups water
Smoked ham bone, if available
Freshly ground pepper
1-2 teaspoons thyme
2 bay leaves
¼ cup flour
½ cup dry sherry
1 tablespoon red wine vinegar
Salt
Cayenne pepper

Serves 10

• Soak beans overnight unless they are labelled "pre-soaked." Drain.
• Soak pre-soaked beans 30 minutes in 2 cups water.
• Heat olive oil. Cook bacon, carrots, onions, green pepper, celery, and garlic over low heat 15 minutes.
• Add beans with water, beef stock, 2 cups water, ham bone, pepper to taste, thyme, and bay leaves. Simmer until tender over low heat, about 2½ hours.
• Remove ham bone and bay leaves. Purée ¼ to ½ of the beans with flour and a little liquid. Whisk puréed beans back into soup. Simmer a few minutes to cook flour. Season to taste with sherry, vinegar, salt, and cayenne.

Penelope Johnson Wartels

Soups and Breads

Bourride

¾ cup finely chopped onions
2 tablespoons oil
1 cup finely chopped celery
1 cup finely chopped leeks
2 garlic cloves, finely minced
1 teaspoon saffron
1 bay leaf
1 cup dry white wine
2 cups peeled, cubed potatoes
    (¾ pound)
4 cups Fish Stock (see Index)
⅛ teaspoon cayenne pepper
Salt and freshly ground pepper
4 pounds whiteflesh fish fillets (tile,
    haddock, cod)
Garlic Mayonnaise (recipe follows)

Serves 8

- Sauté onions in oil until transparent in heavy saucepan. Add celery, leeks, minced garlic, saffron, bay leaf, wine, potatoes, fish stock, and cayenne. Season with salt and pepper to taste. Bring to a boil. Simmer 30 minutes.
- Cut fish fillets in 2" cubes and arrange in a large heatproof casserole.
- Prepare Garlic Mayonnaise.
- Purée cooked soup in blender or put through food mill to purée the vegetables. Pour soup over fish to cover. Bring to a boil. Simmer 5 minutes, until fish is cooked. Transfer pieces of fish to heated tureen or serving dish.
- Spoon 1 cup Garlic Mayonnaise into a large saucepan. While stirring with a whisk, add hot soup. Heat thoroughly. Do not boil. Pour over fish. Garnish soup with remaining ½ cup mayonnaise.

Betsy Gimpel Mena

Garlic Mayonnaise

2 egg yolks at room temperature
Salt and pepper
2 teaspoons Dijon mustard
1 tablespoon minced garlic
1 tablespoon white wine vinegar
1½ cups olive oil
Tabasco sauce (optional)

1½ cups

- Place egg yolks, mustard, garlic, and vinegar in mixing bowl or food processor. Add salt and pepper to taste. Beat with a whisk. Gradually add oil. When mixture thickens, add oil more rapidly.
- Beat until all the oil is added. Mayonnaise will thicken. Add tabasco to taste, if desired.

Betsy Gimpel Mena

39

Soups and Breads

Broccoli Soup

1 large bunch fresh broccoli
2-3 tablespoons butter
1 medium onion, chopped
1 garlic clove, minced
1 medium potato, peeled and diced
4 cups chicken broth or vegetable
    broth
2 cups milk
½ teaspoon salt
¼ teaspoon freshly ground pepper
1 small lemon, sliced thinly

Serves 6

• Cut flowerets from broccoli stalks. Boil flowerets until tender in small amount of water. Drain and set aside.
• Peel broccoli stalks if tough. Dice. Heat butter in large, heavy saucepan. Add broccoli stalks, onion, and garlic. Cook slowly, stirring frequently, 10 minutes. Add potato and broth. Bring to boil. Simmer 15 minutes or until potato is tender.
• Add milk, salt, and pepper. Purée in blender or food processor. Return to saucepan. Add flowerets. Reheat. Garnish with lemon slices.

Victoria Eastman Ohlandt

Cheddar Cheese Soup

2 tablespoons butter
1 onion, chopped
1 carrot, chopped
1 celery rib, chopped
3 tablespoons flour
1 tablespoon cornstarch
2 cups chicken stock
2 cups milk
1 cup grated very sharp cheddar
    cheese
¾ teaspoon salt
Dash cayenne pepper
½ teaspoon Dijon mustard
1 tablespoon chopped chives
1 tablespoon chopped parsley
⅛ teaspoon baking soda

Serves 6-8

• Melt butter in heavy soup pot. Add vegetables. Sauté over moderate heat until soft and golden. Add flour and cornstarch. Stir well.
• Heat stock and milk in saucepan. Add to vegetables. Cook over moderate heat until mixture thickens.
• Purée soup in blender. Return to soup pot. Blend in cheese. seasonings. and herbs. Heat. stirring to melt cheese. Before serving. add baking soda.

Keene Harrill Rees

40

Soups and Breads

Frijole Cheese Soup

Serves 8

1 pound bacon
2 large onions, chopped
1 can (28 ounces) and 1 can
   (1 pound) tomatoes
1½ cups water
6-8 celery ribs, chopped
1 pound cheddar cheese, shredded
3 cans (20 ounces) white kidney
   beans or pinto beans, drained
1-2 teaspoons vinegar
Salt and pepper to taste
Dash tabasco sauce

• Cut bacon in small pieces. Fry until crisp. Drain well. Reserve 3 tablespoons drippings. Sauté onion in reserved drippings until soft. Drain.
• Combine bacon, onion, undrained tomatoes, water, celery, and cheese in large saucepan. Cook over low heat until cheese melts, stirring frequently.
• Purée beans. Add to soup with vinegar. Season with salt, pepper, and tabasco.

Ann Keyser Griffin

Chilled Cucumber Soup

Serves 6

3 tablespoons butter
1 medium onion, chopped, or 1 leek,
   cubed
2 medium cucumbers, peeled and
   diced (2-2½ cups)
1 cup watercress leaves
1 large potato, peeled and diced
3 cups chicken broth
3 sprigs parsley
½ teaspoon salt
¼ teaspoon freshly ground
   pepper
¼ teaspoon dry mustard
1 cup heavy cream
Chopped cucumber, parsley, and
   radishes for garnish

• Melt butter. Sauté onion until transparent. Add remaining ingredients except heavy cream and chopped vegetables for garnish. Bring to boil. Simmer 15 minutes or until potatoes are tender.
• Purée in blender or food processor. Taste to correct seasonings. Chill. Before serving, stir in heavy cream. Garnish with combination of chopped cucumber, parsley, and radishes.

Victoria Eastman Ohlandt

Soups and Breads

Cucumber Borscht

2 medium cucumbers
1 pound cooked beets, fresh or
    canned
1 small onion, halved
1 tablespoon chopped parsley
6 cups chicken broth
Salt and pepper to taste
6 tablespoons sour cream
3 sprigs dill, chopped; or 1½-2
    teaspoons dried dill weed

Serves 6

• Peel cucumbers. Cut lengthwise. Remove seeds with spoon. Drain beets. Cut in half. Shred cucumbers and beets in food processor or with hand grater. Remove to bowl.
• Chop onion. Add to bowl with beets and cucumber. Add parsley.
• Heat chicken broth. When hot, pour over shredded beets and cucumbers. Mix well. Add salt and pepper to taste. Chill at least 2 hours. Skim fat from surface.
• Serve chilled soup with 1 tablespoon sour cream and a sprinkle of fresh dill in each bowl.

Penelope Johnson Wartels

Cream of Carrot Soup

1 pound carrots
½ pound potatoes
2 tablespoons butter
¾ cup coarsely chopped onion
6 cups chicken broth
½ teaspoon dried thyme
1 bay leaf
1 cup heavy cream
½ teaspoon worcestershire sauce
½ teaspoon sugar
¼ teaspoon tabasco sauce
Salt and freshly ground pepper to
    taste
1 cup cold milk

Serves 6-8

• Trim and peel carrots and potatoes. Cut carrots into rounds. Cube potatoes.
• Heat butter. Add onion. Cook briefly. Add carrots, potatoes, and broth. Bring to boil. Add thyme and bay leaf. Simmer 30-40 minutes until carrots and potatoes are tender.
• Put mixture in blender or food processor. Blend until smooth. If serving hot, bring to a boil. Add remaining ingredients. If serving cold, add remaining ingredients to blended mixture. Stir well and chill thoroughly.

Donna Chisholm Clark

42

Soups and Breads

Chinese Velvet Chicken Soup with Sweet Corn

¼ pound minced raw chicken
1 teaspoon dry sherry
1 tablespoon salt
2 egg whites, lightly beaten
2½ quarts chicken broth, salted to taste
1 can (17 ounces) cream style corn
½ teaspoon monosodium glutamate
Sliced green onions for garnish

Serves 10

● Mince chicken. Mix well with wine, salt, and beaten egg whites.
● Bring chicken broth to a boil. Add corn and chicken mixture. Bring to a boil again. Add monosodium glutamate. Serve hot, garnished with green onions.

Lucie Ling Campbell

Crab Bisque

6 tablespoons butter
4 tablespoons finely chopped onion
4 tablespoons finely chopped green pepper
1 green onion, chopped with stem
2 tablespoons chopped parsley
1 cup sliced fresh mushrooms
2 tablespoons flour
1½ cups milk
1 teaspoon salt
¼ teaspoon ground mace
⅛ teaspoon freshly ground pepper
Dash tabasco sauce
1 cup half-and-half
1½ cups cooked fresh crabmeat or 2 packages (6 ounces) thawed frozen crabmeat
3 tablespoons dry sherry

Serves 4

● Heat *4 tablespoons* butter. Add vegetables. Sauté until soft but not brown.
● Heat remaining 2 tablespoons butter. Remove from heat. Stir in flour. Gradually add milk. Cook, stirring constantly, until thickened and smooth. Stir in seasonings.
● Add sautéed vegetables and half-and-half. Bring to a boil, stirring. Reduce heat and add crabmeat. Simmer, uncovered, 5 minutes. Stir in sherry before serving.

Madeleine Galanek Egan

Soups and Breads

Gazpacho

2 large tomatoes, peeled
1 large cucumber, pared
1 medium onion
1 green pepper
1 pimiento, drained
3 cups tomato juice
⅓ cup olive oil
⅓ cup vinegar
¼ teaspoon tabasco sauce
1½ teaspoons salt
⅛ teaspoon freshly ground pepper
2 garlic cloves (optional)
½ cup croutons (optional)

Serves 6

● In blender or food processor, combine 1 tomato, ½ cucumber, ½ onion, ¼ green pepper, pimiento, and ½ cup tomato juice. Purée. Combine mixture in large bowl with remaining tomato juice, ¼ cup olive oil, vinegar, tabasco, salt, and pepper. Cover and chill.
● Rub skillet with garlic. Add rest of oil and heat. Sauté bread cubes until browned.
● Chop remaining tomato, cucumber, onion, and pepper. Serve in separate bowls. Use as garnish with croutons.

Suzanne Rich Beatty

Leek and Potato Soup

2 large leeks
6 tablespoons butter
5 cups chicken broth
4 medium potatoes, peeled and
    thinly sliced
4 slices bacon, fried and crumbled,
    or 1 ham bone
1 cup milk
Salt
¼ teaspoon freshly ground pepper
½ cup heavy cream

Serves 6-8

● Cut off all but 1" of the greens from the leek tops. Peel leeks and wash well. Slice thinly. Cook in butter in large pot until limp. Add chicken broth, potatoes, and bacon or ham bone.
● Cover. Bring to a boil then reduce heat. Cook slowly for an hour. Remove ham bone, if used.
● Purée soup in blender or food processor. Return to pan. Add milk, salt, and pepper. Bring to a boil, stirring. Stir in cream before serving. Best made a day ahead. Serve hot or cold.

Suzanne Rich Beatty

Soups and Breads

Mulligatawny Soup

1 roasting chicken (4-5 pounds), cut in pieces
⅓ cup flour
⅓ cup butter
1½ cups chopped onion
2 cups chopped celery
2 cups chopped carrot
1½ cups chopped tart apple
4 teaspoons salt
1-1½ tablespoons curry powder
¾ teaspoon mace
¼-½ teaspoon freshly ground pepper
¼ teaspoon chili powder
¾ cup shredded coconut
6 cups cold water
1 cup apple juice
1 cup light cream
1½ cups hot cooked rice

Serves 8-10

● Wash chicken. Pat dry. Shake in paper bag with flour, to coat completely. Reserve remaining flour. Sauté chicken in butter in large kettle or dutch oven until well browned. Remove chicken. Add vegetables, apple, and remaining flour. Cook, stirring, 5 minutes. Add seasonings, coconut, cold water, and chicken. Bring to a boil. Reduce heat. Simmer, covered, for 2 hours. Stir occasionally.

● Remove from heat. Cool. Skim fat from broth. Remove chicken meat from bones. Cut into large pieces. Return chicken pieces to soup pot, along with apple juice. Chill or freeze until ready to serve.

● To serve, reheat. Add cream. Put a large spoonful of hot cooked rice in each soup bowl. Pour soup over it.

Mary Hegarty Seaman

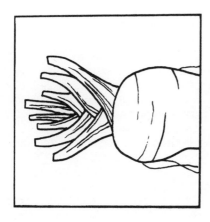
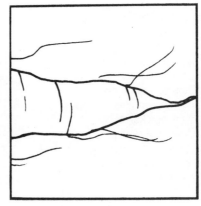

Soups and Breads

French Onion Soup

3 tablespoons butter
1 tablespoon oil
1½ pounds onion, thinly sliced
1 teaspoon salt
½ teaspoon sugar
3 tablespoons flour
1 tablespoon Bovril
2 quarts boiling beef broth
½ cup dry white wine or vermouth
French bread
6 ounces grated swiss cheese
Salt and pepper

Serves 8

● Melt butter in a large, heavy skillet. Add oil and heat mixture. Add onions. Cover and cook slowly for 15 minutes. Remove cover. Add salt and sugar. Cook 30 minutes, stirring often, until onions are light brown.
● Sprinkle flour over onions. Stir in well. Remove pan from stove. Add onions and Bovril to boiling beef broth. Add wine or vermouth. Salt and pepper to taste. Simmer, partially covered, 30-40 minutes.
● Prepare ½" slices of French bread by drying them out at room temperature. At serving time, fill individual ovenproof ramekins with boiling soup. Add 1 slice of French bread to each ramekin. Press it into soup to soak. Sprinkle grated cheese heavily over bread and soup. Place under broiler until cheese melts and bubbles.

Marcia Petersen Sandner

Pumpkin Soup

4 green onions, chopped with stems
1 onion, chopped
2 carrots, peeled and sliced
4 tablespoons butter, melted
1 can (29 ounces) pumpkin
5 cups chicken stock
¼ teaspoon salt
½ teaspoon minced garlic
2 tablespoons flour
1 cup heavy cream

Serves 6-8

● In large pot, sauté all onions and carrots in *3 tablespoons* butter until tender. Add pumpkin and *all but 2 tablespoons* chicken stock. Blend well. Add salt and garlic. Simmer 25 minutes.
● In small cup, mix flour and 2 tablespoons reserved cool broth. Stir into hot soup. Bring back to boil. Add remaining 1 tablespoon butter. Purée in blender if desired. Return soup to pot and stir in cream. Boil again before serving.

Jane Miller Moritz

46

Soups and Breads

Potage Senegalese

2 tablespoons butter
1 onion, finely chopped
1 small unpeeled apple, sliced
4 tablespoons flour
2 teaspoons curry powder
Salt
Chile peppers
Cayenne pepper
3 cups chicken broth
½ cup cooked fresh or frozen peas,
    puréed
1½ cups cream
½ cup finely diced chicken white
    meat

Serves 6

• Melt butter. Add chopped onion and apple slices. Cook very slowly until soft. Stir in flour and curry powder. Cook slowly over very low heat for 5 minutes.

• Add salt, cayenne, and chile peppers to taste. Stir the broth until smooth. Add purée of cooked peas. Stir over medium heat until soup comes to boil.

• Purée soup in blender or press through fine strainer. Add cream and diced chicken. Serve hot.

• Chill for cold Senegalese. Add cream and diced chicken before serving.

Katharine Lynne Peckham

Spinach Chowder

2 cups chopped spinach
1 cup boiling water
3 medium potatoes, peeled and
    sliced
4 slices bacon
½ cup sliced onion
3 tablespoons flour
1 cup evaporated milk
1 teaspoon salt

Serves 6-8

• Add spinach to boiling water. Cover. Simmer 3-5 minutes over low heat. Drain, reserving liquid.

• Cook potatoes in salted water to cover until tender. Drain, reserving liquid.

• Fry bacon in dutch oven until brown. Drain bacon. Crumble. Reserve drippings.

• Sauté onion in bacon drippings to brown lightly. Blend in flour. Gradually add milk, spinach liquid, and potato water. Cook, stirring constantly, until mixture begins to boil and thickens. Add salt, spinach, and potatoes. Bring to boil. Lower heat. Simmer 5 minutes. Garnish each serving with bacon.

Victoria Eastman Ohlandt

47

Soups and Breads

Fresh Tomato Soup

Serves 8-10

4 tablespoons butter
2 tablespoons olive oil
4 medium onions, sliced
2-3 leeks
2 garlic cloves, minced (optional)
2 carrots, peeled, trimmed, and sliced
2-3 celery ribs with leaves, trimmed
    and sliced
2 teaspoons coarse salt
Freshly ground pepper
Pinch cayenne pepper
Pinch chopped fresh or dried
    tarragon or basil
3-4 parsley sprigs, coarsely chopped
4 pounds ripe tomatoes (about 12
    medium)
½ teaspoon sugar
Small pinch nutmeg (optional)
1 tablespoon tomato paste (optional)
5 cups fresh or canned chicken broth

- In large pot, heat butter and oil until sizzling. Add onions. Toss to coat with fat. Cover pot. Cook slowly over medium heat about 5 minutes, tossing occasionally.
- Trim leeks leaving 2"-3" of green. Split lengthwise. Leave root end intact. Wash carefully. Slice crosswise ½" thick.
- Add leeks and garlic to onions. Cook, covered, 3 more minutes. Add carrots, celery, salt, peppers, tarragon or basil, and parsley. Toss and cover again. Cook 5 minutes until vegetables are slightly soft.
- Peel tomatoes if using blender or food processor. If using food mill, leave skins on. Cut out stems and cores with small sharp knife. Halve crosswise. Squeeze out seeds and cut in half.
- Add tomato quarters to pot. Stir. Add sugar, nutmeg, and tomato paste. Heat uncovered. Lower heat when soup comes to boil. Simmer, stirring occasionally for 10 minutes. Add chicken broth. Bring to boil and lower heat again. Simmer, partially covered, 15 minutes more, still stirring occasionally.
- If using unpeeled tomatoes, put soup through food mill using medium disc. Otherwise, purée soup in a blender or food processor.

Soups and Breads

continued

● Return to pot. Correct seasonings with salt, pepper, and cayenne. Serve hot, garnished with parsley, tarragon, or basil. Do not use dried herbs. Serve with homemade croutons.

Variation: *Cream of Tomato Soup:* After soup is puréed, stir in ½-⅔ cup heavy cream. Simmer 10 minutes. Correct seasonings. Garnish with herbs. Serve with croutons.

Nancy Beck Hoggson

Tomato Bouillon

2 cans (28 ounces) tomatoes, or 8 ripe tomatoes
1 large onion, finely chopped
Juice of 2 lemons
4 cups chicken stock
½ teaspoon seasoned salt
¼ cup sherry
Chopped chives for garnish

Serves 8

● If using garden tomatoes, peel them. Place tomatoes in blender or food processor until puréed. Add onion. Purée again.
● Place tomato-onion mixture in large, heavy saucepan. Add lemon juice, chicken stock, and seasoned salt. Simmer 45 minutes. Add sherry. Heat again. Serve piping hot, garnished with chopped chives.

Margaret Muncie

Cold Strawberry Soup

1 cup halved strawberries
1 cup orange juice
¼ cup sour cream
½ cup sweet white wine
Strawberry slices and mint leaves for garnish

Serves 4

● Put all ingredients except garnish in blender. Purée and chill.
● Blend again before serving. Top with strawberry slices and mint leaves.

Cheryl Giffin Carter

Soups and Breads

Spicy Tomato Soup

Serves 4-6

1 tablespoon butter
1 medium onion, sliced
1 can (1 pound) tomatoes, cut up
2 cups chicken broth
Dash ground cloves
½ teaspoon basil
1 teaspoon paprika
1 teaspoon sugar
1 bay leaf
⅛ teaspoon ground nutmeg
⅛ teaspoon salt
⅛ teaspoon freshly ground pepper
2 tablespoons chopped parsley
½ cup heavy cream, whipped

• Melt butter. Add onion. Cook until limp. Add tomatoes and their liquid. chicken broth. cloves. basil. paprika. sugar. bay leaf. nutmeg. salt. and pepper. Simmer. covered. 30 minutes. Remove from heat. Discard bay leaf.
• In blender or food processor. puree soup adding small amounts at a time. Cover and chill. Before serving. stir in parsley and reheat. Add salt to taste. Top with whipped cream.

Penelope Crabb Baylis

Hearty Vegetable Soup

Serves 6-8

3 onions, chopped
2 tablespoons butter
1 pound lean ground beef
1 garlic clove, minced
3 cups beef broth
2 cans (1 pound, 14 ounces) tomatoes
1 cup diced potatoes
1 cup diced carrots
1 cup diced celery
1 cup broken green beans
1 cup dry white wine
2 tablespoons chopped parsley
½ teaspoon basil
¼ teaspoon thyme
Salt and freshly ground pepper

• Sauté onions in butter until golden. Stir in ground beef and garlic. Cook, stirring, until beef is browned.
• Add remaining ingredients. Bring to a boil. Reduce heat. Simmer 1-1¼ hours. Purée 1 cup of vegetables in blender or food processor. Add to soup to thicken slightly before serving.

Anne Ruthrauff Seltzer

50

Soups and Breads

Watercress Soup

3 large potatoes
1 large onion
6 cups chicken broth
2 bunches watercress
¾-1 teaspoon salt
¼ teaspoon freshly ground pepper
3 egg yolks
1 cup heavy cream

Serves 8

● Peel potatoes and onion. Cut in quarters. Place in a saucepan and cover with chicken broth. Bring to a boil and lower flame. Simmer 20 minutes, until potatoes are tender.

● Wash watercress. Dry well and trim. Set aside 8 small sprigs for garnish. Place rest in blender or food processor in small batches. Chop finely.

● When potatoes and onions are tender, transfer with a slotted spoon into blender or food processor. Add 3 tablespoons or more of chicken broth. Purée mixture.

● Spoon potato-onion purée into heavy saucepan. Add chopped watercress. Pour chicken broth over all. Bring soup to boil, stirring constantly with wooden spoon over low heat. Add salt and pepper to taste. Turn heat very low.

● Mix egg yolks in blender or food processor. Add ½ cup of heavy cream. Mix well with egg yolks. Stirring constantly, add egg-cream mixture to soup. Heat 3-4 minutes but do not let soup boil. Gently stir in remaining heavy cream.

● Chill overnight. Serve hot or cold.

Diana Moody Huston

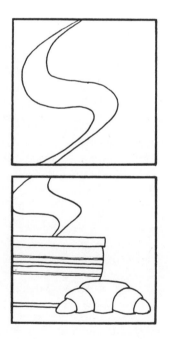

Soups and Breads

Zucchini Tarragon Soup

2 tablespoons butter
1 pound zucchini, diced
1 cup carrots, diced
1 medium onion, chopped
1 garlic clove, minced
2 cups chicken broth
2 cups milk
1 teaspoon tarragon
1/2-3/4 teaspoon salt
1/8 teaspoon freshly ground pepper
Chopped parsley (optional)

Serves 4

● Melt butter. Sauté zucchini, carrots, onion, and garlic over medium heat for 10 minutes, stirring frequently. Add chicken broth, milk, tarragon, salt, and pepper. Simmer 25 minutes.
● Purée in blender or food processor, a few cups at a time. Serve warm, garnished with chopped parsley.

Karin Best Garson

Curried Zucchini Soup

3 tablespoons butter
2-3 medium onions, thinly sliced
1 tablespoon curry powder
8 medium zucchini
2-3 teaspoons salt
Freshly ground pepper
3 cups chicken broth
Cayenne pepper
Lemon juice
2 cups heavy cream
1½ tablespoons dark rum or brandy

Serves 6-8

● Melt butter. Add onions. Cook until soft over low heat. Do not brown. Stir in curry powder. Cook very slowly for 2 minutes.
● Scrub zucchini. Slice 1/4" thick, without peeling. Add to butter and curry. Cook 6 minutes over low heat. Add salt and pepper to taste. Add chicken broth. Cover. Raise heat slightly. Simmer 8 minutes, until zucchini is tender but still crisp.
● Purée soup in food processor or blender, using off-and-on technique to avoid making purée too smooth. Season with salt, cayenne, and lemon juice to taste. Chill.
● Before serving, stir in cream and rum or brandy. Can also be served hot.

Nancy Beck Hoggson

Soups and Breads

Cheese Blintzes

8 ounces cream cheese, softened
½ cup sugar
1 egg yolk
1 loaf soft white bread
Melted butter
Cinnamon and sugar

3 dozen

● Mix cheese, sugar, and egg yolks. Cut crusts from bread. Roll bread flat. Spread cheese mixture on flattened bread and roll. Dip in melted butter, then in cinnamon-sugar. Refrigerate or freeze until firm.
● To serve, heat in 350° oven for 20 minutes. Good with sour cream.

Kathleen Kayser Dixon

Special Muffins

1 cup flour
1½ teaspoons baking powder
2 tablespoons sugar
½ teaspoon salt
1 egg
½ cup milk
2 tablespoons melted shortening

12 muffins

● Preheat oven to 425°. Sift flour. Measure 1 cup. Sift again with baking powder, sugar, and salt.
● Beat egg. Add milk and melted shortening.
● Make a well in flour mixture. Pour in combined liquid ingredients. Stir to blend. Do not overbeat.
● Stir in blueberries, caraway seeds, fruit, nuts, or crumbled bacon. Bake 15-20 minutes in greased muffin cups.
Variations: Add 1 cup well-drained fresh or frozen blueberries,
or 1 tablespoon caraway seeds,
or ½ cup raisins or chopped dates,
or 1 cup finely chopped nuts.

Mary Vance Watson

Soups and Breads

Blueberry Bran Muffins

2 eggs, beaten
½ cup vegetable oil
¾ cup sugar
4 tablespoons maple syrup
1½ cups milk
2 cups flour
1 tablespoon baking powder
½ teaspoon salt
½ cup bran
1 cup blueberries (if frozen, thaw
  before using)

2 dozen
- Preheat oven to 375°.
- In large bowl, combine eggs, oil, sugar, and syrup. Mix well. Stir in milk.
- Combine flour, baking powder, and salt. Add to liquid mixture. Fold in bran and blueberries.
- Pour into well-greased muffin tins. Bake 25 minutes until brown.

Barbara Smith Suval

Cherry Muffins

2 cups flour
¾ cup sugar
2 teaspoons baking powder
¼ teaspoon salt
¾ cup milk
2 eggs, slightly beaten
2 tablespoons butter, melted
2 cups pitted tart cherries, fresh,
  frozen, or canned (drained)

1 dozen
- Preheat oven to 400°. Mix *1½ cups* flour, sugar, baking powder, and salt. Beat milk, eggs, and butter. Stir into flour mixture until moistened.
- Toss cherries with remaining ½ cup flour. Fold into batter.
- Fill each greased muffin cup ⅔ full. Bake 20 minutes until brown.

Madeleine Galanek Egan

Raisin Bran Muffins

¾ cup sugar
¼ cup oil
1 cup raisin bran
1 egg
1 cup buttermilk
1¼ cups flour
1½ teaspoons baking soda
½ teaspoon salt
¼ teaspoon vanilla

12 muffins
- Preheat oven to 400°. Combine ingredients in order listed. Grease muffin pans or line with paper liners.
- Pour batter into muffin pans. Bake 20 minutes.

Susan Sample Marx

Soups and Breads

Scotch Scones

1 tablespoon vinegar
2 cups milk
4 cups sifted flour
1 teaspoon salt
¼ cup sugar
3 tablespoons baking powder

2 dozen
- Preheat oven to 275°.
- Add vinegar to milk. Let stand to sour. Sift together flour, salt, sugar, and baking powder. Gradually add sour milk. Dust sticky dough with flour. Roll lightly to ½" thickness.
- With knife, cut rolled dough into biscuit-sized shapes. Place on ungreased baking sheet. Bake 30-40 minutes. Scones should be lightly browned. If not, increase temperature to 325° and bake longer. Serve hot.
- Freezes well. Reheat as needed. Scones are delicious split, toasted, and spread with sweet butter and jam.

Susan Kross Cowan

Apple Currant Bread

2 cups unbleached flour
1 tablespoon baking powder
1 teaspoon baking soda
1 teaspoon salt
1 teaspoon cinnamon
¼ teaspoon freshly grated nutmeg
⅔ cup dried currants
2 tart apples, peeled, cored, and
   quartered
2 teaspoons grated lemon zest
   (outer yellow rind)
1¼ cups sugar
3 eggs
½ cup butter, at room temperature
1 tablespoon fresh lemon juice
1 teaspoon vanilla

2 loaves
- Lightly flour 2 greased bread pans (8"). Preheat oven to 350°.
- Place metal blade in food processor. Add dry ingredients and currants. Process 2 seconds. Remove to bowl.
- Replace metal blade. Add apples and lemon zest. Chop coarsely. Purée 30 seconds.
- Add sugar. Process 30 seconds. Add eggs. Mix 1 minute. Cut butter in 4 pieces. Add butter, lemon juice, and vanilla. Process 1 minute.
- Add dry ingredients until flour disappears. Spoon batter into prepared pans. Smooth tops.
- Bake 40-45 minutes until loaves are browned. Cool 10 minutes. Turn out onto wire rack. Allow to cool.

Penelope Johnson Wartels

Soups and Breads

Apple Coffee Cake

4 cups pared, sliced apples
5 tablespoons sugar
5 teaspoons cinnamon
3 cups flour
1½ cups sugar
3 teaspoons baking powder
1 teaspoon salt
4 eggs
¼ cup orange juice
1 cup corn oil

Serves 12-16

● Preheat oven to 375°. Toss apples with sugar and cinnamon to coat.

● Mix flour, sugar, baking powder, and salt. Make a well in dry ingredients. Add eggs, orange juice, and oil. Stir to blend.

● Grease a 10″ bundt or tube pan. Layer ⅓ the batter, ½ the apple mixture, ⅓ the batter, then remainder of apple mixture and batter. Bake 30-45 minutes.

● Cool 6 hours or overnight before removing from pan.

Judith Freyermuth Rex

Fresh Apple Bread

2 cups flour
2 teaspoons baking powder
1 teaspoon salt
½ teaspoon cinnamon
¼ teaspoon grated nutmeg
½ cup butter, softened
1¼ cups sugar
2 eggs
1½-2 cups peeled, finely grated
     tart apples
¾ cup chopped walnuts

1 loaf

● Preheat oven to 350°. Sift together first five ingredients.

● Cream together butter and sugar. Beat in eggs one at a time. Stir in alternately flour mixture and apples. Add nuts.

● Pour into well-greased 9″ loaf pan. Bake 1 hour. Cool 10-15 minutes in pan. Turn onto wire rack. Cool completely before slicing.

Stephanie Fay Arpajian

Soups and Breads

Banana Nut Bread

2 cups sifted flour
1 teaspoon baking soda
½ teaspoon salt
½ cup butter
1 cup sugar
2 eggs
2 medium bananas, mashed (1 cup)
⅓ cup milk
1 teaspoon lemon juice
½ cup chopped nuts

1 loaf

• Preheat oven to 350°.
• Sift flour with baking soda and salt. Cream butter. Gradually add sugar. Cream well. Add eggs and bananas. Blend thoroughly.
• Combine milk and lemon juice. Add alternately with dry ingredients to banana mixture. Begin and end with dry ingredients. Blend well after each addition. Stir in nuts.
• Grease bottom of 9" loaf pan. Pour in batter. Bake 60-70 minutes. Remove from pan and cool on wire rack.

Carolyn Nielsen Creavy

Beer Bread

2½ cups self-rising flour
1½ tablespoons sugar
1 can (12 ounces) beer, at room
    temperature

1 loaf

• Preheat oven to 350°. Mix all ingredients. Pour batter into 9" x 5" x 3" buttered loaf pan. Bake 1 hour.

Carole Kruse Long

Soups and Breads

Quick Brown Bread

3 cups whole wheat flour
1 teaspoon salt
1 teaspoon baking powder
¼ teaspoon baking soda
1½ cups buttermilk

1 loaf

• Preheat oven to 425°. Mix flour, salt, baking powder, and baking soda. Add buttermilk.
• Knead dough into a ball. Place in floured iron pan, skillet, or baking sheet. Flatten into a 7" circle with your hand. Cut deep cross from side to side on top of dough with sharp knife dipped in flour. This will allow bread to expand.
• Bake 40 minutes until bread is crusty or sounds hollow when tapped. Cool before slicing.

Mary Vance Watson

Brown Sugar Coffee Cake

½ cup butter
1 cup sugar
2 eggs
2 cups flour
1 teaspoon baking powder
1 teaspoon baking soda
½ teaspoon salt
1 cup yogurt or sour cream
1 teaspoon vanilla
⅓ cup brown sugar
1½ teaspoons cinnamon
1 cup chopped walnuts or pecans

Serves 10-12

• Cream butter and ¾ cup sugar. Beat until fluffy. Add eggs one at a time. Beat after each addition.
• Sift together flour, baking powder, baking soda, and salt. Add to above mixture alternately with yogurt or sour cream. Add vanilla. Blend well.
• Preheat oven to 325°. Pour half of batter into greased, floured 9" x 13" baking pan or 10" bundt pan. Combine brown sugar, remaining ¼ cup white sugar, cinnamon, and pecans. Sprinkle half this mixture over batter.
• Top with remaining batter. Sprinkle with remaining topping mixture. Bake 40 minutes.

Donna Chisholm Clark

Soups and Breads

Autumn Bundt Bread

2 cups flour
1 tablespoon baking powder
½ teaspoon baking soda
½ teaspoon salt
½ teaspoon cinnamon
½ teaspoon freshly grated nutmeg
¼ teaspoon ground cloves
¼ teaspoon ground ginger
½ cup plus 2 tablespoons butter, at
    room temperature
1½ cups sugar
2 eggs
1 cup canned pumpkin
2 cups shredded unpeeled tart
    apples
1 cup chopped pecans
2 tablespoons confectioners sugar
    (optional)

Serves 12-16
● Generously grease 10" bundt pan.
Preheat oven to 350°.
● Combine first eight ingredients.
Cream butter and sugar. Beat in eggs
and pumpkin. Mix until fluffy. Add apples and pecans. Blend thoroughly.
Mix in dry ingredients.
● Turn into prepared pan. Bake 50-55
minutes until bread pulls away from
sides of pan. Cool in pan on wire rack 5
minutes. Invert onto rack. Cool completely. Dust bread with sifted confectioners sugar. if desired. Freezes well.

Nancy Beck Hoggson

Chocolate Applesauce Bread

⅓ cup butter
2 squares (2 ounces) unsweetened
    chocolate
1½ cups flcur
1¼ cups sugar
1 teaspoon baking soda
¼ teaspoon baking powder
½ teaspoon salt
½ teaspoon cinnamon
¼ teaspoon nutmeg
2 eggs, slightly beaten
½ cup sweetened applesauce
½ cup chopped walnuts or pecans

1 loaf
● Lightly grease and flour a 9" loaf pan.
Preheat oven to 350°.
● In small saucepan or double boiler.
heat butter and chocolate over low
heat until melted. Stir to mix and remove from heat.
● Mix flour. sugar. and other dry ingredients. Add eggs. applesauce. nuts.
and melted chocolate mixture. Stir with
wooden spoon until well blended. Pour
into prepared pan. Bake 50-60 minutes.
● Cool 10 minutes in pan on wire rack.
Remove from pan. Serve warm or
cooled.

Ann Dodds Costello

59

Soups and Breads

Cranberry Nut Bread

6 tablespoons butter
¾ cup sugar
2 eggs
1 teaspoon lemon juice
Rind of 1 orange, chopped
¼ cup fresh orange juice
1⅓ cups flour
1 teaspoon baking soda
1¼ teaspoons baking powder
½ teaspoon salt
1¼ cups fresh cranberries
1 cup walnuts

2 loaves

• Preheat oven to 350°. Cream butter and sugar together until fluffy. Beat in eggs one at a time. Still beating, add lemon juice, chopped orange rind, and orange juice.

• Sift together dry ingredients. Add gradually to butter and sugar combination. Stir in cranberries and walnuts. Pour into two well-greased 8" loaf pans. Bake 1 hour.

Susan Hendrickson Eden

Eggnog-Cherry Nut Loaf

2½ cups flour
¾ cup sugar
1 tablespoon baking powder
1 teaspoon salt
1 egg, beaten
1¼ cups dairy or homemade eggnog
⅓ cup oil
½ cup chopped pecans
½ cup chopped maraschino cherries

2 loaves

• Preheat oven to 350°. Stir together flour, sugar, baking powder, and salt.

• Mix egg, eggnog, and oil. Stir into dry ingredients and mix well. Fold in nuts and cherries.

• Pour into 2 greased 8" loaf pans or 4 small loaf pans. Bake 45-50 minutes. Cool 15 minutes. Remove from pans.

   Note: *Homemade Eggnog.* Beat together 2 eggs, 1 cup light cream or half-and-half, ¼ cup sugar, and ¼ teaspoon nutmeg.

Madeleine Galanek Egan

60

Soups and Breads

Gougère

1 cup water
¼ pound butter
1 cup flour
½ teaspoon salt
5 eggs
1½ cups cubed swiss cheese

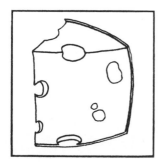

1 loaf

• Preheat oven to 400°. Bring water and butter to boil. Sift flour and salt together. Beat all at once into boiling mixture over low heat until mixture leaves sides of pan and forms a ball.
• Remove from heat. Beat in eggs one at a time. Beat well after each addition. Fold in cheese.
• Shape dough into 12" circle on greased baking sheet. Bake 25 minutes. Reduce oven temperature to 350°. Bake 30-40 minutes longer, until light and dry. Serve hot. Freeze and reheat if desired.

Anne Ruthrauff Seltzer

Johnny Cake

1 cup flour
¼ cup sugar
3 teaspoons baking powder
1 teaspoon baking soda
½ teaspoon salt
1 cup stone ground cornmeal
1 egg
1 cup buttermilk
3 tablespoons butter, melted

Serves 6-8

• Preheat oven to 350°. Sift flour, sugar, baking powder, baking soda, and salt into bowl. Stir in cornmeal. Mix well. Beat egg and add to dry mixture along with buttermilk. Stir in butter.
• Pour into greased 8" square pan. Bake 20 minutes.

Betsy Gimpel Mena

61

Soups and Breads

Jumble Bread

2½ cups sugar
1¼ cups salad·oil
4 eggs
½ cup water
1 cup canned pumpkin
1 cup grated carrots
¾ cup raisins
¾ cup chopped walnuts
3 cups flour
2 teaspoons baking soda
¼ teaspoon baking powder
1½ teaspoons salt
1½ teaspoons cinnamon
½ teaspoon ground cloves
½ teaspoon nutmeg

2 loaves
● Preheat oven to 350°. Grease 2 loaf pans (9").
● Mix sugar and oil. Add eggs, beating well after each addition. Add water, pumpkin, and carrots. Fold in raisins and nuts.
● In another bowl, mix flour, baking soda, baking powder, salt, and spices.
● Combine both mixtures. Pour into prepared pans. Bake 1 hour.

Judith Torrisi Wintermuth

Glazed Lemon Bread

1 cup sugar
6 tablespoons butter
Grated rind and juice of 1 lemon
2 eggs
1½ cups flour
½ teaspoon salt
1 teaspoon baking powder
½ cup milk
½ cup chopped walnuts
¼ cup sugar (scant)

1 loaf
● Preheat oven to 325°.
● Cream sugar and butter. Add grated lemon rind. Beat in eggs. Sift flour, salt, and baking powder together. Add to sugar and butter mixture alternately with milk, beginning and ending with flour. Stir in nuts.
● Pour into greased 9" loaf pan. Bake 45-60 minutes. Dissolve sugar in lemon juice. Pour over hot bread. Allow to cool in pan. Slice when cold. Warm to serve, if desired.

Nancy Gould Pinkernell

Soups and Breads

Nut Bread

1 cup flour
2 cups whole wheat flour
½ cup sugar
2½ teaspoons baking powder
¾ teaspoon baking soda
1¾ teaspoons salt
½ cup molasses
¾ cup buttermilk
¾ cup water
¾ cup nuts
½ cup chopped dates or cranberries
   (optional)

1 loaf
● Preheat oven to 350°. Sift flours, sugar, baking powder, baking soda, and salt. Stir in molasses, buttermilk, and water. Mix well.
● Stir in nuts and fruit. Pour into buttered 9″ loaf pan. Bake 1 hour.

Betsy Gimpel Mena

Oatmeal Raisin Bread

1 cup rolled oats
1 cup buttermilk
½ cup firmly packed dark brown
   sugar
1 egg, well beaten
1 cup whole wheat flour
1 teaspoon baking powder
1 teaspoon salt
½ teaspoon baking soda
6 tablespoons butter, melted and
   cooled
½ cup golden raisins

1 loaf
● Soak oats in buttermilk at least an hour. Stir in brown sugar and beaten egg.
● Preheat oven to 400°. In another bowl, mix dry ingredients. Combine the two mixtures. Stir in melted butter and raisins. Spoon batter into well-greased 8″ loaf pan. Bake 40 minutes until bread has risen and is well browned.

Nancy Beck Hoggson

Soups and Breads

Orange Bread

2 cups whole wheat flour
¾ cup sugar
1 tablespoon baking powder
½ teaspoon salt
2 eggs, beaten
1 cup fresh orange juice
3 tablespoons vegetable oil
1 cup Candied Orange Peel (see Index)

1-2 loaves
- Preheat oven to 350°.
- Combine flour, sugar, baking powder, and salt.
- Beat together eggs, orange juice, and oil. Add to flour mixture. Beat well. Stir in candied orange peel.
- Turn into greased loaf pans (one 9" pan or two 8" pans). Bake 40-50 minutes.
- Cool 5 minutes. Remove from pans and cool on rack.

Nancy Beck Hoggson

Popovers

Oil
1 cup milk, at room temperature
2 eggs, at room temperature
1 cup flour
½ teaspoon salt
⅓ cup grated parmesan cheese (optional)

12 popovers
- Preheat oven to 450°. Put ¼ teaspoon oil in each section of a 12-cup muffin pan. Place in oven to heat oil while mixing popovers.
- Place milk and eggs in blender or food processor. Beat 5 seconds. Add flour, salt, and cheese, if desired. Blend on high speed 5 seconds. Stir and blend again. Let mixture stand 5 minutes.
- Pour even amounts of batter into oiled muffin pan. Bake 15 minutes. Reduce oven heat to 375°. Bake additional 20 minutes.

Betsy Gimpel Mena

64

Soups and Breads

Raisin Caraway Bread

2 cups buttermilk
1 egg
⅛ tablespoon baking soda
3½ cups flour
1 teaspoon salt
1 cup raisins
¼ cup sugar
¼ cup caraway seeds
1 tablespoon plus 1 teaspoon baking
    powder

1 loaf

● Preheat oven to 375°. Combine all ingredients. Spoon batter into greased and floured 9″ loaf pan. Bake 45 minutes.

Ann Keyser Griffin

Tomato Bread

2 cups flour
1 tablespoon baking powder
1 teaspoon baking soda
1 teaspoon salt
1 teaspoon fresh ginger, peeled and
    minced
½ cup fresh basil leaves, tightly
    packed, or ¼ cup dried basil
1 green onion, cut in 1″ pieces
3 medium tomatoes, cored,
    quartered, and seeded
1 tablespoon tomato paste
1¼ cups sugar
3 eggs
½ cup butter, at room temperature

2 loaves

● Preheat oven to 350°. Grease and lightly flour 2 bread pans (8″).
● Mix first four ingredients in food processor for 2 seconds to sift.
● Place ginger, basil, and green onion in work bowl. Process 2 seconds with metal blade. Add tomatoes and tomato paste. Purée 30 seconds. Purée should measure 1½ cups. Add sugar and process 30 seconds longer. Add eggs and process 1 minute.
● Cut butter in 4 pieces. Add to work bowl. Process 1 minute. Add dry ingredients. Turn machine on and off 5 times until flour disappears.
● Spoon batter into prepared pans, spreading evenly with spatula. Bake 40-45 minutes until browned. Cool 10 minutes in pans. Turn out onto wire rack to cool completely.

Diana Moody Huston

Soups and Breads

Zucchini-Nut Spice Bread

2 cups sugar
3 eggs
½ cup oil
2 cups shredded zucchini, raw and unpeeled
1 teaspoon vanilla
1 cup chopped nuts
3 cups flour
½ teaspoon baking powder
1 teaspoon baking soda
1 teaspoon salt
1 teaspoon cinnamon
½ teaspoon ginger
½ teaspoon cloves

2 loaves

• Preheat oven to 350°. Beat sugar, eggs, oil, zucchini, and vanilla until blended. Sift together flour, baking powder, baking soda, salt, cinnamon, ginger, and cloves. Add dry ingredients to zucchini mixture. Add nuts.

• Pour into 2 greased 9" loaf pans. Bake 50-60 minutes. Freezes well and doubles nicely.

Jean Hoy Novak

Zucchini Wheat Germ Bread

3 eggs
1 cup oil
1 cup honey
1 cup brown sugar
2 cups coarsely grated zucchini
2½ cups flour
½ cup wheat germ
2 teaspoons baking soda
2 teaspoons salt
½ teaspoon baking powder
1 teaspoon cinnamon
1 cup chopped walnuts or pecans
Sugar

2 loaves

• Beat eggs, oil, honey, and brown sugar until foamy. Gently stir in zucchini with a spoon.

• Preheat oven to 350°. Sift together flour, wheat germ, soda, salt, baking powder, and cinnamon. Stir into zucchini mixture, along with nuts.

• Divide batter between 2 greased and flour-dusted 8" pans. Sprinkle loaves with sugar. Bake 1 hour, or until done.

Ann Keyser Griffin

Soups and Breads

Braided Breakfast Bread

2 loaves

1 cup milk
⅔ cup sugar
1 cup plus 1 tablespoon butter
1 teaspoon salt
2 packages (¼ ounce) dry yeast
½ cup warm water
3 eggs, beaten
6-7 cups sifted flour
1 egg white, beaten with 1
    tablespoon water
Sugar
Chopped nuts and cinnamon
    (optional)

• Scald milk. Pour over sugar, *1 cup* butter, and salt in large mixing bowl. Cool.

• Sprinkle yeast into warm water. Let stand a few minutes. Stir until dissolved. Add to cooled milk mixture. Add beaten eggs and *3 cups* flour. Beat until smooth. Stir in remaining flour to make dough. Turn onto lightly floured board and knead well.

• Place in greased bowl, turning dough so greased side is up. Cover and place in warm spot until double in bulk, about 1 hour. Punch down and turn onto board. Divide dough in half. Cut each half into 3 equal parts. Roll into strips 18″ long. Braid and place on greased baking sheet. Repeat with other half of dough. Melt remaining 1 tablespoon butter. Brush each braid with melted butter. Sprinkle with sugar.

• Let rise until doubled in bulk. Preheat oven to 375°. Brush with egg white and water. Sprinkle with cinnamon and nuts, if desired. Bake 30-35 minutes. Brush twice while baking with egg white and water. Bread sounds hollow when done. Freezes well.

Alice Van Nuys Sessa

67

Soups and Breads

Brown and Serve Rolls

18 rolls

1 package (¼ ounce) active dry yeast
¾ cup warm water (105-115°F)
¾ cup lukewarm milk, scalded and cooled
4 tablespoons sugar
2¼ teaspoons salt
4 tablespoons vegetable shortening
4½ cups flour

• Dissolve yeast in warm water. Set aside. Add sugar, salt, and vegetable shortening to milk and scald. Cool mixture to lukewarm. Place 2½ cups flour in food processor and add, with machine on, the yeast mixture and the lukewarm milk mixture. Add 1 more cup flour gradually and combine in processor. Turn dough out onto heavily floured surface. Add additional flour while kneading to make dough smooth and elastic. Knead about 7-10 minutes. Place dough in greased bowl and turn greased side up.

• Cover. Let rise in warm place until doubled in bulk, about 1½ hours.

• Punch down dough. Turn onto lightly floured board. Divide in 24 equal pieces. Shape each piece into a smooth ball. Place 3" apart on greased baking sheet. Cover and let rise until doubled, about 45 minutes.

• Preheat oven to 275°. Bake rolls 20 minutes. Do not brown. Remove from baking sheet. Cool at room temperature.

• Place rolls in plastic bags. Store in refrigerator several days, or freeze. To serve, brown rolls in a 400° oven for 7-10 minutes.

Carol Wenger Losey

Soups and Breads

Dill Bread

1 package (¼ ounce) active dry
    yeast, or 1 cake compressed
    yeast
¼ cup warm water
1 cup (½ pound) cream-style cottage
    cheese
2 tablespoons sugar
1 tablespoon minced onion
2 teaspoons fresh dill weed, or 1
    teaspoon dried dill weed
1 teaspoon salt
¼ teaspoon baking soda
1 egg
2½ cups sifted flour
Butter
Coarse salt

1 loaf

● Dissolve yeast in warm water in large bowl. With compressed yeast, water should be lukewarm. Heat cottage cheese until lukewarm. Stir into yeast mixture. Blend in sugar, onion, dill, salt, baking soda, and egg. Mix well. Beat in flour gradually, scraping down sides of bowl, then beat vigorously for 20 strokes. Dough will be sticky and heavy. Cover with clean towel. Let rise in warm, draft-free place 1 hour, or until doubled in bulk.

● Stir down dough. Butter a round 6-cup baking dish. Spoon in dough. Cover with towel. Let rise in warm, draft-free place for 45 minutes, or until doubled in bulk.

● Preheat oven to 350°. Brush top with butter. Sprinkle with coarse salt. Bake 50 minutes until golden brown. Remove from dish and cool.

Joan Williams Erhard

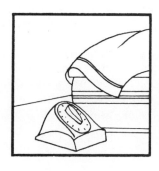
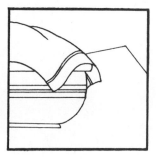

69

Soups and Breads

Mexican Bread Ring

1 loaf

2 cups water
1½ tablespoons sugar
1 tablespoon sea salt
1 tablespoon butter
1 rounded tablespoon dry yeast
6 cups unbleached wheat flour
1 teaspoon cornstarch
½ cup cold water

- Combine *2 cups* water with sugar and sea salt in saucepan. Heat to dissolve sugar. Add butter. Heat mixture slowly to 115° on a thermometer. Pour into mixing bowl. Add yeast and allow to stand a few minutes until bubbly. Stir to dissolve yeast completely.
- Stir in flour. Turn dough onto floured board. Knead for 10 minutes until velvety smooth.
- Grease large bowl. Add dough, turning it so greased side is up. Cover with plastic wrap. Let rise in warm place until nearly doubled in size, about 1½ hours.
- Punch dough down to release air bubbles. Turn out onto floured board. Cut off a 4-ounce ball of dough and reserve. Divide remaining dough in thirds. Form each third into balls. Cover and let rest on board for 10 minutes.
- Roll each of the 3 dough balls into a strip ½" in diameter and 4½' long, using palms of hands. Braid the strips together.
- Grease 14" baking sheet. Place in its center a round 8" baking pan which has been greased on the outside. Place braided dough on baking sheet encircling the pan. Trim ends, overlapping neatly. Stick ends together with a drop of water.

Soups and Breads

continued

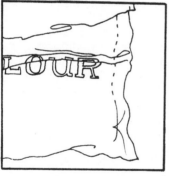

• To make bow, roll out reserved ball of dough into a strip ½" in diameter and 28" long. Shape into bow. Cut off tips of each end of dough "ribbon." Roll them into a strip 6" long, ⅛" thick, and ½" wide. Wrap this tightly around the middle of bow. Shape and pinch ends together securely. Place bow on wreath to cover the joined ends. Cover bread ring. Store in warm place to rise until almost doubled in size, 1 hour.

• Preheat oven to 375°. In saucepan, dissolve cornstarch in cold water. Heat to boiling, stirring. Cool slightly. Brush this glaze on dough wreath. Bake for 35-40 minutes until golden brown and hollow when tapped. A shallow pan filled with boiling water and placed on lower oven shelf will assure a very crisp bread.

• Cool baked wreath ring on wire rack. Wrap securely in plastic or foil to freeze.

• Reheat for 20 minutes in 350° oven before serving. Brush bread with water.

Betsy Gimpel Mena

Soups and Breads

Mediterranean Bread

1½ packages (⅜ ounce) yeast
1 tablespoon sugar
2 cups warm water
1 tablespoon salt
5 cups flour
Cornmeal
1 tablespoon water
1 egg white

2 loaves

• Dissolve yeast and sugar in warm water. Add salt and flour. Mix until stiff. Add more flour if necessary.
• Knead vigorously on floured board for 10-12 minutes, until dough is no longer sticky. Place dough in generously buttered bowl. Spread additional butter over top of dough. Cover and let rise in warm place until doubled in bulk, 2 hours.
• Punch dough down. Divide in half. Shape in 2 long loaves, like French or Italian bread. Place on baking sheet, sprinkled with cornmeal. Slash each loaf diagonally in 2 or 3 places.
• Cover dough and let rise for 5 minutes. Brush with mixture of 1 tablespoon water and 1 egg white.
• Place loaves in cold oven. Put pan of boiling water on shelf under bread to produce extra-crisp crust. Turn oven temperature to 400°. Bake bread for 35-45 minutes until golden brown and hollow-sounding when tapped. Freezes well.

Carole Kruse Long

72

Soups and Breads

Oatmeal Bread

2 cups boiling water
1 cup quick-cooking oats
½ cup whole wheat flour
½ cup brown sugar
2 tablespoons butter
1 tablespoon salt
1 tablespoon dry yeast
½ cup warm water
5 cups unbleached flour

2 loaves

● Pour boiling water over oats, whole wheat flour, sugar, butter, and salt. Stir mixture. Cool to lukewarm.
● Dissolve yeast in ½ cup warm water. Add to above batter.
● Add unbleached flour. Blend well. Knead 5-10 minutes on floured surface.
● Place dough in greased bowl, turning so greased surface of dough faces up. Cover and let rise in warm place until doubled in bulk, 1½ hours.
● Punch dough down. Shape in two loaves, placing each in a greased 9″ loaf pan. Cover and let rise in warm place until double in bulk, 1½ hours.
● Preheat oven to 350°. Bake loaves for 20-30 minutes. For glass pans, reduce oven temperature to 325° and bake for 30 minutes.

Susan Smith Cooley

pasta, cheese, and eggs

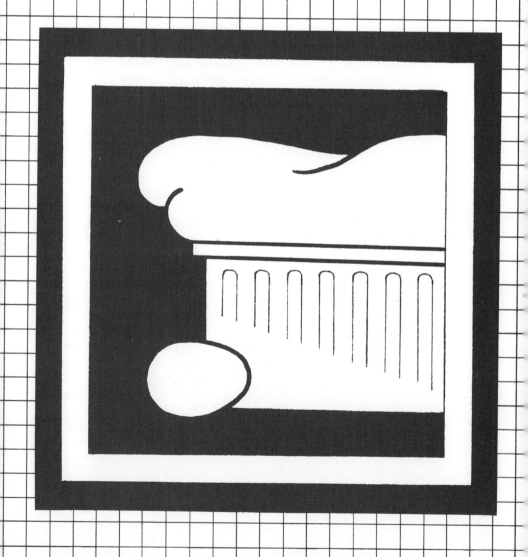

A Gourmet Omelet

These instructions for omelet making will seem simple enough. However, they should be memorized thoroughly before the actual cooking takes place. Preparation will go very quickly, leaving you with little time to glance at your cookbook.

1. For easiest preparation and clean-up, use an omelet pan with a non-stick finish and sloping sides, measuring 6″ or 7″ across the bottom and 9″ or 10″ across the top.

2. Make only small omelets. Use no more than 2 or 3 eggs in the size pan described above. For one omelet you will need:

1 tablespoon butter	Salt and pepper
2 large eggs	Filling—tomatoes, cheeses, sour
1 tablespoon water	cream, fresh berries

3. Beat eggs, seasonings, and water in bowl. Beat only until whites and yolks are blended.

4. Heat omelet pan over high heat. It is ready to use when a drop of water bounces when sprinkled on pan. Add butter, which must melt, foam, then stop foaming. If it burns or browns, the pan is too hot and must be removed from the heat. Wipe out burned butter with paper towels. Cool pan and start over.

5. When the butter stops foaming, pour in the egg mixture, shaking the pan with one hand. If your pan is non-stick, there is no need to stir the eggs. They will move around enough from the shaking.

6. When the eggs start to set but are still creamy, add filling. Tip the pan forward, rolling the omelet over with a spatula, beginning at the end of the pan near the handle. The omelet should roll onto itself.

7. Roll the omelet out onto a plate held just beneath the pan. The omelet should be in a neat, smooth roll, with edges tucked underneath.

8. Serve immediately. If you are making many individual omelets, wipe the pan with paper towels, reheat, add a tablespoon of butter, and begin again. Small omelets can be assembled from start to finish in a matter of 30 seconds.

Pasta, Cheese, and Eggs

Cappelletti with Fish Stuffing in Shrimp Sauce

Serves 4-6

Green Pasta
½ pound spinach, cooked,
    well-drained, and squeezed dry
1½ cups flour
½ teaspoon salt
1 egg, at room temperature
1 tablespoon water

• Place spinach in food processor and chop finely. Remove and set aside. Add flour and salt to processor bowl. Turn on and off to mix. Add egg and chopped spinach. Process until mixture resembles fine meal.
• Add water and process until dough forms a ball.
• Remove from processor. Knead slightly on a floured board. Roll out dough, using a pasta machine, and increasing tension as you go.
• Cut out circles of cappelletti. Set aside, covered.

Court Bouillon
2 tablespoons vinegar
1 small carrot
1 small onion
2 cups water
Bouquet garni: 3 parsley sprigs, 2
    green celery tops, 1 large bay
    leaf, 1 thyme sprig, 1 clove, 6
    peppercorns, and ½ teaspoon
    salt, tied in cheesecloth

• Combine all ingredients in a saucepan for Court Bouillon.

Stuffing
¾ pound fillet of sole, flounder, or
    sea bass
2 egg yolks
3 tablespoons grated parmesan
    cheese
2 tablespoons vinegar
¼ teaspoon grated nutmeg
⅛ teaspoon marjoram
Dash freshly ground pepper

• Poach fish in court bouillon with 2 tablespoons vinegar until cooked through. Drain well. Mash with a fork.
• Add remaining ingredients. Mix thoroughly until smooth.
• Spoon a little filling in the center of each cappelletti round. Twist to seal. Let dry at room temperature for 1 hour, or freeze until you wish to cook the cappelletti.

77

Pasta, Cheese, and Eggs

continued

• To cook, drop in boiling water for 4-5 minutes. Drain well. Serve with Shrimp Sauce (recipe follows).

Shrimp Sauce
2 garlic cloves, speared with
    toothpicks
⅓ cup olive oil
1½ tablespoons tomato paste
½ cup white wine
¼ pound shelled and deveined
    shrimp
Salt and freshly ground pepper
1 cup heavy cream
2 tablespoons chopped parsley

• Sauté garlic cloves in hot oil. Mix tomato paste with wine and add to garlic. Cook a few minutes, then add shrimp. Cook over high heat 2-3 minutes. Season with salt and pepper.
• Discard garlic cloves. Remove shrimp from sauce to food processor. Purée shrimp. Return to pan and add cream. Reduce heat slightly. Cook and stir until sauce is piping hot. Do not boil.
• Pour over hot pasta and serve. Garnish with chopped parsley.

Marcia Petersen Sandner

Cappelletti in Cream Sauce

8 ounces cappelletti or tortellini
1 tablespoon oil
2 tablespoons butter, melted
1 cup heavy cream
½ cup grated parmesan cheese
Salt and pepper
Cooked peas and minced prosciutto
    (optional)

Serves 2-4
• Cook cappelletti or tortellini until tender in boiling, salted water with the oil. Oil prevents pasta from sticking together.
• Melt butter in a heavy saucepan. Add cream and simmer until mixture thickens slightly. Add grated parmesan and seasonings. Cook a moment longer. Add pasta, cooked peas, and prosciutto.
    Note: This sauce is delicious with fettuccini noodles.

Peggy Swanson Smith

Pasta, Cheese, and Eggs

Fettuccine with Cognac

2 tablespoons olive oil
¼ cup butter
2 cups finely chopped onions
1 teaspoon minced garlic
1 pound ground round or sirloin
Salt and freshly ground pepper to taste
1 can (2 pounds, 3 ounces) tomatoes with tomato paste
¾ cup beef broth
1 hot, dried red pepper (optional)
2 tablespoons finely chopped parsley
1 pound fettuccine or other pasta
2 tablespoons cognac
½-1 cup sour cream
¾ cup grated parmesan cheese

Serves 4

● Heat oil and butter. Add onions and garlic, stirring. Cook until onions wilt and begin to brown. Add meat, salt, and pepper. Continue to cook until meat is lightly browned, tossing in pan. Add tomatoes, broth, red pepper, and parsley. Cook, stirring occasionally, 45 minutes to 1 hour, until sauce thickens.
● Cook fettuccine al dente.
● Add cognac to thickened spaghetti sauce. Bring to a boil. Serve fettuccini immediately topped with sauce. Garnish with sour cream and grated parmesan.

Victoria Eastman Ohlandt

Fettuccine with Double Cheese Sauce

1 pound fettuccine noodles
1 cup melted butter
1 cup freshly grated parmesan cheese
1 cup grated gruyère cheese
¾ cup heavy cream
Freshly ground pepper

Serves 6

● Cook pasta al dente in boiling salted water, then drain. Place hot, drained pasta in a heat-proof casserole over low heat. Add butter, cheeses, and cream, tossing after each addition.
● Sprinkle with pepper and serve.

Eugenia McCuen Thomason

Pasta, Cheese, and Eggs

Lasagne à la Française

Serves 8

1 chicken, 2½-3 pounds
1 carrot, sliced
2 celery ribs with leaves
1 onion, sliced
1 tablespoon tarragon
Salt and freshly ground pepper
2 pounds fresh spinach or 2-3
    packages (10 ounces each)
    frozen chopped spinach
½ cup butter
3 cups combined grated parmesan,
    swiss, and provolone cheeses
½ cup chopped onions
½ cup flour
2 cups chicken broth
1-1½ cups milk
⅔ cup dry white wine
¾ pound lasagne noodles
2 cups tomato sauce

• Cook chicken with sliced carrot, celery ribs, onion, tarragon, salt, and pepper in water to cover. When tender, remove chicken from broth and cool. Break meat in large pieces. Strain broth and refrigerate until fat can be skimmed from top.
• Cook, drain, and chop spinach. Season with 2 *tablespoons* butter and salt and pepper to taste.
• Mix together all the grated cheeses. Set aside.
• Prepare **Bèchamel Sauce:** Melt remaining 6 tablespoons butter in saucepan. Add chopped onions. Cook until golden. Add flour. Cook about 2 minutes, stirring constantly. Heat broth and milk together in a saucepan. Remove from heat. Add about ⅔ of the hot broth-milk mixture to butter-onion-flour roux. Add more, beating constantly with a wire whisk. Reserve ½ cup of the broth-milk mixture. Add wine. Return sauce to the burner. Cook about 5 minutes, stirring constantly. Add remaining hot liquid to thin the cooked sauce, if necessary.
• Cook lasagne noodles al dente. Drain and run under cold water. Place cooked noodles over colander until used, or leave in ice water. Drain and blot at the last minute before placing in casserole.
• Oil a lasagne pan. Layer cooked lasagne noodles, Bèchamel Sauce, spinach, cheeses, and chicken. Top with more sauce.
• Repeat layers. Sprinkle tomato sauce over Bèchamel Sauce. Top with a thick layer of cheeses.

Pasta, Cheese, and Eggs

continued

• Bake 30-40 minutes at 350° until bubbling. Remove from oven. Let stand 10 minutes before serving.

Mary Hegarty Seaman

Lasagne with Uncooked Noodles

¼ pound sweet Italian sausage
1 pound ground beef
6 cups marinara sauce
2 eggs
1 pound ricotta cheese
½ pound mozzarella cheese
2 cups hot water
¾-1 pound lasagne noodles
¼ cup grated parmesan or asiego cheese

Serves 8

• Remove sausage from casing. Brown sausage meat with ground beef in a skillet over medium heat, breaking up lumps with a fork. Remove meat with a slotted spoon and drain well. Place cooked meat in a large saucepan. Add marinara sauce and mix well. Bring to a simmer. Cook, partially covered, for 1-2 hours. This sauce can be made in advance.

• Beat eggs into ricotta. Dice mozzarella. Preheat oven to 400°.

• Spread a little meat sauce in the bottom of a lightly greased 9" x 13" baking pan. Mix in *1 cup* of hot water.

• Add a layer of uncooked noodles. Spoon some ricotta cheese-egg mixture down the center of each noodle. Cover with sauce and dot with mozzarella. Repeat these layers twice.

• Sprinkle with grated parmesan or asiego cheese. Pour remaining 1 cup hot water evenly over top. Cover tightly with foil and bake 30 minutes. Remove foil. Pasta should be almost tender. There will still be a lot of liquid in the pan.

• Continue to bake, uncovered, another 10-20 minutes. Cheese topping should be browned and most of the liquid will have evaporated. Allow lasagne to stand at room temperature for 15 minutes before serving.

Barbara Smith Suval

Pasta, Cheese, and Eggs

Linguine with Oysters

Serves 4-6

1 quart oysters
Bacon
Tabasco sauce
Salt and freshly ground pepper
Chopped parsley
3 cups Bèchamel Sauce (page 80)
½ pound parmesan cheese, grated
1 pound linguine

● Drain oysters, reserving liquor. Cut bacon strips in half and place an oyster on each. Top with a dash of tabasco, salt, pepper, and chopped parsley. Roll bacon around each oyster and skewer with a toothpick.
● Broil bacon-wrapped oysters until crisp, about 4 minutes on each side. Remove toothpicks. Keep warm.
● Make Bèchamel Sauce, adding oyster liquor, salt, pepper, and grated parmesan.
● Cook linguine in boiling, salted water with 1 tablespoon oil. Drain. Serve tossed with sauce and broiled oysters.

Susan Hendrickson Eden

Linguine with Roast Peppers

Serves 4-6

4 sweet red or green peppers, or a combination of both
1 pound linguine
1 small onion, thinly sliced
¼ cup olive oil
3 garlic cloves, minced
¼ teaspoon dried hot red pepper flakes
1 cup tomato sauce
Salt and freshly ground pepper
¼ cup chopped parsley

● Place whole peppers on a sheet of heavy-duty foil. Broil, turning often, until skins are burned all over. Hold peppers under cold water and pull off skins with your fingers. Cut into julienne strips, making about 1⅓ cups.
● Cook linguine in boiling, salted water.
● Sauté onion in the oil until it begins to brown. Add the garlic and cook briefly. Add roasted pepper strips, pepper flakes, tomato sauce, and salt and pepper to taste. Cook and stir until piping hot. Stir in the parsley.
● Drain linguine and serve hot with sauce.

Betsy Gimpel Mena

Pasta, Cheese, and Eggs

Macaroni in Cream

½ pound elbow macaroni
3 tablespoons butter
¾ cup ground ham, or 2-3 truffles,
    chopped
2 egg yolks
1 cup cream
¾ cup grated swiss cheese
Freshly grated nutmeg
Salt and freshly ground pepper to
    taste

Serves 6

● Boil macaroni in salted water for 12 minutes. Drain.
● Melt butter in a saucepan. Add cooked macaroni and ham or truffles. Mix egg yolks with cream. Add to pan along with cheese and seasonings. Reheat over a very low flame, stirring constantly. Serve immediately.

Nancy Beck Hoggson

Stuffed Manicotti in Tomato Sauce

3 tablespoons oil
2 garlic cloves, minced
1 can (28 ounces) tomato sauce
2 cans (1 pound each) tomatoes
2 tablespoons chopped parsley
½ teaspoon and 1 tablespoon sugar
½ teaspoon basil
Salt and freshly ground pepper to
    taste
1 recipe manicotti shells (recipe
    follows)
2 pounds ricotta cheese
½ pound mozzarella cheese, grated
½ cup grated parmesan and/or
    romano cheese
2 eggs

Serves 8-10

● Heat oil in large saucepan. Sauté minced garlic until lightly browned. Add tomato sauce, tomatoes, parsley, ½ teaspoon sugar, basil, salt, and pepper to taste. Simmer sauce while preparing manicotti shells.
● Combine cheeses with sugar and salt and pepper to taste. Add eggs. Beat well.
● Lightly grease a large, shallow baking dish. Pour in a thin layer of sauce. Place a generous spoonful of cheese mixture on each manicotti shell. Wrap sides of manicotti shell around filling. Arrange shells on sauce in one layer, filling dish completely. Pour remaining sauce over top. Sprinkle with grated parmesan. Bake at 350° for 20 minutes, or until sauce is bubbling.

Anne Ruthrauff Seltzer

83

Pasta, Cheese, and Eggs

Manicotti Shells

4 eggs
1 cup water or milk
1 cup flour
½ teaspoon salt
Oil

18-24 shells
● Beat eggs. Add milk, salt, and flour. Beat until smooth.
● Oil skillet. Pour in enough batter to make a thin 7″ pancake. Let pancake cook about 45 seconds. Do not turn over or let brown.
● Repeat this process, greasing skillet each time.

Judith Torrisi Wintermuth

Green Noodles and Broccoli

½ pound green noodles, cooked
1 cup mayonnaise
2 eggs
½ cup milk
1 tablespoon prepared mustard
Salt and pepper
1 package (10 ounces) chopped broccoli, cooked and drained
½ cup grated parmesan cheese

Serves 4-6
● Preheat oven to 300°. Mix all ingredients except grated parmesan.
● Place in a greased casserole. Sprinkle with grated parmesan. Bake 1 hour, then serve immediately.

Karin Rahm Carlson

Noodles à l'Alsacienne

½ pound fine noodles
Salt and freshly ground pepper to taste
5 tablespoons butter
1 hard-cooked egg, peeled and sieved
½ cup fine, fresh breadcrumbs
¼ cup finely chopped parsley

Serves 4
● Cook noodles in salted water. Drain. Add *1 tablespoon* butter, and salt and pepper to taste.
● Quickly add remaining 4 tablespoons butter to a skillet. When bubbling, add sieved hard-cooked egg and breadcrumbs. Cook about 30 seconds over high heat, shaking skillet and stirring. Add parsley and toss. Pour sauce over noodles. Mix and serve.

Nancy Beck Hoggson

Pasta, Cheese, and Eggs

Noodles with Mushrooms

½ cup butter
⅓ cup minced onion
1 garlic clove, minced
2 tablespoons lemon juice
1 cup sliced mushrooms
3-4 cups chicken broth
1 package (8 ounces) very thin
noodles

Serves 6

● Sauté first 5 ingredients for 6 minutes. Add broth and bring to a boil. Add noodles. Cook until all liquid is absorbed, about 7 minutes.

Susan Bremer Turner

Pasta Primavera

1 pound spaghetti
3 tablespoons olive oil
1½ cups coarsely chopped fresh
broccoli
1½ cups snow peas or 1 cup baby
peas
1 cup sliced zucchini (optional)
6 sliced asparagus stalks
2 medium tomatoes, chopped
3 teaspoons minced garlic
¼ cup chopped parsley
Salt and freshly ground pepper
⅓ cup pine nuts
10 mushrooms, sliced
1 cup heavy cream
½ cup grated parmesan cheese
⅓ cup butter
⅓ cup chopped fresh basil

Serves 6-8

● Cook spaghetti with salt and *1 tablespoon* oil in boiling water until barely tender.
● Blanch broccoli, peas, zucchini, and asparagus by pouring boiling water over. Let stand 3-4 minutes. Rinse in a colander under cold water. Set aside.
● Heat *1 tablespoon* olive oil in skillet. Add tomatoes, *1 teaspoon* garlic, parsley, salt, and pepper to taste. Sauté 2-3 minutes. Set aside and keep warm.
● Heat remaining 1 tablespoon oil in a large skillet. Sauté pine nuts over medium heat. Add remaining 2 teaspoons garlic, mushrooms, and blanched vegetables. Cook 3-5 minutes. Add cooked, drained spaghetti, cream, grated parmesan, butter, and basil. Mix gently with a fork. Top with sautéed tomatoes and serve immediately.

Sonia Collom Oram

Pasta, Cheese, and Eggs

Pasta with Broccoli-Pesto Sauce

1 small bunch broccoli
1 pound small shell pasta or
   vermicelli
1 tablespoon olive oil
1 large garlic clove, peeled
2 medium tomatoes, peeled and cut
   in 1" chunks, or 16 cherry
   tomatoes, halved
⅔ cup pesto sauce, at room
   temperature (see Index)
Salt and freshly ground pepper
½ cup freshly grated parmesan
   cheese

Serves 8

• Cut flowerets from broccoli. Slice stems crosswise in ¾" slices. Bring 2 quarts water to a boil. Add salt and all the broccoli. Cook 3-5 minutes. Drain and rinse in cold water.

• In the same pot, cook pasta al dente.

• Heat olive oil in a large skillet over medium heat. Add garlic and cook until brown. Add broccoli. Toss gently, heating through. Add tomatoes, remove from heat, and cover. Add salt and pepper to taste.

• Drain pasta. Arrange on a large, shallow, heated dish with broccoli and tomatoes on top. Discard garlic. Top with pesto and toss gently. Serve with grated parmesan.

Penelope Johnson Wartels

Spaghetti alla Carbonara

½ pound thickly sliced bacon
⅓ cup dry white wine or dry
   vermouth
1 pound spaghetti
2 eggs, well beaten
½ cup or more freshly grated
   parmesan or romano cheese
Freshly ground pepper

Serves 4-6

• Dice bacon in ½" pieces. Sauté until cooked but not crisp. Drain all but 4 tablespoons bacon fat from pan. Add wine and cook until quantity is reduced by about ⅓.

• Cook spaghetti. Drain and return to pot. Immediately add wine and bacon mixture. Mix well,then add eggs and cheese. Toss in pan as you would a salad, adding pepper to taste. Sprinkle with additional cheese as garnish.

Karin Lawrence Siegfried

Pasta, Cheese, and Eggs

Spaghetti Casserole

2 onions
1½ green peppers
½ cup plus 3 tablespoons butter
1 can (28 ounces) tomatoes
1 teaspoon salt
1 pound thin spaghetti
1 tablespoon oil
3 tablespoons flour
1 cup milk
1 cup cream
1 cup grated cheddar cheese
½ pound mushrooms, chopped
¼ cup chopped ripe olives

Serves 10-12

● Chop onions and green peppers. Sauté in ½ cup butter. Add tomatoes and salt. Bring to a boil and simmer 40 minutes.
● Cook spaghetti in boiling, salted water with 1 tablespoon oil until tender. Drain.
● Prepare cream sauce: Melt remaining 3 tablespoons butter and stir in flour until smooth. Gradually stir in milk and cream. Cook, stirring, until thickened. Add grated cheese and stir over heat until melted.
● Combine cooked spaghetti, mushrooms, olives, and tomato mixture. Cover with cream sauce. Bake at 300° for 1 hour.

Adrienne Wheeler Rudge

Spaghetti with Clams

1 tablespoon finely minced garlic
2 tablespoons olive oil
1 tablespoon finely chopped fresh
    basil, or 1½ teaspoons dried
1 teaspoon oregano
4 cups crushed tomatoes
¼ cup chopped parsley
1 dried hot red pepper
Salt and freshly ground pepper to
    taste
1 pound spaghetti or spaghettini
1 can (2 ounces) anchovies, drained
2 tablespoons capers, drained
12 pitted black olives
½ cup bottled clam juice (optional)
18 littleneck clams, scrubbed

Serves 4

● Cook garlic briefly in oil without browning. Add herbs, tomatoes, parsley, and dried pepper. Season to taste with salt and pepper. Bring to a boil, then simmer about 30 minutes.
● Cook spaghetti. Drain and keep warm.
● Chop anchovies and add to sauce. Stir in olives and drained capers. Reheat, stirring. Add clam juice to thin sauce, if necessary. Add clams. Cover pot closely and simmer slowly until clams open, about 5 minutes.
● Serve spaghetti topped with sauce and clams.

Susan Don Lubin

Pasta, Cheese, and Eggs

Spaghettini Rustico

2-3 large whole chicken breasts
4 cups chicken broth
2 sweet Italian sausages
5 tablespoons butter
3 tablespoons flour
½ cup heavy cream
2 cups tomato sauce
1 teaspoon worcestershire sauce
Tabasco sauce
6 tablespoons olive oil
2 cups chopped onion
1 cup chopped green pepper
1 cup chopped celery
1-2 tablespoons minced garlic
¾ pound ground round steak
Salt and freshly ground pepper
1 bay leaf
1 cup thinly sliced mushrooms
½ pound vermicelli or spaghettini
1 cup fresh or frozen green peas
½ pound sharp cheddar cheese, cut
    in small chunks

Serves 10-12

● Simmer chicken breasts in broth until tender, about 20 minutes. Drain, reserving broth. Separate cooled meat from bones, and cut in bite-sized pieces.

● Fry sausages until cooked through. Drain and reserve.

● Melt *3 tablespoons* butter. Whisk in flour. Add *1 cup* of reserved chicken broth. Cook and stir until thickened. Add cream and tomato sauce. Season to taste with worcestershire and tabasco.

● Heat oil in a large skillet. Sauté onion, green pepper, and celery until just tender. Add garlic and ground meat. Cook, stirring, until the meat loses its red color. Add tomato-cream sauce. Season to taste with salt, pepper, and bay leaf.

● Sauté sliced mushrooms in remaining 2 tablespoons butter. Add them to sauce. Slice sausage in ¼″ rings and set aside.

● Meanwhile, cook vermicelli or spaghettini in boiling, salted water for 4-5 minutes. Drain in a colander, and run under cold water.

● To assemble casserole, spoon a thin layer of sauce into the bottom of a deep baking dish. Add half each of the spaghettini, the chicken, the sausage, the peas, the cheese, and the sauce.

● Repeat layers. Stir with a fork to blend ingredients. Add 1½ cups of the remaining broth.

● Refrigerate, or bake now for 25-35 minutes in a 350° oven, until hot and bubbly. Add more broth during baking if necessary to keep pasta moist.

Elizabeth Raub Matisoo

Pasta, Cheese, and Eggs

Spaghetti with Mushrooms and Shrimp

½ cup butter
25-30 small frozen shrimp, or 6 very
  large fresh shrimp, cleaned and
  diced
1 small garlic clove, minced
4 large or 8 small mushrooms, sliced
  or chopped
1 pound thin spaghetti
3 tablespoons grated romano cheese
½ teaspoon salt
Freshly ground pepper

Serves 4

● Melt butter. Add shrimp, garlic, and mushrooms. Cook slowly for 5 minutes.

● Cook and drain spaghetti. Add to mixture in pan, tossing gently to mix. Sprinkle with romano cheese, salt, and pepper.

Susan Sample Marx

Spaghetti with Prosciutto

4 tablespoons butter
1 cup heavy cream
½ pound ham or prosciutto, diced
1 pound spaghetti
4 eggs, beaten
1 garlic clove, minced
½ teaspoon salt
⅛ teaspoon freshly ground pepper
2 tablespoons chopped chives
½ cup grated parmesan cheese

Serves 4

● Melt butter and add cream. Simmer 15 minutes over very low heat to reduce cream. Add ham. Simmer 2 more minutes.

● Cook spaghetti in boiling, salted water with 1 tablespoon oil. Drain.

● Gradually blend eggs and garlic into cream and ham mixture. Heat 1-2 minutes over very low heat. Do not overcook.

● Season with salt, pepper, and chives. Serve over hot, drained spaghetti with grated parmesan.

Leslie May Marra

Pasta, Cheese, and Eggs

Italian-Style Spaghetti Sauce

¼ cup finely chopped onion
1 garlic clove, minced
2 tablespoons olive oil
1 can (28 ounces) Italian tomatoes
2 cans (6 ounces) Italian tomato
  paste
¾ cup hot water
½ cup chopped parsley
¼ cup grated parmesan or romano
  cheese
1 tablespoon oregano
1½ teaspoons salt
½ teaspoon basil
¼ teaspoon sugar
1 cup fresh mushrooms, sliced
  (optional)

2 cups

• Sauté onion and garlic slowly in oil for about 5 minutes.
• Crush tomatoes coarsely with hands and add to onion and garlic. Stir in tomato paste and hot water. Add remaining ingredients except mushrooms. Cook, covered, for at least 4 hours. Stir often to prevent scorching.
• Add mushrooms for the last 15 minutes of cooking. Thin sauce with wine or water if it is too thick.

Donna Chisholm Clark

Quick Spaghetti Sauce

1 small onion, minced
1 garlic clove, minced
2 tablespoons olive oil
2 cups spaghetti sauce
16 green or black olives, pitted and
  sliced
1-2 tablespoons drained capers
1 tablespoon oregano
Salt and freshly ground pepper

2 cups

• Sauté onion and garlic in olive oil until softened. Add spaghetti sauce, olives, drained capers, oregano, salt, and pepper.
• Simmer 10-15 minutes.
  Variations: Add quartered slices of pepperoni, browned sausage meat, drained canned clams or well-scrubbed fresh clams, if desired. (Fresh clams will open as they cook in the sauce.)

Ann Dodds Costello

Pasta, Cheese, and Eggs

Uncooked Tomato Sauce

Serves 4-6

1-1½ pounds fresh, ripe tomatoes, skinned, seeded, and diced
½ cup olive oil
2 garlic cloves, minced
2-3 tablespoons chopped fresh basil and/or parsley
Salt and freshly ground pepper
1 pound vermicelli, spaghetti, or other pasta

● At least 2 hours before serving, place tomatoes with all their juices in a glass or porcelain dish. Add olive oil and toss. Add garlic and herbs. Marinate 2-4 hours at room temperature. Season to taste with salt and pepper.
● Stir gently and serve over 1 pound of hot, drained pasta.

Nancy Beck Hoggson

Tortellini with Parsley and Anchovy Cream Sauce

Serves 2-4

6 quarts water
1 tablespoon oil
1 tablespoon salt
½ pound fresh, meat-filled tortellini or cappelletti
2 garlic cloves
6 tablespoons clarified butter
⅓ cup minced parsley
¼ cup freshly grated parmesan cheese
4 teaspoons minced anchovy fillets
1 tablespoon minced fresh basil, or 1 teaspoon dried basil
¾ cup heavy cream

● In a large kettle, bring water to a boil with oil and salt. Drop in tortellini and boil for 15 minutes.
● While tortellini are cooking, sauté garlic in clarified butter until golden. Add parsley, grated parmesan, anchovies, and basil. Stir in heavy cream. Cook over moderate heat. Do not boil.
● When tortellini are cooked, drain in a colander and put back in cooking pot. Add sauce. Cook 5 minutes over low heat. Serve immediately.

Harmony Traulsen Stern

Pasta, Cheese, and Eggs

Beer and Cheese Soufflé

Serves 6

¼ cup butter, at room temperature
2 tablespoons Dijon mustard
10 slices day-old white bread, crusts
    removed
4 eggs, separated
¾ cup milk
Salt and freshly ground pepper
½ pound cooked ham, cut in ½"
    cubes
½ pound sharp cheddar cheese,
    grated
½ cup chopped green onion
½ cup beer
Pinch cream of tartar
⅛ teaspoon salt

• Generously butter a 1½-quart soufflé dish.
• Cream butter with mustard. Spread
each bread slice. Cut bread in 1"
cubes.
• Beat egg yolks with milk, salt, and
pepper. Add bread cubes, ham,
cheese, and chopped onion. Toss
lightly. Let stand about 15 minutes at
room temperature.
• Preheat oven to 350°. Stir beer into
bread mixture. Beat egg whites until
foamy. Add cream of tartar and salt.
Continue to beat until stiff. Fold about
¼ of the beaten egg whites into bread-
beer combination. Gently fold in rest of
the egg whites. Turn into prepared
soufflé dish. Bake 45 minutes until
puffed and golden brown. Serve immediately.

Diana Moody Huston

Cheese and Spinach Pie

Serves 6-8

¼ pound mushrooms, sliced
1 medium zucchini, thinly sliced
1 small onion, chopped
2 garlic cloves, minced
5 tablespoons butter
1 cup ham, cooked and cubed
1 package (10 ounces) frozen
    chopped spinach
1 pound ricotta cheese, drained
1 cup mozzarella cheese, grated
3 eggs, lightly beaten
2 tablespoons oil
1 teaspoon dill weed
Salt and freshly ground pepper to
    taste

• Sauté mushrooms, zucchini, onion,
and garlic in *3 tablespoons* butter until
vegetables are soft. Add ham and
sauté 2 minutes. Let mixture cool.
• Cook spinach. Drain and squeeze
dry. Preheat oven to 350°.
• In a bowl, combine ricotta, mozzarella, eggs, oil, and seasonings with
ham mixture. Add cooked, drained
spinach. Transfer mixture to an oiled
10" pie plate. Melt remaining 2 tablespoons butter. Drizzle over top of pie.
Bake 45-60 minutes in preheated
oven, or until knife inserted in center
comes out clean.

Leslie May Marra

Pasta, Cheese, and Eggs

Cheese Fondue

1 garlic clove, split
1 pound imported gruyère cheese, grated (4 cups)
Dash each salt and freshly ground pepper
1-1½ cups dry white wine
4 tablespoons cornstarch
2 tablespoons kirsch
2 tablespoons cold water
1 loaf crusty French bread

Serves 8-10

• Rub bottom and sides of a deep baking dish with garlic. Add cheese, salt, and pepper. Add wine almost to cover. Cook over medium heat, stirring constantly until cheese melts.

• Make a smooth paste with cornstarch, kirsch, and cold water. Stir cornstarch mixture into melted cheese and wine, using a wire whisk. Cook over medium heat, stirring, for 2-3 minutes, until fondue is creamy and thick.

• Cut bread in 1" cubes to serve with fondue. Keep warm over a candle burner, stirring occasionally.

Betsy Gimpel Mena

Cheese Strata

8 slices white bread
8 ounces cheddar cheese
¼ cup butter, melted
3 eggs
1 teaspoon salt
½ teaspoon freshly ground pepper
¾ teaspoon dry mustard
2 cups milk

Serves 6-8

• At least 4 hours before serving, or the night before, trim crusts from bread. Cut bread in 1" squares. Cut cheese into bite-sized pieces. In a greased shallow casserole (about 1½ quarts), alternate bread and cheese. Pour melted butter over top.

• Beat together eggs, seasonings, and milk. Pour over bread and cheese. Cover and refrigerate 4-8 hours.

• An hour before serving time, put covered casserole in a 350° oven. Bake 30 minutes. Uncover and bake 30 minutels more, until top is golden and puffy.

Ann Keyser Griffin

Pasta, Cheese, and Eggs

Chile Rice Casserole

¾ pound monterey jack cheese
3 cups sour cream
2 cans (4 ounces each) green chiles, chopped and partially seeded
½ teaspoon salt
3 cups cooked rice
½ cup grated cheddar cheese

Serves 8

● Cut jack cheese in strips. Mix sour cream and chiles with salt.
● In a buttered 1½-quart casserole, layer rice, cheese strips, and sour cream-chile mixture. Top with grated cheddar.
● Bake at 350° for 35 minutes.

Susan Sample Marx

Green Enchiladas Casserole

2 dozen corn tortillas
1 cup oil
2 cups grated cheddar cheese
1 cup chopped onion

Green Sauce
1 package (10 ounces) frozen chopped spinach
2 cans (10¾ ounces) cream of chicken soup
4 green onions, minced
2 cans (4 ounces each) chopped green chiles
2 cups sour cream
¼ teaspoon salt
1½ cups grated cheddar cheese

Serves 8-10

● Dip each tortilla in very hot oil. Drain and spread with grated cheese and chopped onion. Roll each filled tortilla and place in a shallow baking dish. When dish is full, cover tortillas with Green Sauce.
● To prepare Green Sauce, cook and drain spinach. Add soup, onions, and chiles. Purée in blender or food processor. Add sour cream and salt to taste, and mix well. Set aside.
● To freeze casserole, pour a little Green Sauce over filled enchiladas. Freeze remaining sauce separately to pour on at baking time.
● To bake, pour sauce over enchiladas. Sprinkle with remaining grated cheese. Cover and bake at 350° for 15 minutes.

Susan Sample Marx

94

Pasta, Cheese, and Eggs

Tortilla Torte

10 flour tortillas
½ pound grated monterey jack
    cheese
½ pound grated cheddar cheese
1 can (7 ounces) diced green chiles,
    drained
⅔ cup thinly sliced green onions
¼ cup sliced pitted olives, drained
    (optional)
2-3 tablespoons chili powder
    (optional)
3 tablespoons butter, melted

Serves 6-8

● Place 1 tortilla on a lightly greased, rimmed baking pan. Sprinkle evenly with ½ cup of each grated cheese, 1 tablespoon each of chiles and onions, and 1 teaspoon olive slices. Add chili powder, if desired.
● Cover with another tortilla. Repeat layers until you have used 4 tortillas. Top pile with 1 more tortilla. Brush with melted butter.
● Make another stack with remaining 5 tortillas, layering as above. Bake uncovered in a 400° oven until browned, about 25 minutes. Cut in wedges.

Susan Sample Marx

Baked Onion and Bacon Custard

3 tablespoons butter
2 large Spanish onions, finely
    chopped
6 eggs
8 slices bacon, cooked, drained,
    and crumbled
1 cup heavy cream
¼ cup milk
1 teaspoon salt
½ teaspoon freshly grated nutmeg
Freshly ground white pepper

Serves 4

● Generously butter a shallow 4½-cup baking dish. Preheat oven to 300°.
● Melt butter over medium heat. Add onion. Cover with a circle of wax paper and cook 10 minutes. Discard paper. Reduce heat to medium-low. Cook onion until completely soft but not brown, shaking pan occasionally.
● Beat eggs. Add sautéed onion, bacon, and remaining ingredients. Combine well, but do not overmix. Taste and adjust seasonings.
● Pour mixture into prepared dish. Bake 55-60 minutes, until puffed and browned. Let stand at room temperature about 10 minutes before cutting.

Nancy Beck Hoggson

Pasta, Cheese, and Eggs

Baked Eggs en Croustade

4-5 slices white bread, quartered
¼ cup butter, cut in 4 pieces
½ teaspoon salt
½ teaspoon sage
¼ teaspoon freshly ground pepper
1 egg white
6 eggs, at room temperature

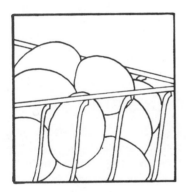

Serves 6

● Preheat oven to 375°. Chop bread coarsely in food processor. Spread crumbs on a cookie sheet and bake 10 minutes. Let crumbs cool. Return them to processor. Add butter and seasonings. Turn machine on and off several times until mixture is crumbly.

● Beat egg white until foamy. Stir in crumb mixture.

● Grease a 6-cup muffin pan. Divide crumb mixture among muffin tins, pressing against sides and bottoms to form ⅛″ crusts. Bake 8 minutes.

● Cover eggs with very hot tap water. Let stand 10 minutes, so whites and yolks will bake quickly and evenly.

● Crack eggs into baked crusts. Return pan to oven and bake 6 minutes. Whites sould be softly set and yolks runny.

● To remove. run a thin knife carefully around each cup. Transfer to a serving dish.

Variations: Add about 1 teaspoon of any creamed or chopped vegetable to bottom of pre-baked crusts before adding eggs.

Nancy Beck Hoggson

Pasta, Cheese, and Eggs

Brunch Eggs

2 cups diced cheddar cheese
¼ cup butter
1 cup light cream
2 teaspoons prepared mustard
½ teaspoon salt
½ teaspoon freshly ground pepper
12 eggs, beaten
Chopped fresh parsley or chives for
　　garnish, if desired

Serves 6
● Preheat oven to 325°. Spread cheese in greased casserole. Dot with butter. Combine cream, mustard, salt, and pepper. Pour half this mixture over cheese. Pour in eggs, then remaining cream mixture.
● Bake 40 minutes. Garnish with chopped fresh parsley or chives.

Katharine Knapp Sherwood

Crêpes à la Spinach Quiche

Crêpes
3 eggs
⅔ cup plus 3 tablespoons flour
½ teaspoon salt
1 cup milk
Oil

Filling
1½ cups shredded cheddar cheese
3 tablespoons flour
3 eggs, slightly beaten
⅔ cup mayonnaise
6 bacon slices, fried and crumbled
1 package (10 ounces) spinach,
　　thawed and drained
½ teaspoon salt
Dash freshly ground pepper

10 crêpes
● Mix crêpe batter. Let stand in refrigerator for 30 minutes. Brush crêpe pan with oil before cooking each crêpe. Cook 10 crêpes, each 6″ in diameter.
● To make quiche filling, toss cheese with flour. Add remaining ingredients. Mix well.
● Preheat oven to 350°. Place cooked crêpes in greased muffin cups. Fill to top with spinach mixture. Bake 30-40 minutes. A knife inserted in the center will come out clean when custard is set.

Karen Rudge Richards

97

Pasta, Cheese, and Eggs

Frittata

3 large leeks with green tops, peeled
1 large green pepper, seeded
1 medium zucchini, scrubbed
½ pound mushrooms, scrubbed, with
    stem tips trimmed
5 tablespoons butter
3 tablespoons olive oil
1 dozen eggs
¼ cup light cream
¼ teaspoon baking powder
Salt and freshly ground pepper
Fresh or dried basil
½ cup diced mozzarella cheese
Chopped parsley

Serves 4-6
● Chop vegetables coarsely. Melt *4 tablespoons* butter in a skillet. Sauté vegetables gently until cooked but still crisp. Add remaining butter and oil to pan with salt and pepper to taste. Remove from heat. Place in a 9″ x 13″ pan or a large oven-proof skillet.
● Preheat oven to 375°. Beat eggs with cream, baking powder, a dash of salt and pepper, and basil to taste. Place vegetable mixture back on medium heat. When it begins to sizzle, pour in egg mixture. Add mozzarella. Sauté 3-4 minutes.
● Bake for 15 minutes until brown and cooked through. Garnish with parsley.

Ann Dodds Costello

Hashed Brown Omelet

4-6 slices bacon
2 cups shredded potatoes
¼ cup chopped onion
4 eggs
¼ cup milk
½ teaspoon salt
Freshly ground pepper
1 cup shredded sharp cheddar
    cheese

Serves 4-6
● Cook bacon until crisp, then drain and crumble. Leave drippings in skillet. Mix potatoes and onion. Pat into skillet and cook over low heat until bottom is crisp and brown.
● Blend eggs, milk, salt, and pepper. Pour over potatoes. Top with cheese and crumbled bacon. Cover and cook over low heat for 20 minutes.

Marilyn Seltzer Clark

98

Pasta, Cheese, and Eggs

Apple Pancake

8 extra-large eggs
1 cup flour
2 tablespoons sugar
1 teaspoon baking powder
⅛ teaspoon salt
2 cups milk
¼ cup butter, melted
2 teaspoons vanilla extract
½ teaspoon freshly grated nutmeg
½ cup butter
1⅓ cups sugar
1 teaspoon cinnamon
2 large, tart apples, peeled, halved,
    cored, and thinly sliced

Serves 8-10

● Combine eggs, flour, sugar, baking powder, salt, and milk in a mixing bowl. Blend until smooth. Add melted butter, vanilla, and ¼ *teaspoon* nutmeg. Blend thoroughly. Let stand at room temperature for 30 minutes, or in refrigerator overnight.

● Preheat oven to 425°. Melt ½ cup butter in oven in two 10″ ovenproof skillets. Brush butter to coat sides of pans. Remove from oven.

● Combine sugar, cinnamon, and nutmeg. Sprinkle ⅓ cup of this mixture over melted butter in each skillet. Divide apple slices evenly between the two pans, arranging in a layer. Sprinkle apples with the rest of the cinnamon sugar.

● Place pans over medium-high heat until mixture bubbles. Divide batter evenly, pouring half into each pan. Place in oven for 15 minutes, then reduce heat to 375° and bake 10 minutes longer. Slide onto heated serving platters, cut into wedges, and serve immediately.

Donna Chisholm Clark

Pasta, Cheese, and Eggs

Puff Pancake

4 tablespoons butter
2 eggs
½ cup flour
½ cup milk
Pinch nutmeg
Topping: Grated cheese, or lemon
    juice and confectioners sugar, or
    cinnamon sugar

Serves 2-3

● Preheat oven to 425°. Place butter to melt in oven in a heavy, large oven-proof skillet or 9" round cake pan.
● Beat eggs. Beat in flour, milk, and nutmeg. Pour batter into sizzling butter in pan. Bake 20 minutes until puffed and brown. Sprinkle with topping, cut in wedges, and serve immediately.

Variation: With cheese topping, this is like a Yorkshire pudding. With sweet toppings, it is good for breakfast or brunch.

Josephine Lane van der Hoeven

Souffléed Pancakes

½ cup cornmeal
1 tablespoon sugar
½ teaspoon salt
1 cup boiling water
2 eggs, separated
1 cup flour
1 tablespoon baking powder
1 cup milk or buttermilk
¼ cup vegetable oil

Serves 4-6

● Combine cornmeal, sugar, and salt in a saucepan. Pour boiling water over mixture, stirring constantly with a whisk. Cook, stirring, about 2 minutes. Let cool, then add egg yolks.
● Sift together flour and baking powder. Stir into batter. Add milk and oil.
● Beat egg whites until stiff. Fold in. Let batter sit at room temperature about 15 minutes before cooking.
● Lightly oil a griddle or skillet. Heat until water sprinkled on the surface dances in little balls. Ladle pancakes onto hot skillet and brown. Turn and cook the other side.

Note: This batter can be refrigerated and used the next day. The pancakes will be thinner, but still light. Cook all the batter and freeze pancakes as you would freeze crêpes. separating them with wax paper. Pop cooked pancakes in toaster to reheat.

Nancy Beck Hoggson

Pasta, Cheese, and Eggs

Chicken-Broccoli Quiche

1 unbaked 9" or 10" pastry shell
1¼ cups boned cooked chicken
8 medium mushrooms
1 small onion, peeled and quartered
1 tablespoon butter
¼ pound imported gruyère or swiss
    cheese, grated
1 package (10 ounces) frozen
    chopped broccoli, defrosted and
    squeezed dry
4 eggs
1½ cups heavy cream
1½ teaspoons salt
¼ teaspoon dried tarragon
¼ teaspoon freshly grated nutmeg
Freshly ground pepper to taste

Serves 6

● Preheat oven to 450°.

● Coarsely chop chicken, mushrooms, and onion. Sauté in butter over moderate heat until most of the moisture evaporates. Remove from heat.

● Sprinkle half the grated cheese over the pastry. Spread broccoli over cheese in an even layer. Spread chicken-mushroom-onion mixture over all. Sprinkle with remaining cheese.

● Mix eggs, cream, and seasonings and pour into pastry shell. Bake 10 minutes. Reduce oven temperature to 325°. Bake 20-25 minutes longer, until filling is brown and firm. Let stand 10 minutes before serving.

Nancy Beck Hoggson

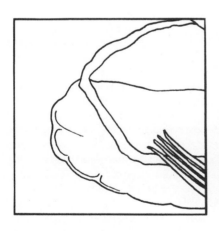
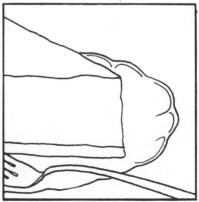

Pasta, Cheese, and Eggs

Spinach Quiche

2 unbaked 8″ pastry shells
1 tablespoon soft butter
1 pound bacon
4 eggs
2 cups heavy cream
¾ teaspoon salt
Pinch nutmeg
Pinch sugar
Pinch cayenne pepper
⅛ teaspoon freshly ground pepper
1 package (10 ounces) frozen
    chopped spinach, thawed
1 cup grated swiss cheese

Serves 8-10

● Preheat oven to 425°. Rub soft butter over surface of pastry shells.
● Fry bacon until crisp. Drain and crumble.
Combine eggs, cream, seasonings, and well-drained, thawed spinach. Mix thoroughly. Sprinkle crumbled bacon and grated cheese in pastry shells. Pour in cream mixture.
● Bake 15 minutes, then reduce oven temperature to 300° and bake 40 minutes more.

Robin McNevin Robertson

Broccoli Quiche

1 unbaked 9″ pastry shell
1 package (10 ounces) frozen
    broccoli, or fresh
¼ cup butter
4 tablespoons flour
2 cups light cream
½ teaspoon salt
¼ teaspoon dry mustard
Dash each cayenne and white
    pepper
2 eggs, lightly beaten
1 cup grated swiss cheese

Serves 4-6

● Preheat oven to 450°. Prick unbaked pastry with a fork to prevent bubbling. Bake 5 minutes.
● Cook broccoli in ½″ of boiling, salted water just until stalks are separated. Drain, chop coarsely, and set aside.
● Melt butter. Remove from heat and blend in flour. Cook 1 minute. Remove from heat and add cream, stirring until smooth. Return to heat. Stir and cook until thickened. Add seasonings and stir. Blend a little of this hot sauce into the beaten eggs. Add immediately to rest of sauce. Add cheese and continue to stir until cheese melts.
● Place chopped broccoli in pastry shell. Pour cheese mixture over. Bake 10 minutes. then reduce oven temperature to 350°. Bake 15-20 minutes more.

Laura Treadway Moreno

Pasta, Cheese, and Eggs

Tomato Quiche

1 unbaked 9″ pastry shell
¾ cup grated parmesan cheese
½ cup sliced green onions, tops included
1 large tomato, peeled and sliced
Flour
½ cup sliced black olives
3 egg yolks
1½ cups heavy cream
½ teaspoon salt
Freshly ground pepper to taste

Serves 4-6

• Preheat oven to 400°. Sprinkle unbaked pastry with ¼ *cup* grated parmesan and *half* the green onions. Dust tomato slices with flour. Add to pie. Add another ¼ *cup* parmesan and the rest of the green onions. Sprinkle sliced olives over all.

• Beat egg yolks. Stir in cream, salt, and pepper. Add to quiche and sprinkle with remaining ¼ cup grated parmesan.

• Bake 35-45 minutes until golden brown.

Karin Lawrence Siegfried

Zucchini and Ham Quiche

1 unbaked 10″ pastry shell
1¼ pounds zucchini, trimmed and shredded (about 5 cups)
2 tablespoons butter
¼ cup finely chopped onion
1 small garlic clove, minced
Salt and freshly ground pepper
¾-1 cup finely diced ham
4 eggs
¾ cup milk
½ cup heavy cream
¼ cup grated parmesan cheese

Serves 6-8

• Preheat oven to 350°. Prick pastry with a fork. Line with foil. Add rice or beans to prevent bubbling. Bake 20 minutes. Do not brown. Remove foil and beans from pastry. Turn up oven heat to 375°. Let pastry cool.

• Shred zucchini and place in a colander. Sprinkle with salt. Squeeze in the corner of a towel to remove excess moisture.

• Heat butter in a skillet. Add onion and garlic. Cook, stirring, until soft. Add salt, pepper, and zucchini. Taste and adjust seasonings. Cook for three minutes, then blend in ham and remove from heat.

• Beat eggs with milk and cream. Stir into zucchini mixture. Pour zucchini custard into pastry shell. Sprinkle with grated parmesan.

• Bake 30 minutes. Reduce oven heat to 350° and bake 15 minutes more until done.

Joan Cooley May

103

Pasta, Cheese, and Eggs

Scotch Eggs

1 pound bulk sausage
6 hard-cooked eggs, peeled
2 eggs, beaten
2 cups well-seasoned fine
    breadcrumbs
Oil for frying

Serves 6

• Divide sausage meat in 6 portions. Pat dry peeled, hard-cooked eggs. Wrap sausage meat evenly around each egg by molding it and patting into place with damp hands. Meat should be about ½″ thick all around, and eggs should be completely covered.

• Dip in beaten egg. Roll in bread-crumbs to coat well. Heat 3″ of oil in a large skillet. Lower eggs into skillet with a spoon and deep fry 3-4 minutes, turning. Let cool on paper towels. Halve or quarter the eggs and serve at room temperature.

Cheryl Giffin Carter

Bacon Omelet Soufflé

6 slices bacon, diced
6 eggs
3 tablespoons heavy cream
⅛ teaspoon salt
Freshly ground pepper

Serves 4

• Sauté bacon until lightly colored. Transfer to paper towels with a slotted spoon. Divide bacon fat among 4 round baking dishes about 1½″ deep, or pour into a 1½-quart casserole. Heat baking dishes in 400° oven.

• Separate eggs. Beat yolks with cream, salt, and pepper. Beat egg whites with salt until they hold stiff peaks. Stir ¼ of the whites into yolk mixture, then fold in remaining whites and bacon. Gently pour mixture into baking dishes and bake at 400°, 10 minutes for individual soufflés, 30 minutes for large soufflé.

Nancy Beck Hoggson

Pasta, Cheese, and Eggs

Broccoli Soufflé

Serves 4

1 small bunch broccoli, or 1 package
   (10 ounces) frozen chopped
   broccoli
3 tablespoons butter
3 tablespoons flour
1 cup milk
3 eggs, separated
½ teaspoon salt
¼ teaspoon freshly ground pepper

● Cook and drain broccoli.
● Melt butter over medium heat. Stir in flour until smooth. Add milk, stirring constantly until thick and bubbly. Remove from heat and add egg yolks one at a time. Mix in salt, pepper, and drained broccoli.
● Preheat oven to 350°. Beat egg whites until they hold soft peaks. Fold into broccoli mixture. Turn into an ungreased 1-quart soufflé dish.
● Bake for 45 minutes, until puffed and brown.

Susan Sample Marx

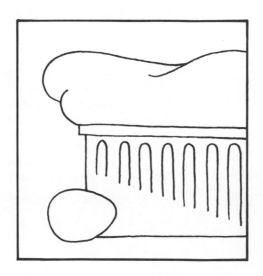

Pasta, Cheese, and Eggs

Cheese Soufflé

4 tablespoons butter
½ cup finely grated parmesan
    cheese
3 tablespoons flour
1 cup milk
6 tablespoons grated gruyère cheese
4 egg yolks
½ teaspoon salt
Dash nutmeg
Dash cayenne pepper
5 egg whites
Pinch cream of tartar

Serves 6

● Brush the inside of a 1½-quart soufflé dish or 6 individual 1-cup soufflé dishes with *1 tablespoon* melted butter. Dust lightly with *2 tablespoons* grated parmesan cheese.

● Melt remaining 3 tablespoons butter in a heavy pan. Add flour. Cook gently, stirring until smooth. Remove from heat. Scald milk and add to butter-flour mixture. Beat with a whisk until smooth. Return to heat and cook, stirring, until thickened.

● Add remaining grated parmesan along with gruyère cheese. Mix until dissolved. Cool slightly. Beat in egg yolks one at a time. Add seasonings. If desired, cover with plastic wrap until about 1 hour before serving time.

● Preheat oven to 400°. Beat egg whites until foamy. Add cream of tartar. Continue to beat until definite peaks are formed. Fold 2 tablespoons of beaten egg whites into the soufflé mixture, then fold in the rest of the beaten egg whites.

● Spoon into prepared dishes until ⅔ full. Dust lightly with grated parmesan. Place in oven and immediately reduce heat to 375°. Bake 15 minutes if using 1-cup soufflé dishes and 30 minutes if using a 1½-quart soufflé dish.

Nancy Beck Hoggson

Pasta, Cheese, and Eggs

Romaine Soufflé

1 medium head romaine lettuce
4 tablespoons butter
3 green onions, chopped
3 tablespoons flour
1 cup milk or light cream
4 eggs
1 cup shredded cheddar cheese
½ teaspoon worcestershire sauce
1 teaspoon salt
2-3 dashes tabasco sauce
Grated parmesan cheese

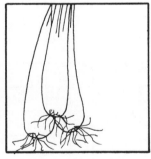

Serves 4-6

● Cut bottom from lettuce. Wash thoroughly, then chop coarsely. Put in a heavy saucepan with ½" water in the bottom, and cook until wilted. Drain well, then chop very finely.

● Melt *1 tablespoon* butter in a skillet. Cook onions until soft but not brown. Add chopped romaine and cook, stirring, until moisture has evaporated.

● Melt remaining 3 tablespoons butter. Add flour. Cook 2-3 minutes, stirring. Heat milk and add, stirring over medium-low heat until sauce thickens.

● Separate eggs. Beat yolks into hot sauce one at a time. Add shredded cheese and cook until smooth. Stir in lettuce and onions to blend well, then add worcestershire, salt, and tabasco. This can wait several hours until you are ready to assemble and bake the soufflé.

● Butter a 1½-quart soufflé dish generously. Sprinkle sides and bottom with grated parmesan. Shake out excess. Butter a foil collar and attach.

● Preheat oven to 400°. Beat egg whites until they hold soft peaks. Stir about ⅓ of the whites into lettuce mixture, blending thoroughly. Add remaining egg whites and fold in loosely.

● Pour into prepared soufflé dish and smooth top. Sprinkle with grated parmesan, and place in oven. Immediately reduce oven temperature to 375° and bake 25-30 minutes.

Mary Vance Watson

salads and
salad dressings

Salad Makings

Arrange orange or grapefruit sections with thin onion slices on a bed of lettuce. Drizzle with Poppy Seed Dressing (see Index).

Try a rice wine vinegar or walnut oil for a new twist to a classic vinaigrette dressing.

Briefly cook whole green beans. Drain. While they are still warm, toss with homemade vinaigrette. Add chopped green onions, dill, or parsley. Refrigerate and serve on lettuce.

Make a simple dressing for fruit salads by beating 1 cup softened vanilla ice cream with 3 tablespoons mayonnaise. (Under no circumstances is bottled "salad dressing" interchangeable with mayonnaise.)

Steam broccoli stalks until tender. Top with paper-thin shavings of radish and homemade vinaigrette.

Toast walnuts or pecans in homemade garlic-butter. Use to accent a green salad.

Combine sections of pink grapefruit and crumbles of roquefort cheese on lettuce. Add oil and vinegar dressing (3 parts oil to 1 part vinegar).

When adding tomatoes to a salad, slice them vertically so they weep less. Dress them separately and add to the salad at the last moment.

Rub a stale heel of bread with a split garlic clove. Add this *chapon* to the bowl with salad ingredients and dressing. Toss, then remove the bread. Serve the salad at once.

Rather than iceberg lettuce, try romaine, bibb, boston, leaf lettuce, or spinach in combination with chicory, endive, watercress, or arugula.

Shred cooked beets and add to chicory, endive, arugula, or watercress.

Marinate thinly sliced fresh vegetables in vinaigrette. Add to a green salad.

Salads and Salad Dressings

Artichoke-Rice Salad

2 cups chicken broth or bouillon
1 cup uncooked white rice
2 green onions, chopped with stems
½ green pepper, chopped
12 pimiento-stuffed olives
1 jar (6 ounces) marinated artichoke
    hearts, drained
¾ teaspoon curry powder
3 tablespoons mayonnaise
Fresh lemon juice to taste

Serves 6
● Boil chicken broth. Add rice. Simmer 15-20 minutes until rice is tender.
● Add green onions, green peppers, olives, artichokes, curry powder, and mayonnaise. Stir in lemon juice. Serve warm or chilled.

Jane Miller Moritz

Asparagus Salad

2 pounds fresh asparagus (about 4
    cups), cut diagonally
2 tablespoons sesame seed oil
3 tablespoons light soy sauce
½ teaspoon sugar
10 drops sesame seed oil with chili

Serves 6-8
● Bring to a boil enough salted water to cover asparagus. Drop in asparagus and return to boil. Cook 1-2 minutes. Drain and rinse immediately in cold water to stop cooking. Drain again. Chill.
● Mix sesame seed oil, soy sauce, sugar, and chili-flavored oil. Toss with asparagus. Adjust seasonings.

Deborah Morrow Hunter

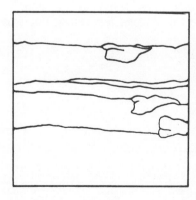

Salads and Salad Dressings

Avocado Mousse with Shrimp

Serves 8-10

2 large or 3 medium avocados
5 ounces chicken bouillon
Juice of half a lemon
1 tablespoon finely chopped onion
2 teaspoons worcestershire sauce
½ teaspoon salt
2 envelopes unflavored gelatin
½ cup cold water
1¼ cups mayonnaise
½ cup heavy cream, whipped
¾ pound shrimp, cooked and shelled
Catsup, worcestershire sauce, and
    Dijon mustard
Chopped fresh parsley

● Peel, quarter, and pit avocados. Purée with chicken bouillon, lemon juice, onion, worcestershire, and salt.
● Sprinkle gelatin on cold water. Set in a pan of hot water until gelatin is dissolved. Blend into mousse mixture. Fold in ½ *cup* mayonnaise and the whipped cream. Pour into greased 1-quart ring mold. Chill several hours or overnight.
● Mix shrimp with remaining ¾ cup mayonnaise, catsup, worcestershire, and Dijon mustard to taste. Chill until serving time.
● Unmold mousse. Fill center with shrimp mixture. Sprinkle with chopped parsley.

Donna Chisholm Clark

French Beef and Mushroom Salad

Serves 4

½ cup olive oil
3 tablespoons white wine vinegar
4 teaspoons chopped capers, rinsed
    and drained
4 teaspoons minced fresh parsley
2 teaspoons Dijon mustard
½ teaspoon chopped fresh tarragon
Salt and freshly ground pepper
Chilled, cooked flank steak or
    London broil, cut in matchstick
    strips
½ pound mushrooms, sliced
Lettuce leaves
Tomato wedges, stuffed eggs, olives,
    cornichons, marinated artichoke
    hearts, or tiny dill pickles for
    garnish

● Combine first 6 ingredients with salt and pepper to taste. Blend well in a mixing bowl. Add beef and mushrooms. Toss to coat. Cover and marinate 1 hour at room temperature.
● Line 4 plates with lettuce and divide salad evenly.

Nancy Beck Hoggson

Salads and Salad Dressings

Broccoli Dome

2 bunches broccoli (about 2 pounds)
⅓ cup fresh lemon juice
1-2 teaspoons Dijon mustard
Salt to taste
Freshly ground white pepper to taste
1 cup olive oil
3 tablespoons drained capers
1 jar (4 ounces) pimientos
¼ cup sliced stuffed olives
2 tablespoons minced parsley
4-6 anchovy fillets
Parsley sprigs and stuffed olives for
    garnish

Serves 6

● Trim flowerets from broccoli, leaving 2" stems. Rinse and drain. Steam broccoli until barely tender, about 6 minutes. Do not overcook. Drain and rinse in cold water.
● Place broccoli flowerets head down in the bottom of a large mixing bowl. When bottom is lined, work broccoli up the sides of the bowl. Place all flowerets with stems toward center of bowl and heads against sides. Fill center of bowl with any remaining pieces. Cover with a plate set into bowl to pack broccoli together. Cover and refrigerate for several hours.
● To make vinaigrette, mix lemon juice and mustard with salt and pepper. Beat oil in slowly, mixing until smooth and thick. Stir in capers, 3 tablespoons diced pimientos, sliced olives, and minced parsley. Let stand several hours.
● To serve, invert a plate over the bowl of broccoli and broccoli will unmold. Garnish with strips of remaining pimientos, anchovy fillets, more stuffed olives, and parsley sprigs.
● Mix vinaigrette. Taste for seasonings and pour into a serving bowl. Serve with broccoli.

Penelope Johnson Wartels

Salads and Salad Dressings

Our Favorite Caesar Salad

2-3 garlic cloves, crushed
½ teaspoon dry mustard
½ teaspoon worcestershire sauce
6 tablespoons grated parmesan
    cheese
2 tablespoons wine vinegar
2 tablespoons lemon juice
½ cup olive oil
2 egg yolks
1 large head romaine lettuce
½ cup croutons (see Index)

Serves 6-8

● Mix garlic, mustard, worcestershire, and *1 tablespoon* parmesan in a large, clear bowl (not wooden). Beat in vinegar, lemon juice, and olive oil. Add egg yolks. Mix well. Let stand 30 minutes at room temperature.
● Wash and dry lettuce. Tear into large pieces. Add lettuce to dressing in bowl. Sprinkle with remaining parmesan and croutons, and toss.

Judith Freyermuth Rex

Caponata

1 eggplant, unpeeled and diced
1 large onion, chopped
½ green pepper, chopped
2 garlic cloves, minced
⅓ cup olive or salad oil
1 can (6 ounces) tomato paste
½ cup stuffed olives, sliced
¼ pound mushrooms, chopped
¼ cup capers
¼ cup red wine vinegar
¼ cup water
1 tablespoon sugar
1 teaspoon salt
½ teaspoon basil
½ teaspoon oregano
Tabasco sauce to taste

2 cups

● Combine eggplant, onion, green pepper, garlic, and oil in a large skillet. Cover and simmer 10 minutes. Add remaining ingredients. Simmer covered for 20-25 minutes. Chill before serving.

    Note: Good as a dip or salad. Cut vegetables in larger chunks for the latter and serve on lettuce. Freezes well.

Barbara Smith Suval

Salads and Salad Dressings

Carrots Vinaigrette

2 pounds carrots, sliced
1 cup condensed tomato soup
1 cup sugar
¾ cup vinegar
½ cup salad oil
1 teaspoon dry mustard
Dash salt
1 large green pepper, diced
1 small onion, diced

Serves 6
● Steam carrot slices 5-8 minutes. Carrots should be crisp.
● Combine soup, sugar, vinegar, oil, mustard, and salt. Mix well. Stir in diced green pepper and onion. Pour over warm carrots. Chill.
● Drain carrots before serving.

Barbara Byrne Esau

Chick Pea Salad

1 can (20 ounces) chick peas, rinsed
    and drained
¼ cup tarragon vinegar
½ cup olive oil
1 garlic clove, crushed
½ teaspoon salt
Freshly ground pepper
½ cup stuffed olives, sliced
¼ pound sliced hard salami, cut in
    thin strips
Salad greens
3 tablespoons chopped scallions
2 tomatoes, peeled, seeded, and
    diced

Serves 6
● Rinse and drain chick peas.
● Combine vinegar, oil, garlic, salt, and pepper in bowl. Stir in chick peas, olives, and salami. Mix lightly. Chill several hours.
● To serve, turn into a bowl lined with salad greens. Sprinkle with scallions. Garnish with tomatoes.

Victoria Eastman Ohlandt

115

Salads and Salad Dressings

Crunchy Hot Chicken Salad

4 whole chicken breasts, cooked and
  skinned
3 hard-cooked eggs, sliced
½ can condensed cream of chicken
  soup
2 cups finely cut celery
1 cup mayonnaise
1 cup sour cream
1 can (8 ounces) water chestnuts,
  drained and sliced
1 can (4 ounces) mushroom pieces,
  drained
½ cup slivered almonds
2 tablespoons minced onion
2 tablespoons lemon juice
1 teaspoon salt
¼ teaspoon pepper
1 cup grated cheddar cheese
1 can (3½ ounces) fried onion rings,
  slightly crushed

Serves 10-12

● Cut chicken in 1″ pieces. Mix with remaining ingredients, except cheese and onion rings. Turn into a lightly greased 9″ x 13″ casserole. Top with cheese and bake at 350° for 30 minutes. Sprinkle onion rings over top. Bake 15 minutes longer.

Linda Cantrell Lindon

Salads and Salad Dressings

Curried Chicken Salad with Avocado and Bacon

1 tablespoon butter
1 tablespoon flour
1 cup chicken stock
1 cup light cream
2 teaspoons curry powder, to taste
Salt and freshly ground pepper
1 beaten egg yolk
4 cups diced cooked chicken or turkey
1 cup green seedless grapes
½ cup coarsely chopped celery
½ cup sliced green onions
¼ cup coarsely chopped walnuts
Romaine lettuce, torn in small pieces
1 avocado, peeled and thinly sliced
½ pound bacon, cooked and crumbled

Serves 4-6

● Melt butter over medium heat. Stir in flour. Cook 2 minutes, stirring constantly. Heat stock and add a little at a time. Stir vigorously. Add cream, curry powder, salt, and pepper. Add beaten egg yolk, stirring constantly. Cook until thick. Pour over chicken or turkey. Add grapes, celery, green onions, and walnuts. Chill.

● Toss lettuce with chilled chicken salad to serve. Garnish with avocado strips and crumbled bacon.

Pamela Neill Collins

Indian Melon Chicken Salad

2 cups coarsely chopped chicken or turkey
1 can (8 ounces) water chestnuts, thinly sliced
½ pound seedless green grapes (optional)
½ cup chopped celery
1 cup mayonnaise
½ teaspoon curry powder
1 tablespoon lemon juice
¼ teaspoon salt
¼ teaspoon pepper
1 teaspoon soy sauce
1 cup honeydew melon balls
1 cup cantaloupe melon balls
4-5 lettuce leaves

Serves 4

● Combine chicken, chestnuts, grapes, and celery.

● Mix mayonnaise with curry powder, lemon juice, salt, pepper, and soy sauce. Combine mayonnaise and chicken mixtures. Chill well to blend flavors.

● Add melon balls to chicken salad. Serve in lettuce cups. Use additional melon balls for garnish.

Susan Necarsulmer Dallin

Salads and Salad Dressings

Layered Chicken Salad

2 cups cubed cooked chicken
½ teaspoon curry powder
¾ teaspoon salt
¼ teaspoon paprika
Dash pepper
2 cups shredded iceberg lettuce
2 cups shredded romaine lettuce
1 large cucumber, sliced
1 cup small shell macaroni, cooked
   and drained
1 small green pepper, chopped
1½ cups mayonnaise
2 tablespoons milk
2 tablespoons lemon juice

Garnish:
2 tomatoes, cut in wedges
2 tablespoons chopped parsley

Serves 8

● Combine chicken, curry, ¼ *teaspoon* salt, paprika, and a dash of pepper. Toss to coat well.

● In a large clear salad bowl, layer lettuce, chicken, cucumber, macaroni, and green pepper. Stir mayonnaise with milk, lemon juice, remaining ½ teaspoon salt, and a dash of pepper. Spread over all.

● Cover and chill several hours or overnight. Garnish with tomato wedges and parsley.

Robin Collins Vermylen

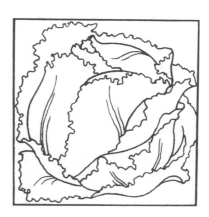

Salads and Salad Dressings

Piquant Chicken Rice Salad

1 chicken (2½-3 pounds) or 2 whole
    chicken breasts
1 small onion
1 celery rib
Salt and pepper
1 cup long-grain white rice
¾ cup olive oil
¼ cup red wine vinegar
2 teaspoons Dijon mustard
½ teaspoon salt
Freshly ground pepper
½ cup chopped red pepper
½ cup coarsely grated swiss cheese
⅓ cup sour gherkins, capers, or
    artichoke hearts
¼ cup sliced, pitted ripe black olives

Serves 4-6

● Cook chicken in water to cover with onion, celery, salt, and pepper until tender, 30-45 minutes. Strain stock, removing chicken. Reduce stock by boiling vigorously for 20 minutes.
● When chicken has cooled, remove skin and bones. Cut meat into bite-sized pieces. Cover and refrigerate.
● Bring to a boil *2 cups* of chicken broth. Add rice. Cook 15-20 minutes, until rice is tender. Remove from heat and let stand 5 minutes.
● Put oil, vinegar, mustard, salt, and pepper to taste in small, screw-top jar. Cover and shake to mix. Mix hot rice and chicken with dressing. Toss gently to mix. Add remaining ingredients. Toss again. Serve warm or at room temperature.

Nancy Beck Hoggson

Surprise Chicken Salad

⅓ cup mayonnaise
¼ cup diced celery
2 tablespoons horseradish
2 tablespoons milk
10-12 slices bacon, fried and
    crumbled
¾ pound cooked, diced chicken
½ pound swiss or jarlsberg cheese,
    cut in ½" cubes
4 large tomatoes
½ head iceberg lettuce, shredded

Serves 4

● Combine mayonnaise, celery, horseradish, milk, and bacon. Save a little bacon for garnish. Gently fold in chicken and cheese cubes until well coated. Chill until serving time.
● To serve salad, cut each tomato into 8 wedges, but not quite through. Spread wedges apart. Spoon chicken mixture into each tomato. Sprinkle with reserved bacon. Serve over shredded lettuce.

Helen Schreiner Bradley

Salads and Salad Dressings

Blue Cheese Cole Slaw with Almonds

1 cup sour cream
¾ cup bottled blue cheese salad
    dressing
3 ounces blue cheese, crumbled
2 teaspoons freshly ground black
    pepper
8 cups shredded cabbage
1 onion, finely chopped
2 tablespoons minced parsley
6 ounces slivered almonds, toasted

Serves 12

● Combine sour cream, blue cheese dressing, crumbled cheese, and pepper. Toss cabbage, onions, and *half* the parsley with dressing. Place in serving dish and chill.
● Before serving, garnish with toasted almonds and remaining parsley.

Victoria Eastman Ohlandt

Cranberry Mold

1 can (9 ounces) crushed pineapple
1 package (3 ounces) cherry flavored
    gelatin
½ cup sugar
1 cup hot water
1 tablespoon lemon juice
1 cup ground fresh cranberries
1 cup chopped celery
1 small orange, seeded and ground
    with skin
½ cup chopped walnuts

Serves 8-10

● Drain pineapple, reserving syrup. Add enough water to pineapple syrup to make ½ cup. Dissolve gelatin and sugar in 1 cup hot water. Add reserved pineapple syrup-water and lemon juice. Chill until partially set.
● Add remaining ingredients. Pour into lightly greased 1-quart mold. Chill overnight.

Valerie Korn Luther

Salads and Salad Dressings

Cucumbers with Dill

4 large cucumbers
2 tablespoons salt
1 cup white vinegar
¼ cup sugar
½ teaspoon white pepper
2 tablespoons snipped fresh dill

Serves 6-8

• The day before serving, scrub cucumbers with vegetable brush. Wipe dry with paper towels. Cut unpared cucumbers into thin slices. Toss lightly with salt. Cover cucumbers with plate. Weight down plate with heavy can. Let stand at room temperature 2 hours.

• Drain cucumbers well. Pat dry with paper towels. Place in medium-sized bowl.

• Combine vinegar, sugar, and pepper. Mix well. Pour over cucumber slices. Cover and refrigerate overnight, until well chilled.

• To serve, drain cucumber slices well. Turn into serving dish. Sprinkle with dill.

Note: This makes a delicious appetizer served on sesame crackers.

Madeleine Galanek Egan

Dutch Cucumbers

½ cup vinegar
½ cup water
¼ cup sugar
¾ teaspoon salt
Generous dash pepper
2 cups thinly sliced unpared
    cucumbers
1 cup thinly sliced onion

Serves 4-6

• Combine vinegar, water, sugar, salt, and pepper. Pour over cucumber and onion slices. Let stand overnight.

Violet Kozdra Galanek

121

Salads and Salad Dressings

Fish Mousse

1 envelope unflavored gelatin
2 tablespoons lemon juice
½ cup boiling chicken broth
½ cup mayonnaise
¼ cup milk
2 tablespoons chopped parsley
1 tablespoon minced green onion
1 teaspoon prepared mustard
1 teaspoon dried dill
¼ teaspoon pepper
1 can (7 ounces) tuna, salmon, or
    crabmeat
½ cup shredded cucumber

Serves 4

● Soften gelatin in lemon juice in large mixing bowl. Add broth. Stir to dissolve gelatin. Add next 7 ingredients. Beat until well mixed.
● Chill 20-30 minutes, or until slightly thickened. Beat until frothy. Fold in fish and cucumbers. Turn into lightly greased 2-cup mold. Chill until firm.

Holley Hicok Schroeder

Salmon Mousse with Sour Cream Dill Sauce

1 envelope (1 tablespoon) unflavored
    gelatin
¼ cup cold water
½ cup boiling water
½ cup mayonnaise
2 tablespoons lemon juice
1 tablespoon grated onion
1 teaspoon salt
½ teaspoon tabasco sauce
¼ teaspoon paprika
2 cups salmon, drained and finely
    chopped
½ cup heavy cream
1-3 cups cottage cheese
Watercress and lemon slices for
    garnish
Sour Cream Dill Sauce (recipe
    follows)

Serves 8-10

● Soften gelatin in cold water. Add boiling water and stir until gelatin is dissolved. Cool and add mayonnaise, lemon juice, onion, salt, tabasco, and paprika. Mix well.
● Chill to consistency of unbeaten egg white. Add salmon and beat well.
● Whip cream and fold into salmon mixture. Turn into an oiled 1-2 quart mold. Add cottage cheese to fill mold. Chill until set.
● Unmold and garnish with watercress and lemon slices. Serve with Sour Cream Dill Sauce.

Constance Foti Stewart

122

Salads and Salad Dressings

Sour Cream Dill Sauce

1 egg
2 tablespoons finely cut dill
4 teaspoons lemon juice
1 teaspoon grated onion
1 teaspoon salt
Freshly ground pepper
⅛ teaspoon sugar
1½ cups sour cream

1½ cups
● Beat egg. Add remaining ingredients, blending in sour cream last. Stir until well blended. Chill.

Constance Foti Stewart

Molded Fruit Salad

2 packages (3 ounces each)
  fruit-flavored gelatin—strawberry,
  cherry, or raspberry
2 cups boiling water
1 package (10 ounces) frozen
  strawberries
1 package (10 ounces) frozen
  blueberries
1 package (10 ounces) frozen
  raspberries
1 large banana, sliced
½ pint sour cream
⅓ cup chopped walnuts

Serves 6-8
● Dissolve each package of gelatin in a separate bowl, pouring *1 cup* boiling water over each. Stir to dissolve well. Add strawberries and blueberries to one bowl of gelatin. Add raspberries, banana, and walnuts to the other bowl. Pour one mixture into lightly greased 1½-quart mold. Chill until firm. Leave other bowl at room temperature.
● Spread sour cream evenly on set fruited gelatin. Pour on remaining fruit mixture. Chill until serving time for at least 3 hours.

> Note: Substitute any fruits, fresh or frozen, except pineapple.

Carol Mansi Crikelair

123

Salads and Salad Dressings

Gorgonzola and Walnut Salad

5 tablespoons olive oil
1 tablespoon wine vinegar
Salt to taste
Freshly ground pepper
¼ pound gorgonzola cheese,
   crumbled
1 cup walnuts, coarsely chopped
1 head romaine lettuce

Serves 6
• In large salad bowl, place olive oil, vinegar, salt, pepper, and half the cheese. Mix together to make a paste. Add walnuts.
• Wash and dry lettuce. Tear into bite-sized pieces. Add dressing and toss thoroughly. Top with remaining cheese.

Mary Ellen Donovan Weinrib

Greek Salad

2 green peppers
4 large tomatoes
2 cucumbers
1 Spanish onion
¾ pound feta cheese
1 can (1 pound) pitted black olives
¼ teaspoon oregano
6 tablespoons olive oil
2-3 tablespoons wine vinegar, to
   taste

Serves 10
• A day ahead. or early in the day, cut peppers. tomatoes. cucumbers, on-ion. and cheese into chunks. Combine with olives and oregano. Mix olive oil and vinegar and pour over all. Chill, tossing occasionally.
• Remove from refrigerator 30 minutes before serving.

Susan Don Lubin

Salads and Salad Dressings

Kraut Relish

Serves 20

2 cups sugar
1 cup water
2 pounds sauerkraut
2 cups chopped celery
1 cup chopped onion
1 cup chopped green pepper

● Boil sugar and water together until sugar is dissolved. Cool and pour over vegetables. Refrigerate overnight. Good with barbecued meat.

Suzanne Rich Beatty

Ten Layer Salad

Serves 8-10

1 large head iceberg lettuce, shredded
½ cup finely chopped green onions
¼ cup chopped celery
1 can (6 ounces) water chestnuts, sliced
2 packages (10 ounces) frozen peas
2 cups mayonnaise
1 tablespoon sugar
1 pound bacon, fried, drained, and crumbled
4 hard-cooked eggs, chopped
4 tomatoes, peeled, seeded, and diced
Grated parmesan and romano cheese
Chopped fresh parsley for garnish

● A day ahead, place shredded lettuce in large shallow serving bowl. Sprinkle green onions, chopped celery, and water chestnuts in layers. Break apart frozen peas. Sprinkle on top without defrosting. Spread mayonnaise over top like frosting. Sprinkle with sugar. Cover and refrigerate overnight.
● Before serving, add layers of crumbled bacon, eggs, and tomatoes. Sprinkle with grated cheeses. Do not toss. To serve, spoon from bottom of bowl to taste all layers.

Josephine Lane van der Hoeven

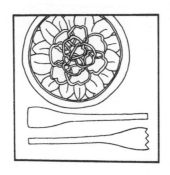

125

Salads and Salad Dressings

Lentil Salad

1 pound lentils, picked over and
    washed
5 cups cold water
1 bay leaf
1½ teaspoons salt
2 onions, each stuck with 2 whole
    cloves
⅔ cup olive oil
¼ cup wine vinegar
¼ teaspoon dry mustard
¼ teaspoon sugar
1 garlic clove, minced
½ teaspoon worcestershire sauce
Tabasco sauce
Freshly ground pepper
½ cup finely chopped green onions
3 tablespoons chopped parsley
3 hard-cooked eggs, quartered

Serves 12

• Place lentils, water, bay leaf, salt, and onions in heavy saucepan.
• Bring to boil. Cover and simmer 30 minutes until lentils are tender but still retain their shape. Drain excess liquid. Remove onions and bay leaf. Place lentils in bowl.
• Combine olive oil, vinegar, mustard, sugar, garlic, worcestershire, and tabasco. Add salt and pepper to taste. Beat well. Pour over hot lentils. Toss gently.
• Chill several hours or overnight. Add green onions and parsley. Mix well. Garnish with egg quarters.

Elizabeth Raub Matisoo

Cold Dilled Pea Salad

½ cup sour cream
Fresh dill and/or chives, chopped
½-1 teaspoon curry powder
Salt and freshly ground pepper to
    taste
Boston or garden lettuce
2 cups fresh peas, or 2 packages
    (10 ounces) tiny frozen peas,
    defrosted
1 cup fresh snow peas, or 1 package
    (10 ounces) frozen pea pods

Serves 12

• Combine sour cream, dill, chives, curry powder, salt, and pepper to taste in a small bowl. Mix well. Combine with uncooked peas, mixing lightly so peas are not crushed.
• Chill 10-15 minutes in refrigerator, if desired, or serve at room temperature.

Susan Don Lubin

126

Salads and Salad Dressings

Dilled Potato Salad

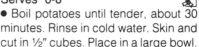

4 medium red potatoes (about 2 pounds)
½ cup sour cream or plain yogurt
½ cup mayonnaise
2 green onions, minced, tops included
1 tablespoon snipped fresh dill, or 1½ teaspoons dried dill weed
2 teaspoons Dijon mustard
1½ teaspoons lemon juice
½ teaspoon salt
Freshly ground pepper
½ pound bacon, fried and crumbled

Serves 6-8

● Boil potatoes until tender, about 30 minutes. Rinse in cold water. Skin and cut in ½" cubes. Place in a large bowl.
● Meanwhile, combine sour cream, mayonnaise, onions, dill, mustard, lemon juice, salt, and pepper to taste in a large bowl.
● Add cooked potatoes to dressing in bowl and toss to coat well. Chill overnight.
● Garnish with crumbled bacon just before serving.

Nancy Reese Corbett

Marinated Potato Salad

6 medium Maine or Long Island potatoes
¼ cup vegetable oil
¼ cup cider vinegar
1 medium onion, chopped
2½ teaspoons salt
¼ teaspoon pepper
¾ cup mayonnaise
¼ cup light cream
3 hard-cooked eggs, peeled and diced
1 cup sliced celery
Boston lettuce
Red pepper slivers for garnish

Serves 6-8

● Cook potatoes for 25 minutes in salted water until tender. Drain and peel potatoes. Cut into thin slices. Place in a large bowl.
● Combine oil, vinegar, onion, salt, and pepper in a covered jar. Shake to mix. Pour dressing over potatoes and toss to blend well. Cover bowl and chill potatoes at least 3 hours.
● Just before serving, stir mayonnaise with cream until smooth. Pour over potatoes and toss to coat. Add diced eggs and celery. Toss lightly. Line a salad bowl with Boston lettuce and fill with salad. Garnish with slivers of red pepper.

Barbara Smith Suval

Salads and Salad Dressings

Salade Julienne

Serves 2-4

¼ pound gruyère or jarlsberg cheese
3 celery ribs
3-4 mushrooms
Vinaigrette Dressing (see Index)
1 tablespoon finely chopped parsley

● Slice cheese very thinly. Cut into julienne strips about 1½" long. Wash and scrape celery if necessary. Cut across rib into sections 1½" long, then into thin julienne strips. Wipe mushrooms with a damp cloth. Slice very thinly.

● Combine above ingredients in a salad bowl with enough dressing to coat lightly, and toss. Allow to stand 15-20 minutes before serving. Garnish with chopped parsley.

Stephanie Fay Arpajian

Salade Niçoise

Serves 6

Lettuce leaves (boston or bibb)
1 can (7 ounces) tuna
1 cup julienne or shredded chicken
   or ham
½ pound crisply cooked fresh
   vegetables (green beans, peas,
   zucchini, broccoli)
½ cucumber, thinly sliced
1 teaspoon chopped parsley
1 teaspoon chopped fresh basil
1 teaspoon chopped fresh tarragon
1 pound firm, ripe tomatoes
1 can (2 ounces) anchovy fillets,
   drained
12 black olives
Vinaigrette Dressing (see Index)

● Line a large bowl with lettuce. Drain and flake tuna. Place on lettuce. Add meat, vegetables, and cucumbers in a circular design. Sprinkle with herbs. Arrange tomato slices or wedges over salad. Make a final design with anchovies and olives.

● Pour vinaigrette over salad just before serving. Do not toss.

Ann Dodds Costello

Salads and Salad Dressings

Salade Provençale

½ cup olive oil
¼ cup vinegar
½ teaspoon chopped olives
½ teaspoon chopped parsley
½ teaspoon chopped gherkins
Salt and freshly ground pepper
3 potatoes, cooked and sliced
1½ pounds fresh green beans,
    cooked
Lettuce
2 cans (7 ounces each)
    water-packed tuna
1 cucumber, sliced
2 tomatoes, sliced
3 hard-cooked eggs, cut in wedges
Black or green olives

Serves 4

● Prepare vinaigrette: Mix oil, vinegar, olives, parsley, and gherkins with salt and pepper to taste. Pour over warm cooked potatoes and green beans. Marinate several hours.
● At serving time, arrange lettuce on a platter. Drain tuna. Arrange with all vegetables, hard-cooked eggs, and black olives to make an attractive platter.

Anne Ruthrauff Seltzer

Marinated Scallop Salad

1 pint fresh bay scallops
½ cup fresh lime juice
1 green pepper, finely diced
1 white celery rib, finely diced
2 green onions, finely chopped with
    stems
2 tablespoons finely chopped Italian
    parsley
2 tablespoons oil
3-4 dashes tabasco sauce, to taste
Salt and freshly ground white pepper
    to taste

Garnish:
1 ripe avocado
Juice of 1 lemon
Parsley sprigs

Serves 4-6

● Marinate scallops in lime juice 1-4 hours, turning occasionally.
● Drain off most of lime juice. Add remaining ingredients except avocado, lemon juice, and parsley. Chill until serving time.
● Garnish with avocado slices sprinkled with lemon juice, and parsley sprigs.

Anne Ruthrauff Seltzer

Salads and Salad Dressings

Shrimp Salad Mexicano

1½ tablespoons fresh lemon juice
½ cup olive oil
Salt and freshly ground pepper
2 cups coarsely chopped cooked
   shrimp
2-3 tablespoons minced onion
1 medium tomato, peeled, seeded,
   and cubed, or 8 cherry tomatoes,
   quartered
1 small avocado
1 tablespoon finely chopped fresh
   coriander or parsley
4 tortilla cups (recipe follows)

Serves 4

• Place lemon juice in a small bowl. Gradually beat in oil with a whisk. Season to taste with salt and pepper. Add shrimp and onion and toss lightly. Let stand about 15 minutes. Add tomato, avocado, and chopped coriander or parsley. Toss lightly.
• Serve in tortilla cups or on lettuce.

Nancy Beck Hoggson

Tortilla Cups

• Place a corn tortilla in a large ladle. Holding it in place with a slightly smaller spoon, fry in hot deep fat or peanut oil (375°) until tortilla is crisp. Or:
• Place tortilla in a Bird's Nest Maker and deep fry until crisp. These can be stored overnight at room temperature.

Nancy Beck Hoggson

Salads and Salad Dressings

Fresh Spinach and Mushroom Salad with Blue Cheese

10 ounces fresh spinach
2 cups sliced mushrooms (about ¼ pound)
½ medium Spanish onion, thinly sliced
½ cup crumbed blue cheese (about 2 ounces)
1 garlic clove, minced
¾ teaspoon salt
¼ teaspoon thyme
6 tablespoons olive oil
2 tablespoons white wine vinegar
Freshly ground pepper

Serves 6

● In a large salad bowl, combine spinach, mushrooms, onion, and blue cheese.
● Combine garlic, salt, thyme, oil, and vinegar in a small jar. Shake well. Pour over salad and toss lightly. Serve immediately with freshly ground pepper.

Anne Ruthrauff Seltzer

Layered Spinach Salad

1 pound fresh spinach
Dash each salt, freshly ground pepper, sugar
1 head iceberg lettuce
½ pound bacon, fried and crumbled
¼-½ pound mushrooms, sliced
6 hard-cooked eggs, chopped
1 package (10 ounces) frozen quick-cooking peas, defrosted, or 1½ cups fresh peas, barely cooked
1 Spanish onion, thinly sliced in rings
2 cups mayonnaise
1 cup sour cream

Serves 8-10

● Wash and dry spinach. Tear into large bite-sized pieces. Sprinkle with salt, pepper, and sugar. Do the same with lettuce.
● Layer spinach. bacon, mushrooms, hard-cooked eggs, lettuce, peas, and onion rings in a deep salad bowl.
● Mix mayonnaise with sour cream. Spread evenly on top of salad. Cover with plastic wrap and refrigerate overnight.
● Each serving should have some of each layer.

Lucie Ling Campbell

Salads and Salad Dressings

Spinach Salad Supreme

1 pound fresh spinach
1 raw egg
2 generous teaspoons grated
   parmesan cheese
2 tablespoons Dijon mustard
Juice of 1 lemon, strained
1 scant teaspoon sugar
1 teaspoon worcestershire sauce
¼ cup salad oil (not olive oil)
Salt and pepper to taste
6-8 slices fried bacon, crumbled
2 hard-cooked eggs, chopped

Serves 6

• Wash spinach several times. Drain thoroughly. Remove stems, strings, and soggy leaves. Dry well.
• In a screw-top jar, beat raw egg with a fork. Add parmesan, mustard, lemon juice, sugar, and worcestershire. Shake to mix thoroughly. Add oil and mix again. Season with salt and pepper.
• Put spinach in salad bowl. Sprinkle with bacon bits and chopped egg. Shake dressing and pour over salad just before serving. Toss thoroughly.

Ann Dodds Costello

Tabouli

⅓-½ cup fresh lemon juice
¼ cup olive oil
1 teaspoon dried mint leaves, or 1
   tablespoon chopped fresh mint
   leaves
1½ teaspoons salt
¼ teaspoon pepper
1 cup medium bulgur wheat
1 cup boiling water
½ cup finely chopped fresh parsley
½ cup minced green onions
2 tomatoes, chopped (about 2 cups)
Lemon slices for garnish

Serves 6-8

• Put ⅓ cup lemon juice in a screw-top jar with oil, mint leaves, salt, and pepper. Cover and shake well to mix.
• Put bulgur into a medium-sized heat-proof bowl. Cover with boiling water. Let stand 10 minutes, until all water is absorbed. Stir gently with a fork to separate grains.
• Shake dressing and pour over bulgur. Toss to coat. Add parsley, onions, and tomatoes. Toss again. Add more seasoning and lemon juice to taste.
• Serve mounded on a serving platter, garnished with lemon slices.
   Variations: This can be stuffed into pita bread, tomatoes, or green peppers.

Betsy Gimpel Mena

Salads and Salad Dressings

Tomato Aspic

1 envelope (1 tablespoon) unflavored
   gelatin
1 can (18 ounces) tomato juice
1 beef bouillon cube
2 tablespoons lemon juice
2 tablespoons grated onion
½ teaspoon worcestershire sauce
½ teaspoon sugar
¼ teaspoon salt
⅛ teaspoon tabasco sauce or ¼
   teaspoon horseradish

Serves 4

• Sprinkle gelatin over ½ cup tomato juice in a saucepan. Add bouillon cube. Place over very low heat and stir constantly until gelatin and bouillon cube are dissolved.
• Remove from heat. Add remaining ingredients and chill in a mold until firm.

Peggy Swanson Smith

Spicy Tomato Aspic

1 can (1 pound, 13 ounces)
   tomatoes
2 small onions
6 whole cloves
6 peppercorns
2 bay leaves
1 envelope (1 tablespoon) unflavored
   gelatin
¼ cup cold water
2 tablespoons vinegar
1½ tablespoons lemon juice
1 teaspoon sugar
½ teaspoon salt, to taste

Serves 4-6

• Cook tomatoes, onions, cloves, peppercorns, and bay leaves together for 20-25 minutes. Tomatoes should be very soft. Press through a sieve or food mill.
• Soften gelatin in cold water. Add to tomato mixture. Add vinegar, lemon juice, sugar, and salt to taste. Pour into a lightly oiled 2-cup mold. Chill until set.

Alice Frauenheim Foley

Marinated Cherry Tomatoes

½ cup olive oil
2 tablespoons white wine vinegar
1 teaspoon Dijon mustard
Salt
Freshly ground pepper
⅔ cup fresh basil, chopped
5 cups cherry tomatoes

Serves 6

• Mix oil, vinegar, mustard, salt, and pepper in serving bowl. Add basil. Wash tomatoes and toss with dressing an hour before serving. Serve at room temperature for best flavor.

Nancy Beck Hoggson

Salads and Salad Dressings

Tomato Mozzarella Salad

2 tablespoons minced basil
1 tablespoon minced parsley
5 tablespoons olive oil
1½ tablespoons red wine vinegar
1 large garlic clove, minced
Salt
Freshly ground pepper
4 large ripe tomatoes, peeled and
    sliced ¼" thick
1 pound mozzarella cheese, thinly
    sliced
1 Spanish onion, peeled, thinly sliced,
    and separated into rings
1 can (2 ounces) flat anchovy fillets,
    drained
Fresh parsley and oil-cured black
    olives for garnish

Serves 4-6

● Blend basil, parsley, oil, vinegar, and garlic. Season with salt and pepper.
● Alternate tomato and mozzarella slices on large platter, overlapping slices. Spoon dressing over salad. Sprinkle with fresh pepper and top with onion rings. Arrange anchovy fillets on top. Garnish with parsley and olives. Chill.

Susan Hendrickson Eden

Crisp Vegetable Salad

1½ pounds fresh green beans or 2
    packages (10 ounces) frozen
    whole green beans
1 medium Spanish onion
2 small celery ribs
1 medium green pepper
4-5 radishes
Vinaigrette Dressing (see Index)
Bibb, boston, or leaf lettuce
1-2 tomatoes
3 tablespoons finely chopped parsley

Serves 6-8

● Cook beans in salted boiling water until tender. Drain. Peel onion and slice thinly. Dice celery. Halve pepper and remove seeds. Cut in thin strips. Wash and trim radishes. Cut into thin rounds.
● Combine all vegetables in a bowl. Pour dressing over salad and mix well. Let stand in refrigerator 2 hours to marinate. Keeps several days.
● Line a large salad bowl with lettuce leaves. Put vegetables in center. Cut tomatoes in wedges and place around edge. Sprinkle with chopped parsley.

Ann Dodds Costello

Salads and Salad Dressings

Perfect Tomato Salad

4 fresh tomatoes
2 teaspoons coarse salt
Freshly ground pepper
6 tablespoons chopped fresh basil or dill
¼ cup chopped fresh parsley, if desired
6 tablespoons olive oil
6 tablespoons wine vinegar

Serves 4-6

● Cut tomatoes in thick slices. Place a layer in the bottom of a glass serving dish. Sprinkle with salt, pepper, and chopped herbs. Add oil and vinegar. Repeat layers.
● Marinate at room temperature for 1 hour before serving.

Catherine Mason Tawes

Ziti Salad

1 tablespoon salt
1 tablespoon olive oil
1 pound ziti
3 tablespoons milk
1 Spanish onion
2 tomatoes
6 sweet pickles
2 small green peppers
1 large shallot
1½ cups mayonnaise
½ cup sour cream
2 envelopes G. Washington Brown Broth, or 2 teaspoons bouillon powder
1 teaspoon salt
Freshly ground pepper
⅛ teaspoon wine vinegar
1 tablespoon pickle juice
Handful fresh dill, chopped

Serves 8-10

● Bring a large pot of water to a boil. Add salt, olive oil, and ziti. Stir with a wooden spoon. Boil 10 minutes until tender but still firm.
● Drain quickly in a colander. Rinse under cold running water and drain again. Blot ziti with paper towels to remove excess moisture. Place in a large bowl and moisten with the milk.
● Chop onion, tomatoes, pickles, and peppers into ¼" dice. Reserve a tablespoon of each for garnish. Mince the shallot.
● Beat mayonnaise and sour cream together until creamy. Add bouillon powder, salt, and pepper. Toss ziti with dressing. Add vegetables, vinegar, and pickle juice. Taste and adjust seasonings. Chill thoroughly. Garnish with reserved vegetables and dill.

  Note: To improve store-bought mayonnaise, add Dijon mustard and lemon juice. It will taste almost like homemade.

Susan Sample Marx

135

Salads and Salad Dressings

Zucchini Salad with Tomato and Herb Dressing

2 pounds small/medium zucchini,
   well scrubbed
¼ cup pine nuts (pignolas)
2 pounds ripe tomatoes
¾ teaspoon salt
1½ teaspoons sugar (to taste)
¼ teaspoon freshly ground pepper
3 tablespoons red wine vinegar
¼ cup olive oil, French, if possible
2 tablespoons finely minced chives
2 tablespoons finely minced parsley

Serves 6

● Drop zucchini into boiling, salted water. Cook 5 minutes, until tender when pressed with finger. Rinse under cold water until cool. Trim ends. Cut zucchini into 2″ x ½″ strips.

● Preheat oven to 300°. Spread pine nuts in a pan. Toast 15 minutes until golden brown. Cool and reserve.

● Drop tomatoes into the same boiling water. Cook 2 minutes and drain. Cool under cold running water. Remove skins. Halve tomatoes crosswise. Remove seeds. Cut flesh in ½″ cubes.

● Blend *half* the diced tomatoes with salt, sugar, pepper, and vinegar. When smooth, add olive oil. Combine tomato purée with *half the remaining* diced tomatoes. Stir in chives and parsley. Adjust seasonings.

● Pour dressing over zucchini strips. Garnish with remaining diced tomatoes. Sprinkle with toasted pine nuts.

Nancy Beck Hoggson

Curry Salad Dressing

2 eggs
1 cup mayonnaise
½ cup grated swiss cheese
2 tablespoons white vinegar
2 tablespoons red vinegar
1½ tablespoons chopped parsley
1 garlic clove, minced
½ teaspoon curry powder
½ teaspoon paprika
½ teaspoon beef bouillon powder
Half-and-half or heavy cream

1¼ cups

● Combine all ingredients except half-and-half or cream in blender or food processor. Blend at high speed. Thin to proper consistency with cream.

Ann Keyser Griffin

136

Salads and Salad Dressings

French Dressing

1 cup vegetable oil
¼ cup olive oil
¼ cup tarragon vinegar
1-2 tablespoons lemon juice
1-2 tablespoons sugar (optional)
2 teaspoons salt
1 teaspoon dry mustard
½ teaspoon finely minced garlic
½ teaspoon pepper

1½ cups
● Mix ingredients and refrigerate.

Holley Hicok Schroeder

Creamy Mustard Dressing

1 teaspoon raw egg yolk
2-3 teaspoons Dijon or Dusseldorf
    mustard
Dash tabasco sauce
½ teaspoon finely chopped garlic
Salt and freshly ground pepper
1 teaspoon vinegar
½ cup olive oil
1-2 teaspoons fresh lemon juice
1 teaspoon heavy cream

1 cup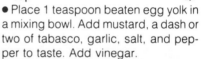
● Place 1 teaspoon beaten egg yolk in a mixing bowl. Add mustard, a dash or two of tabasco, garlic, salt, and pepper to taste. Add vinegar.
● Beat vigorously with a wire whisk to blend ingredients. Still beating, gradually add oil. Continue to beat vigorously until thickened and well blended. Add lemon juice. Beat in heavy cream. Taste to adjust seasonings if necessary.

Nancy Beck Hoggson

Poppy Seed Salad Dressing

1 small white onion
2 cups olive oil
⅔ cup wine vinegar
1½ cups sugar
2 teaspoons salt
2 teaspoons dry mustard
3 tablespoons poppy seeds

2¼ cups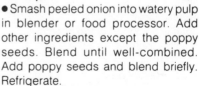
● Smash peeled onion into watery pulp in blender or food processor. Add other ingredients except the poppy seeds. Blend until well-combined. Add poppy seeds and blend briefly. Refrigerate.
    Note: Good with citrus and
    fruit salads.

Ann Dodds Costello

Salads and Salad Dressings

Remoulade

1 cup mayonnaise
¼ cup sour cream
¼ cup catsup
¼ cup minced shallots or green
   onions
¼ cup minced celery
2-4 teaspoons Zataraines Creole
   Mustard
2 tablespoons tarragon vinegar
2 tablespoons chopped dill pickle
1 tablespoon chopped parsley
2 teaspoons anchovy paste
2 teaspoons capers
1½ teaspoons paprika
½ teaspoon dried chervil

2 cups
● Mix all ingredients and chill.
   Note: Excellent with seafood
   salads or as a dip for shrimp and
   raw vegetables.

Holley Hicok Schroeder

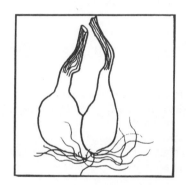

Roquefort Dressing

1 garlic clove, minced
3 tablespoons chopped chives
1 tablespoon lemon juice
½ cup sour cream
1 cup mayonnaise
½ cup crumbled roquefort or blue
   cheese (about 2 ounces)
Salt and freshly ground pepper to
   taste

1½ cups
● Combine garlic, chives, and lemon
juice in bowl. Add sour cream, mayonnaise, and cheese. Blend well. Season
to taste.
● Cover and refrigerate at least 4
hours.

Leslie May Marra

138

Salads and Salad Dressings

Sweet-Sour Salad Dressing

¾ cup sugar
2 tablespoons flour
1½ teaspoons dry mustard
¼ teaspoon salt
1 egg, beaten
¾ cup milk
¾ cup white vinegar
1 tablespoon butter (optional)

2 cups
● Mix dry ingredients in a saucepan. Add egg and milk. Stir in vinegar very gradually. Cook until mixture comes to a boil. Add butter, if desired.
  Note: Make this ahead and store in refrigerator to use in potato salad or deviled eggs. Good combined with mayonnaise.

Margaret Williams Young

Vinaigrette Dressing

6 tablespoons olive oil
2 tablespoons red wine vinegar
1 teaspoon Dijon mustard
1 teaspoon lemon juice
1 teaspoon salt
Freshly ground pepper to taste

½ cup
● Combine all ingredients in a screw-top jar and shake to mix.

Ann Dodds Costello

Winter Vinaigrette

½ cup minced fresh parsley
2 hard-cooked eggs, finely chopped
⅓ cup minced black olives
1 tablespoon capers, crushed
⅓ cup lemon juice
1 cup vegetable oil

2 cups
● Blend parsley, eggs, olives, and capers in a bowl. Add lemon juice, stirring constantly. Add oil in a slow stream. Serve chilled or at room temperature.

Patricia Gates Cioffarri

vegetables

Vegetable Variety

Rather than cooking in water, quickly sauté thinly-sliced mushrooms, zucchini, green peppers, or corn kernels. You may also sauté heavier, thicker vegetables after parboiling them until just tender: cauliflower, brussels sprouts, carrots, green beans, broccoli, turnips, or potatoes. The taste and texture will surprise and delight you.

Instead of crackers, slice unpeeled zucchini into rounds. These are much better as an hors d'oeuvre base than anything from a box.

Try shredded cabbage with a stew instead of noodles. With a food processor shred the cabbage coarsely. Steam 9-10 minutes in 1″ of water with 1-2 tablespoons of butter. Cabbage should be just cooked and still crispy. Drain well. Add more butter and freshly ground pepper.

Use cooked artichoke bottoms as containers for a more colorful vegetable such as carrots, baby peas, or a stiff vegetable purée. Serve as a garnish for roast beef or lamb.

Shred young, unpeeled zucchini. Salt it and press out excess juice. Sauté 5 minutes in butter. Season to taste with salt, freshly ground pepper, parmesan cheese, or a few drops of lemon juice.

Braise brussels sprouts in beef broth. Almost any vegetable will be tastier when cooked in broth.

Cook corn on the cob. Drain and serve with Green Peppercorn Butter (4 tablespoons butter creamed with 1 teaspoon chopped green peppercorns).

Cook *pommes vapeur* (steamed small potatoes), lima beans, cauliflower, squash, corn, or asparagus in a flower-type steamer.

Save celery tops for salads, soups, or stocks. Outer ribs can be sautéed or used for soups. Tender, white inner ribs (also called heart) can be split and braised. The tiny, center-most leaf ribs are lovely in salads and as raw vegetable hors d'oeuvres.

Vegetables

Asparagus Mousse

1 pound fresh asparagus, or 2
    packages (10 ounces each)
    frozen asparagus
2 eggs, beaten
½ teaspoon nutmeg
Salt and freshly ground white pepper
½ cup heavy cream
Parsley sprigs and lemon wedges for
    garnish
Lemon Sabayon Sauce (recipe
    follows)

Serves 6

- Steam asparagus in boiling, salted water until barely tender. Drain cooking liquid, reserving it for Lemon Sabayon Sauce. Cut asparagus in 1" lengths. Purée in blender or food processor.
- Preheat oven to 375°. Blend asparagus purée with eggs and seasonings. Bring cream to a boil and stir in purée. Pour into a 1-quart soufflé dish or individual molds. Cover with foil punctured in several places, to let steam escape during baking.
- Place casserole in oven in a larger pan filled with 2" of water. Bake 45 minutes. Unmold and garnish with parsley and lemon wedges. Serve with Lemon Sabayon Sauce.

Mary Vance Watson

Lemon Sabayon Sauce

½ cup asparagus cooking liquid
3 egg yolks
3 tablespoons lemon juice

1 cup

- If more than ½ cup asparagus cooking liquid remains, cook it down in the top of a double boiler over direct heat until only about ½ cup remains.
- Whisk egg yolks and lemon juice in a small bowl until mixture is light and nearly double in volume. Whisk this mixture into hot asparagus liquid until sauce is thick, cooking just 3 minutes over boiling water.

Mary Vance Watson

Vegetables

Chinese-Style Asparagus

2 pounds fresh asparagus
½ cup finely chopped onion
2 tablespoons oil
1 tablespoon cornstarch
¾ cup chicken broth
1 tablespoon soy sauce
⅛ teaspoon freshly ground pepper
⅓ cup thinly sliced water chestnuts
2 tablespoons slivered, toasted
    almonds

Serves 6

● Cut and peel asparagus stalks. Wash thoroughly. Cut in thin, diagonal slices. Cook with onion in hot oil for 2 minutes just until crisp, stirring constantly.
● Combine cornstarch, chicken broth, soy sauce, and pepper. Add to asparagus. Bring to a boil, then simmer 2 minutes. Stir in water chestnuts and almonds. Serve immediately.

Carole Kruse Long

Spring Asparagus

2 pounds fresh asparagus
Juice of ½ lemon
1 garlic clove, minced
½ cup grated parmesan cheese
4 tablespoons butter

Serves 6

● Preheat oven to 350°. Clean asparagus. Steam 6-7 minutes in salted water. Arrange in a buttered baking dish.
● Squeeze lemon juice over asparagus. Sprinkle with minced garlic and cheese. Dot with butter.
● Bake 10 minutes.

Marjorie Lister Beck

New England Baked Beans

1 pound dry red kidney beans or pea
    beans
¼ pound salt pork, finely sliced or
    diced
½ cup brown sugar
½ cup molasses
2 tablespoons cider vinegar
2 teaspoons dry mustard
1 teaspoon salt
1 teaspoon pepper
¼ teaspoon ginger

Serves 6-8

● Parboil beans according to package directions. or soak overnight in cold water. Drain.
● Cover beans with fresh water. Add all ingredients. Bake in a 300° oven for 8-10 hours.
● Let stand overnight to absorb moisture and to mellow the flavors. Heat and serve.

Cheryl Giffin Carter

Vegetables

Green Beans with Water Chestnuts

2 pound fresh green beans, ends removed
3 tablespoons butter
1 tablespoon oil
1 teaspoon salt
Freshly ground pepper
1 can (8 ounces) water chestnuts

Serves 8

• Steam beans for 5 minutes and drain well. Beans can be set aside to reheat and serve later.
• Add butter and oil to skillet. Add beans, seasoning with salt and pepper. Slice water chestnuts and cut in strips. Add to beans and heat through.

Patricia Farnsworth Kuntz

Baked Lima Beans

1 pound dried baby lima beans
3 teaspoons salt
¾ cup butter
¾ cup brown sugar
1 tablespoon dry mustard
1 tablespoon molasses
1 cup sour cream

Serves 6-8

• Soak lima beans overnight in cold water to cover. The next day, drain and cover them with fresh cold water. Add *1 teaspoon* salt. Cook until tender, about 50 minutes.
• Drain beans and rinse in hot water. Put in a greased casserole. Dot with butter. Mix brown sugar, mustard, and remaining 2 teaspoons salt. Sprinkle on beans. Stir in molasses. Spoon sour cream over all and mix. Bake 1 hour in a 350° oven until bubbling.

Suzanne Rich Beatty

Baked Broccoli

1 garlic clove
2 cups chopped cooked broccoli
3 medium tomatoes, thickly sliced
1 cup grated sharp cheddar cheese
Salt and pepper
1 tablespoon chopped parsley

Serves 4

• Lightly butter a 2-quart casserole. Rub with garlic. Arrange chopped broccoli in dish and place sliced tomatoes on top. Cover with grated cheese, salt, and pepper to taste. Sprinkle with chopped parsley.
• Bake in a 375° oven for 30-35 minutes, until heated through.

Cheryl Giffin Carter

Vegetables

California Broccoli

2 pounds broccoli, or 2 packages
(10 ounces each) frozen
broccoli
⅔ cup finely sliced green onions,
tops included
4 tablespoons butter
2 tablespoons lemon juice
1 teaspoon salt
½ teaspoon pepper

Serves 6-8
● Trim large leaves and lower portion from broccoli stems. Slash stems crosswise. Wash and drain broccoli. Cook until tender, 5 to 10 minutes. Drain.
● Sauté onions in butter in a small skillet for 5 minutes. Remove from heat and add remaining ingredients. Mix and pour over hot broccoli.

Judith Lawson Florence

Broccoli-Cauliflower Panache

1 large head cauliflower
1 large bunch broccoli
2 tablespoons butter
¼ cup sour cream
Salt and freshly ground pepper
⅓ cup breadcrumbs
3 tablespoons grated parmesan
cheese

Serves 6-8
● Wash cauliflower and break into flowerets. Cook covered with boiling salted water for 10 minutes. Drain and place in a buttered 1½-quart casserole.
● Cut flowerets from broccoli stalks. Peel stalks down to tender pith, then chop coarsely. Cook flowerets and chopped stems uncovered in cauliflower water for 8-10 minutes.
● Purée hot, cooked broccoli with butter and sour cream. Season purée to taste with salt and pepper. Spoon over cauliflower. Sprinkle with breadcrumbs and grated parmesan.
● Bake in a 350° oven for 20-30 minutes.

Nancy Beck Hoggson

Vegetables

Carrot Ring

1 cup butter
1 cup light brown sugar
2 eggs
2 cups grated carrots
1 medium sweet potato, grated
1½ cups flour
1 teaspoon lemon juice
½ teaspoon salt
½ teaspoon baking powder
3 cups cooked peas (optional)

Serves 8
● Preheat oven to 350°. Cream butter and sugar. Add eggs. Beat in remaining ingredients. Place in a well-oiled ring mold.
● Bake for 1 hour. Serve with cooked peas in center of ring.

Susan Sample Marx

Dill-Baked Carrots

6-8 carrots
¼ teaspoon salt
⅛ teaspoon freshly ground pepper
1-2 teaspoons snipped fresh dill
1 tablespoon butter
2 tablespoons water

Serves 4
● Scrape carrots. Slice in small julienne strips. Layer in a buttered casserole. Sprinkle each layer with salt, pepper, and dill. Dot with butter
● Add water. Cover tightly and bake in a 350° oven for 40 minutes until tender.

Mary Blake Markoff

Curried Cauliflower

1 head cauliflower, about 2 pounds
¼ cup milk
Salt
1 tablespoon finely chopped shallots
1 teaspoon curry powder
½ cup heavy cream
Freshly ground pepper
1 tablespoon butter

Serves 4
● Break cauliflower into large flowerets. Place in a saucepan with cold water to cover. Add milk and salt. Bring to a boil and simmer 15-20 minutes, until tender.
● Add shallots, curry powder, cream, salt, and pepper to taste. Cook and stir over low heat until hot. Stir in butter.

Anne Ruthrauff Seltzer

147

Vegetables

Creamed Celery with Pecans

2 tablespoons finely chopped onion
¼ cup butter
¼ cup flour
2 cups milk
1 teaspoon salt
⅛ teaspoon freshly ground pepper
5 cups celery, cut in 1" pieces
½ cup heavy cream
¾ cup chopped pecans
½ cup dry breadcrumbs

Serves 6-8

● Sauté onions in *2 tablespoons* butter until soft. Remove from heat and stir in flour. Cook over low heat until flour is golden. Remove from heat. Gradually stir in milk. Add salt and pepper to taste. Bring this mixture to a boil, stirring often. Simmer 15-20 minutes, until thick.

● Steam celery in a little salted water for about 20 minutes. Drain well. Put in a greased 1½-quart casserole.

● Preheat oven to 350°. Stir heavy cream into cream sauce. Pour over celery and sprinkle with pecans. Melt remaining 2 tablespoons butter and mix with breadcrumbs. Sprinkle buttered breadcrumbs over casserole. Bake uncovered for 15-20 minutes.

Judith Lawson Florence

Corn Fritters

2 tablespoons butter
2 cups fresh corn kernels
3 eggs, separated
½ cup heavy cream
1 teaspoon salt
½ teaspoon freshly ground
   pepper
Pinch cayenne pepper
Pinch ground mace
1 tablespoon chopped parsley
1 tablespoon snipped chives
Butter and/or oil for frying

Serves 8

● Melt butter. When foam subsides, add corn. Sauté about 3 minutes, stirring. Reserve.

● Mix egg yolks, cream, salt, pepper, cayenne, mace, parsley, and chives. Stir in sautéed corn kernels. Taste to adjust seasonings.

● About 15-20 minutes before serving, beat egg whites until stiff peaks form. Fold gently into corn mixture.

● Drop from a tablespoon onto a lightly oiled or buttered skillet. Cook 2-3 minutes on each side. Drain on paper towels. Serve hot.

Nancy Beck Hoggson

Vegetables

Fresh Corn Pudding

¼ cup butter
⅓ cup flour
1½ cups light cream
2 eggs, separated
1 teaspoon salt
1½ teaspoons Dijon mustard
Cayenne pepper to taste
2 cups corn kernels, cut from cob, or
    1 package (10 ounces) frozen
    corn
1 tablespoon worcestershire sauce
1 tablespoon chopped parsley
1 cup buttered breadcrumbs
    (optional)

Serves 6

● Preheat oven to 350°. Melt butter in a saucepan. Stir in flour. Gradually blend in cream. Bring to a boil over medium heat, stirring. Remove from heat.

● Beat egg yolks lightly. Add to cream sauce with salt, mustard, cayenne, corn, worcestershire, and parsley.

● Beat egg whites until stiff but not dry. Fold into corn mixture. Turn into a greased 1½-quart casserole. Top with breadcrumbs. Bake 30-45 minutes, until custard is set.

Barbara Smith Suval

Garden Relish

½ small head cauliflower, cut in
    flowerets
2 carrots, sliced
2 celery ribs, sliced diagonally
1 green pepper, diced
1 jar (6 ounces) marinated artichoke
    hearts
1 jar (3 ounces) pitted green olives,
    drained
1 jar (2 ounces) pimientos, cut in
    strips
¾ cup wine vinegar
½ cup salad oil
2 tablespoons sugar
1 teaspoon salt
½ teaspoon oregano
¼ teaspoon pepper

Serves 8

● Put all ingredients in a skillet with ¼ cup water. Bring to a boil and stir.

● Reduce heat and simmer 5 minutes, stirring occasionally. Do not overcook. Drain and serve now or chill overnight. This will keep for several days.

Roberta LaChance Juster

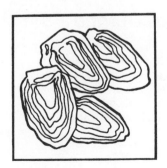

Vegetables

Harvest Casserole

1 large onion, chopped
2 tablespoons butter
2 pounds zucchini
Salt
2 ripe, yet firm tomatoes
3 eggs
½-¾ pound grated cheddar cheese
Freshly ground pepper

Serves 6

● Sauté chopped onion in butter. Wash and trim zucchini. Cut in ½" slices. Cook in boiling, salted water until tender, then drain.

● Quarter tomatoes. Place in a greased ovenproof dish with zucchini and onions.

● Beat eggs. Add grated cheese, salt, and pepper to taste. Mix well with a wire whisk. Pour over vegetables. Bake in a 375° oven for 20 minutes, until custard is set.

Margaret Muncie

Special Squash Casserole

1 cup buttermilk baking mix
4 eggs
½ cup oil
3-4 cups thinly sliced zucchini
2 small onions, chopped
¼ cup grated parmesan cheese
¼ cup grated sharp cheddar cheese
1 garlic clove, minced
½ teaspoon oregano
½ teaspoon salt
¼ teaspoon freshly ground pepper

Serves 8

● Preheat oven to 350°. Blend baking mix with eggs and oil. Stir in remaining ingredients.

● Scrape into a greased 1½-quart casserole or a 10" pie plate. Bake 1 hour until golden brown. Slice in wedges or squares to serve.

Judith Huggard Hubbard

Hot Curried Fruit

1 can (1 pound) peaches
1 can (1 pound) apricot halves
1 can (1 pound) pineapple chunks
⅓ cup melted butter
¾ cup brown sugar
2-3 teaspoons curry powder, to taste

Serves 6-8

● Rinse fruits in colander. Drain and turn into greased casserole. Combine melted butter, brown sugar, and curry powder. Pour over fruit.

● Bake at 250° for 1 hour. Serve with hot or cold meat entrée.

Susan Don Lubin

Vegetables

Chilled Vegetable Curry

Serves 12

1 medium unpeeled eggplant, cut in
   1" cubes
2 medium unpeeled zucchini, cut in
   1" cubes
Salt and freshly ground pepper
6-8 tablespoons olive or vegetable oil
2 cups thinly sliced onion
2 garlic cloves, minced
1 large green pepper, seeded and
   thinly sliced
4 large ripe tomatoes, peeled,
   seeded, and chopped
1 cup thinly sliced pimientos
1½ teaspoons curry powder
1 cup uncooked rice
1-1½ cups chicken broth

● Place eggplant and zucchini in separate colanders. Sprinkle with salt and let drain 30-60 minutes. Drain each vegetable thoroughly on paper towels.
● Heat *4 tablespoons* oil in a heavy skillet. Sauté eggplant until browned. Remove with a slotted spoon and reserve.
● Add a little more oil to the pan. Sauté zucchini for 3-5 minutes until browned. Remove and add to eggplant.
● Add more oil. Sauté onion and garlic until soft. Add peppers, tomatoes, and pimientos. Season with salt and pepper and bring to a boil. Cook uncovered until tomato juices evaporate. Add zucchini and eggplant and cook 3-4 minutes more.
● Blend in curry powder. Add rice and chicken broth, stirring gently with a wooden spoon. Cook until rice is tender. Mound in a serving bowl and cool to room temperature. Chill.

Holley Hicok Schroeder

Stuffed Mushrooms Baked in Cream

Serves 6-8

24 mushrooms
1 onion, finely chopped
4 tablespoons butter
Salt and freshly ground pepper
1 tablespoon chopped parsley
¼ teaspoon tarragon or thyme
½ cup fine fresh breadcrumbs
¾ cup heavy cream

● Remove stems from mushrooms, and place caps in a buttered shallow baking dish.
● Chop stems and onion finely. Sauté in butter. Season to taste with salt, pepper, parsley, and herbs. Add breadcrumbs. Spoon stuffing into mushroom cavities.
● Preheat oven to 350°. Pour cream around mushrooms. Bake until cream is thickened and brown.

Linda Cantrell Lindon

151

Vegetables

Green Pea Purée with Capers

3 pounds fresh green peas in shells, or 2 packages (10 ounces each) frozen peas
½ cup boiling water
Pinch light brown sugar
Salt and freshly ground pepper
2 tablespoons butter
1 tablespoon drained capers, rinsed and dried
Pimiento strips for garnish (optional)

Serves 4-6

● Shell fresh peas. Cook in covered saucepan with boiling water, brown sugar, salt, and pepper. Fresh peas will take 8-10 minutes, frozen peas only 4-5 minutes. Drain peas, reserving cooking liquid. Stir in butter.
● Purée peas until smooth. Adjust seasonings to taste. If purée is too thick, blend in a little of the reserved cooking liquid. Reheat purée. Stir in capers. Serve garnished with pimiento.

Nancy Beck Hoggson

Pommes de Terre Duchesse

6 potatoes (about 1½ pounds)
2 tablespoons butter
2 egg yolks
¼ cup hot milk
Salt and pepper
Nutmeg

Serves 8

● Boil potatoes in their jackets in salted water until tender. Peel. Put through a potato ricer, or mash well. Stir in butter, *1 egg yolk,* and enough hot milk to make a firm purée. Season to taste with salt, pepper, and nutmeg.
● Fit a pastry bag with a large star or rose tube. Pipe potatoes onto a greased baking sheet, making each shape an individual serving. Mix remaining egg yolk with 1 tablespoon cold water. Brush on potatoes. Brown under broiler or in a 450° oven.

Marcia Mead Thomas

Vegetables

Potatoes Anna

6 potatoes, peeled
¾ cup melted butter
Salt and freshly ground pepper
1 cup grated cheese (optional)
2 onions, sliced and sautéed
     (optional)
¼ pound mushrooms, sliced and
     sautéed (optional)
⅓ cup chopped parsley

Serves 6

• Preheat oven to 400°. Slice or julienne potatoes in food processor or by hand. Place in salted, cold water until ready to use.
• Generously butter a round pie plate or casserole. Drain and dry potatoes. Arrange neatly in dish, with slices overlapping. Pour melted butter over each layer. Season with salt and pepper, repeating layers until dish is full. Sprinkle each layer with cheese, onions, and/or mushrooms, if desired.
• Press down with a spatula. Bake 40-50 minutes, until crusty and brown. Invert on a serving dish or serve from baking dish, garnished with chopped parsley.

Mary Ellen Donovan Weinrib

Potatoes Dauphinois

8 potatoes (about 2 pounds)
2 cups milk
1½ cups heavy cream
2 garlic cloves, minced
¾ teaspoon salt
½ teaspoon white pepper
¾ cup grated swiss cheese

Serves 8

• Peel and slice potatoes ⅛" thick. Place in a large saucepan. Add milk, cream, garlic, salt, and pepper. Bring to a boil, stirring with a wooden spoon to prevent scorching. Remove pan from heat.
• Butter a shallow baking dish. Pour in potato mixture. Sprinkle cheese over top and bake in a 400° oven for 1 hour until potatoes are well browned. Reduce oven heat to 375° if potatoes begin to brown too much on the surface. Let stand 15 minutes before serving.

Barbara Smith Suval

Vegetables

Baked New Potatoes

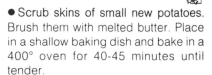

2-3 small potatoes per person
Melted butter
Salt and pepper

● Scrub skins of small new potatoes. Brush them with melted butter. Place in a shallow baking dish and bake in a 400° oven for 40-45 minutes until tender.
● To serve, cut a small "X" in each potato. Press with your fingers until the potato resembles a rosette. Put a piece of butter in each and sprinkle with salt and pepper. Serve hot.

Joan Cooley May

Potato Pudding

6 medium baking potatoes
3 egg yolks, beaten
1 cup grated gruyère or swiss
　　cheese
1 garlic clove, finely minced
½ cup heavy cream
Freshly grated nutmeg
Salt and freshly ground
　　pepper
3 egg whites, beaten to hold stiff
　　peaks
Butter
Breadcrumbs

Serves 6
● Bake potatoes in a 450° oven for 45 minutes, or until soft. Cool and scoop out insides. Mash potatoes and measure. You should have about 4 cups.
● Stir in egg yolks, grated cheese, and garlic, blending well. Add cream, a pinch of nutmeg, salt, and pepper to taste. Beat egg whites to form stiff peaks and fold in.
● Butter sides and bottom of a 2-quart casserole and shake in breadcrumbs to coat bottom and sides. Discard excess crumbs. Turn potato pudding into prepared casserole.
● Bake in a 350° oven for 1 hour, until golden brown. Turn out onto a serving dish or serve from the casserole.

Ann Keyser Griffin

Vegetables

Straw Potatoes with Peas

6-8 potatoes
5 pounds fresh peas, shelled, or 2
   packages (10 ounces each)
   frozen peas
Oil for frying
Butter

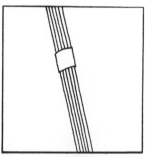
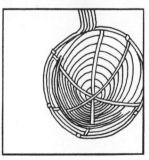

Serves 8-10

● Shred or julienne potatoes. Rinse in cold water. Spread between layers of paper toweling to remove excess water. Dry well.

● Heat oil to 360° in a deep fryer. Lightly oil a Bird's Nest Maker. Cover bottom with julienne potatoes. Press down top of Bird's Nest Maker, and fasten.

● Place basket in hot oil and cook until potatoes are golden brown. Remove basket from oil. Cool 1 minute. Remove top of the Bird's Nest Maker. Turn it over and gently tap the basket. The potatoes will fall out. Continue frying until all potatoes are used.

● Without a Bird's Nest Maker, deep-fry potato straws. Remove from fat with a slotted spoon and drain on paper towels.

● Place cooked potato baskets in a 200° oven while you fry the remainder.

● To serve, steam fresh peas for about 15 minutes. Salt potatoes or baskets. Warm them in a 250° oven. Drain peas. Season with butter, salt, and pepper to taste. Place in the crispy baskets to serve.

Nancy Beck Hoggson

155

Vegetables

Sweet Potato Soufflé

1 cup milk
½ teaspoon salt
2 teaspoons sugar
2 tablespoons butter
2 cups mashed sweet potato
2 eggs, separated
½ cup raisins
½ teaspoon nutmeg
½ cup chopped walnuts
15 marshmallows (optional)

Serves 6

● Scald milk in a saucepan with salt, sugar, and butter. Add to mashed sweet potatoes. Beat well. Beat egg yolks. Add to potato mixture with raisins, nutmeg, and nuts.
● Preheat oven to 325°. Beat egg whites to form stiff peaks. Fold into potato mixture. Turn into a greased 1½-quart casserole. Top with marshmallows and bake 45 minutes or until set.

Madeleine Galanek Egan

Baked Rice Pignola

2 tablespoons butter
2 tablespoons minced onion
¼ teaspoon minced garlic
1 cup uncooked rice
1½ cups chicken broth
2 parsley sprigs
1 fresh thyme sprig, or ¼ teaspoon dried thyme
½ bay leaf
⅛ teaspoon cayenne pepper
¼ cup toasted pine nuts (pignola)

Serves 4

● Preheat oven to 400°. Melt *1 tablespoon* butter in a heatproof casserole. Sauté onion and garlic until onion is translucent. Add rice. Stir briefly over low heat to coat the grains with butter. Stir in chicken broth, parsley, thyme, bay leaf, and cayenne. Cover tightly.
● Bake for 15-20 minutes. Remove cover and discard herbs and bay leaf. Stir in remaining 1 tablespoon butter and pine nuts with a fork. Keep warm until ready to serve.

Karin Lawrence Siegfried

Vegetables

Brown Rice with Pecans

1 cup brown rice
3 cups chicken broth
¼ cup butter
1 medium onion, finely chopped
½ cup finely chopped celery
¼ cup chopped parsley
2 teaspoons monosodium glutamate
1 cup sliced pecans
½ teaspoon poultry seasoning
⅛ teaspoon thyme
Salt and freshly ground pepper

Serves 4-6

● Cook rice in chicken broth over low heat until rice is tender and absorbs all the liquid, about 45 minutes.

● In the meantime, combine butter, onion, celery, parsley, and monosodium glutamate in a skillet. Sauté over low heat until tender.

● Combine sautéed vegetables with cooked rice. Add remaining ingredients, moistening further with broth if needed. Transfer to a casserole and cover with foil. Refrigerate at this point, if desired. Bring to room temperature before baking.

● Preheat oven to 325°. Bake rice for 30 minutes.

Victoria Eastman Ohlandt

Curried Rice

1 small apple
½ cup chopped onion
1 garlic clove, minced
3 tablespoons butter
1 cup uncooked rice
1-3 teaspoons curry powder
½ bay leaf
1½ cups chicken broth

Serves 4

● Core and slice apple. Stack slices. Cut them in ½" strips, then into ¼" cubes.

● Sauté onion and garlic in *2 table-spoons* butter until soft. Add apple cubes, rice, curry powder to taste, bay leaf, and broth.

● Cover. Bring to a boil and cook 15-20 minutes. Add remaining 1 tablespoon butter and fluff rice with a fork.

Nancy Gould Pinkernell

157

Vegetables

Risotto

1 pound Italian (Arborio) rice (about
    2 cups)
2 quarts chicken or beef broth
3 tablespoons butter
1¼ cups freshly grated parmesan
    cheese
Salt and freshly ground pepper

Serves 6

• Remove any dark grains from the rice. Bring broth to a boil in a large pot. Cover and let simmer.

• Melt *2 tablespoons* butter in another saucepan with a heavy bottom. Add rice and stir over moderately high heat until grains are evenly coated with butter, about 2 minutes.

• Stir in ¾ cup of the simmering broth. Lower heat under the rice and simmer. Stir constantly with a wooden spoon until most of the liquid is absorbed. Then add broth to cover but not submerge the rice. Continue to stir and simmer. Add the same amount of broth each time the rice is nearly dry (every 3-5 minutes).

• Bite into a grain of rice after 20 minutes of cooking. It should be almost tender but still have a fairly hard center. Add *1 cup* grated parmesan, a sprinkling of salt and pepper, and more broth. Cook 5 minutes more. Serve al dente, sprinkled with the additional ¼ cup grated parmesan.

Mary Vance Watson

Risotto with Lemon

• Grate the zest from half a lemon. Mix with 1 egg yolk and juice from the lemon half.

• Stir this slowly into cooked Risotto. Return to pot. Stir for another minute. Serve immediately.

Mary Vance Watson

Vegetables

Spinach Ramekins

2 tablespoons minced green onions, tops included
1 tablespoon butter
1 package (10 ounces) fresh spinach, cooked, drained, and chopped
1 egg, well beaten
1 egg yolk, well beaten
½ cup half-and-half
¼ cup dry breadcrumbs
2 tablespoons grated parmesan cheese
¼ teaspoon salt
Dash white pepper
Pinch grated nutmeg
8 sautéed mushroom caps (optional)

Serves 4

● Butter 4 ramekins (6 ounces each), or a 3-cup casserole. Line bottom with buttered wax paper.
● Sauté onions in butter until soft. Mix with remaining ingredients except mushrooms. Spoon mixture into prepared ramekins or casserole.
● Place ramekins or casserole in a large baking pan. Pour 1" of water into pan. Bake in a 350° oven for 20-30 minutes, until set.
● To serve, unmold on a serving platter. Remove wax paper and turn over carefully. Garnish with mushroom caps. Drizzle with olive oil and lemon juice if served cold.

Nancy Beck Hoggson

Candied Acorn Squash

2 medium acorn squash
4 tablespoons butter
2 tablespoons light brown sugar
Salt and pepper
Breadcrumbs

Serves 4

● Halve acorn squash lengthwise. Remove seeds and fibrous material. Place halves cut side down on a rack in a shallow baking pan. Pour hot water halfway up sides of the pan. Bake squash in a 350° oven for 40 minutes, until soft. Remove from oven and cool slightly.
● Scoop out insides, being careful not to puncture skins. Mix cooked squash with butter, brown sugar, salt, and pepper. When smooth, taste and adjust seasonings as needed.
● Mound purée in scooped out shells. Sprinkle each with breadcrumbs. Bake now or refrigerate until 40 minutes before serving time.
● Bake 15-20 minutes in a 350° oven until warm, or 30 minutes if refrigerated.

Barbara Smith Suval

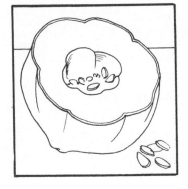

Vegetables

Yellow Squash Scallop

1½-2 pounds yellow squash, washed and sliced
1 small onion, chopped
1 tablespoon butter
4 ounces cream cheese
Cracker crumbs
Salt and pepper
4-5 slices bacon, fried and crumbled (optional)

Serves 8

● Cook squash with salt, pepper, and chopped onion in boiling water. When tender, drain, add butter and cream cheese. Stir until melted.

● Turn mixture into a greased baking dish. Top with crumbs and crumbled bacon. Bake in a 350° oven for 30 minutes.

Robin McNevin Robertson

Baked Tomatoes with Herbs and Breadcrumbs

6 medium tomatoes
1 teaspoon salt
Freshly ground pepper
¾ cup fine fresh breadcrumbs
1½ teaspoons dried basil
1½ tablespoons chopped parsley
½ teaspoon dried thyme
1 garlic clove, minced
1 tablespoon olive oil

Serves 6

● Remove cores from tomatoes. Halve them crosswise. Scoop out seeds leaving flesh intact. Sprinkle cut surfaces with salt and pepper. Place tomatoes, cut sides down, on a rack while preparing topping.

● Mix breadcrumbs with herbs, garlic, salt, and pepper. Arrange tomato halves in a greased baking dish, cut side up. Spoon crumb mixture on each tomato half and into indentations where seeds were removed. Drizzle with olive oil.

● Bake in a 425° oven for 20-30 minutes until topping is golden brown. Tomatoes will be cooked through but still intact.

Anne Ruthrauff Seltzer

Vegetables

Cherry Tomato Sauté

24 firm, ripe cherry tomatoes
2 tablespoons olive oil
1 teaspoon finely chopped garlic
2 tablespoons finely chopped parsley
2 tablespoons chopped tarragon,
    basil, chervil, or chives

Serves 4

● Rinse tomatoes. Pat dry with a paper towel.

● Heat oil in a skillet or baking dish in a 400° oven. Add garlic. Sauté briefly or place in oven for 5 minutes. Add tomatoes. Sprinkle with parsley and herbs to taste.

● Shake skillet while cooking for about 2 minutes, or bake 6-8 minutes in oven. The tomatoes are cooked when heated through and beginning to soften. Sprinkle with salt and pepper.

Barbara Smith Suval

Creamed Green Tomatoes

4 green tomatoes, at room
    temperature
1 cup flour
1 tablespoon salt
Freshly ground pepper
3 tablespoons butter
1 tablespoon oil
1-2 tablespoons brown sugar
¾ cup heavy cream

Serves 4

● Slice tomatoes ½" thick. Season flour with salt and pepper. Dredge tomato slices in this mixture.

● Heat butter and oil in a large skillet. When foaming stops, add tomato slices. Sauté over medium-high heat until browned, about 3 minutes on each side. Remove to a platter and keep warm while frying remaining tomato slices.

● Add brown sugar to juices in pan. Stir briefly until melted. Mix in cream. Pour this sauce over tomato slices on the platter and serve immediately.

Nancy Beck Hoggson

161

Vegetables

Navets Anna

6 white turnips (about 1½ pounds)
5 tablespoons butter
Salt and freshly ground pepper
Chopped parsley

Serves 6

● Preheat oven to 400°. Peel turnips and slice ⅛" thick.
● Heat *4 tablespoons* butter in a skillet, and add sliced turnips. Sprinkle with salt and pepper to taste. Cook 10 minutes over medium heat, turning slices gently.
● Rub a round 8" or 9" cake pan with remaining 1 tablespoon butter. Arrange sautéed turnip slices in pan. Cover and bake 15 minutes.
● Uncover and bake 25-30 minutes longer. Invert on a serving platter. Garnish with chopped parsley.

Susan Don Lubin

Cheese-Stuffed Zucchini

2 medium zucchini (about 1 pound)
¼ cup finely chopped onion
1 tablespoon butter
¾ cup cream-style cottage cheese
⅔ cup cooked rice
1 egg, beaten
1 tablespoon snipped parsley
1 teaspoon salt
⅛ teaspoon dried basil, crushed
2 slices (2 ounces) cheddar cheese,
    cut in 16 strips

Serves 4

● Trim ends from zucchini. Cook in a small amount of boiling, salted water for 8 minutes until tender. Halve lengthwise, scoop out centers, and dice.
● Cook onion in butter until golden. Stir in zucchini, cottage cheese, rice, egg, parsley, salt, and basil.
● Lightly salt zucchini shells and fill with cottage cheese mixture. Place in a greased 11" x 7" baking dish. Cover and bake in a 350° oven for 25 minutes.
● Place 4 cheese strips on each zucchini half. Bake, uncovered, for 5 minutes.

Nancy Gould Pinkernell

Vegetables

Zucchini Custard

6 medium zucchini, grated
Salt
1½ cups heavy cream
3 egg yolks
1 small white onion, chopped
1 tablespoon chopped fresh parsley
1 teaspoon chopped chives
¼ teaspoon freshly ground white
    pepper
Pinch nutmeg
½ cup grated swiss or gruyère
    cheese

Serves 6

● Preheat oven to 375°. Toss grated zucchini with salt and put in a colander. Let sit at least 30 minutes to extract moisture. Squeeze thoroughly dry in a potato ricer or tea towel. Place zucchini in a greased shallow baking dish.
● Mix cream with egg yolks, onion, parsley, chives, pepper, and nutmeg. Pour over zucchini in baking dish. Sprinkle with grated cheese.
● Bake 25-30 minutes, until custard is set and top is golden brown.

Penelope Johnson Wartels

Zucchini Pancakes

3 cups grated zucchini (about 1½
    pounds)
½ cup flour
1 teaspoon baking powder
Salt and freshly ground pepper
1 egg, beaten
Oil for frying
Melted butter
Grated parmesan cheese

Serves 4-6

● Mix zucchini with flour, baking powder, salt, and pepper to taste. Add egg. Stir to blend ingredients well.
● Lightly oil a griddle. Heat until drops of water dance across the surface. Drop zucchini mixture onto griddle with a large tablespoon. Cook to brown on both sides. Serve with melted butter and grated parmesan.

Nancy Beck Hoggson

entrees

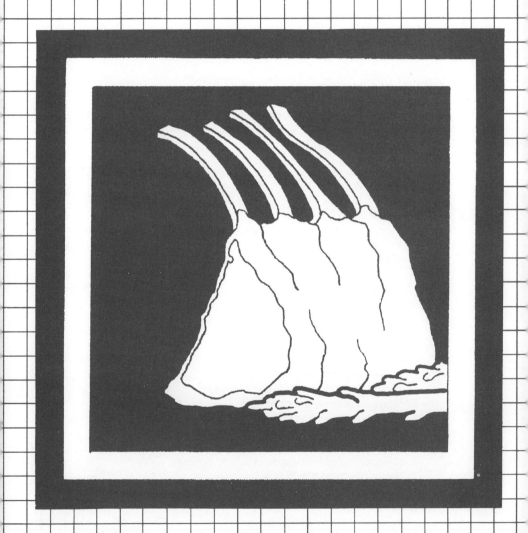

A Fish Story

Allow ⅓ to ½ pound fish fillet or ¾-1 pound whole fish per serving.

When buying whole fish, select those which smell only slightly fishy. The flesh should spring back when pressed.

Prepare fresh fish as soon after buying as possible.

Allow 10 minutes cooking time for each 1″ of thickness, whether broiling, frying, or baking.

Bake fish at a high temperature—450°.

Broil whole fish 2″-4″ from heat source, large fish 4″-6″ from heat. Fish fillets should be broiled 3″ from heat. Frozen fillets can be broiled without thawing by doubling the cooking time.

Cook fish only until the translucent flesh becomes opaque and flakes when tested with a fork.

Make a holder when broiling or grilling delicate fish fillets by lightly oiling a strip of aluminum foil. Place the fillet on the foil on the broiler rack or grill leaving the ends free to use as handles. Lift cooked fish off the rack with these handles and gently tilt onto serving platter.

Thaw frozen fish in milk to replace the distinctly frozen taste with a freshly caught flavor.

Perk up the butter used to dot a fish fillet under the broiler by adding one of the following for each ½ cup of butter.
   —2 tablespoons chopped fresh chives
   —2 teaspoons Dijon mustard
   —½ cup browned, finely chopped almonds
   —2 tablespoons finely chopped fresh parsley or watercress
   —1 tablespoon fresh lemon juice
   —1 teaspoon grated lemon peel
   —1 teaspoon anchovy paste
   —2 tablespoons finely chopped, sautéed onions
   —¼ cup finely diced shellfish

Entrees

Stuffed Filet of Beef

3 large onions, thinly sliced
6 tablespoons olive oil
4 tablespoons butter
2 garlic cloves, minced
18-20 pitted black olives, coarsely
    chopped
½ cup chopped cooked ham
Salt and freshly ground pepper
1 teaspoon thyme
2 egg yolks, beaten
2 tablespoons chopped parsley
1 beef filet, about 7 pounds

Serves 8-10

● Sauté onions in oil and butter until limp. Add garlic, olives, ham, and 1 teaspoon each salt, pepper, and thyme. Cook until well blended. Stir in beaten egg yolks and parsley. Cook about 3 minutes.
● Cut filet not quite through in 1" slices. Spread stuffing between slices. Place on a rack in a roasting pan. Brush with additional oil or butter. Roast about 50 minutes at 300° or until internal temperature is 125°F. Let rest 10 minutes before serving.

Marcia Petersen Sandner

Standing Rib Roast

Any size rib roast
Salt and freshly ground pepper

● About 5 hours before serving time, preheat oven to 375°. Salt and pepper the beef. Roast uncovered for 1 hour.
● After 1 hour, turn off oven. Do not open oven door.
● An hour before serving, turn oven temperature to 300°. Cook as follows:
    45 minutes for rare
    50 minutes for medium-rare
    55 minutes for medium
● Keep oven door closed until you are ready to remove roast from oven. Allow to stand 5-10 minutes before carving.

Judith Huggard Hubbard

Entrees

Steak and Bacon Tournedos

1 flank steak, about 1½ pounds
Freshly chopped garlic
Freshly ground pepper
Finely chopped parsley
Soy sauce
½ pound bacon
Betsy's Marinade (see Index)

Serves 4-6

● Pound steak until thin. Lay flat and score diagonally, making diamond-shaped cuts. Sprinkle cut side with garlic, pepper, parsley, and soy sauce.
● Cook bacon until crisp. Lay bacon strips lengthwise on steak and roll up like a jelly roll, starting at the narrow end. Skewer at 1" intervals with wooden toothpicks.
● Mix ingredients for marinade, and pour over rolled steak in a dish. Marinate 2 days in refrigerator, basting frequently.
● Sear in a buttered skillet on all sides, then roast for 15 minutes in a 450° oven. To cook on the grill, sear each side for 2 minutes, then grill 6 more minutes on each side.

Ann Keyser Griffin

Steak with Green Peppercorns

1 sirloin steak, 1-1½" thick (about 3 pounds)
1 tablespoon cognac or whisky
1 tablespoon drained green peppercorns
¼ cup heavy cream
½ teaspoon Dijon mustard

Serves 3-4

● Cut a piece of fat from steak, and render in a heavy skillet. Pan-fry steak in this fat. Season with salt and transfer to a warm platter. Keep warm.
● Remove any excess fat from skillet. Add cognac or whisky and heat, stirring constantly. Crush green peppercorns with a mortar and pestle. Add with cream to skillet. Simmer and stir in mustard. Pour sauce over steak.

Nancy Beck Hoggson

Entrees

Sukiyaki

3 celery ribs
1 large Bermuda onion
½ pound mushrooms
12 green onions
1 can (5 ounces) water chestnuts,
    drained
¾-1 pound fresh spinach
1 tablespoon oil
2-2½ pounds round or sirloin steak,
    sliced in very thin strips
1 cup beef bouillon
½ cup soy sauce
¼ cup dry vermouth
1 tablespoon sugar

Serves 6
● Slice celery, onion, mushrooms, green onions, and water chestnuts.
● Heat oil in wok or large skillet. Brown meat and push to side of pan. Add all vegetables except spinach. Stir in remaining ingredients. Let cook 5 minutes.
● Add spinach, cover, and cook 5 minutes more. Serve with boiled rice.

Anne Ruthrauff Seltzer

Savory Steak Strips

1 beef round steak, sirloin tip or eye
    round roast (2-3 pounds)
¼ cup flour
1 teaspoon salt
¼ teaspoon freshly ground pepper
¼ teaspoon paprika
3 tablespoons bacon drippings
1 medium onion, thinly sliced
⅔ cup beef consommé
1 tablespoon worcestershire sauce
¼ cup mushrooms, sautéed
½ cup chopped green pepper
1 cup sour cream

Serves 6
● Cut steak into ½" strips, then cut these strips into 3" x ¼" pieces.
● Combine flour, salt, pepper, and paprika. Dredge steak strips in seasoned flour. Brown in bacon drippings and pour off fat. Add onion, consommé, and worcestershire. Cover and cook slowly for about 45 minutes. Stir frequently, adding more consommé if needed to keep from sticking.
● Add mushrooms and green pepper. Continue to cook 30 minutes longer, stirring occasionally.
● Stir a small amount of steak mixture into sour cream. Add sour cream to steak strips. Cook just to heat through.

Suzanne Rich Beatty

Entrees

Downing Street Beef and Kidney Pie

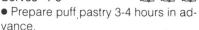

Puff Pastry (see Index)
2 pounds lean beef, cut in 1" cubes
3 lamb kidneys, cleaned and cut in
    pieces
2 rounded tablespoons flour
Salt, freshly ground pepper, and
    chopped parsley
1 medium onion, sliced
2 garlic cloves, minced
2 tablespoons oil or bacon fat
¼ pound mushrooms
1 cup boiling water
3 beef bouillon cubes
¼ cup walnuts
1 egg beaten

Serves 4-6

- Prepare puff pastry 3-4 hours in advance.
- Toss steak and kidney in flour seasoned with salt, pepper, and chopped parsley. Sauté onion and garlic in oil or fat until golden. Push to side of pan and add meat, kidneys, and mushrooms. Brown 5 minutes, stirring often.
- Pour boiling water over bouillon cubes and stir to dissolve. Add to pan, taste, and adjust seasonings. Cover and simmer 2-2½ hours.
- Add walnuts to stew and turn into a casserole. Preheat oven to 425°. Cover with puff pastry. Brush with beaten egg. Make a hole to allow steam to escape. Bake 25-30 minutes.

Betsy Gimpel Mena

Chinese Beef with Vegetables

½ pound flank steak
1 tablespoon cornstarch
1 tablespoon soy sauce
1 tablespoon sherry
½ teaspoon sugar
3 tablespoons peanut oil
1 pound mixed fresh
    vegetables—onions, broccoli, red
    pepper, Chinese or regular
    mushrooms
1 garlic clove, minced
1 slice fresh ginger root
1 green onion, cut in 1" pieces
½ teaspoon salt
½ cup beef broth

Serves 4-6

- Slice beef thinly across the grain. Combine cornstarch, soy sauce, sherry, and sugar, stirring smooth. Add to beef and toss to coat. Let stand at least 30 minutes, turning occasionally.
- Wash vegetables and slice or dice as desired. Heat 1½ tablespoons oil. Add garlic, ginger, and green onion. Stir-fry for 2 minutes, then add beef and stir-fry 2 minutes more. Remove from pan.
- Heat remaining 1½ tablespoons oil. Add vegetables and stir-fry 1-2 minutes. Add salt, then stock. Cover and cook until vegetables are barely tender. Return beef to wok or skillet and stir-fry to reheat and blend flavors. Add seasoning to taste.

Deborah Morrow Hunter

Entrees

Barbequed Beef

4 pounds beef chuck
4 onions, chopped
1 tablespoon salt
¼ teaspoon pepper
½ cup water
½ cup chopped green pepper
1½ cans (6 ounces each)
    tomato paste
1 can (8 ounces) tomato sauce
¼ cup vinegar
¼ cup brown sugar
3 tablespoons worcestershire sauce
2 tablespoons chili powder
1 tablespoon dry mustard
1 tablespoon Liquid Smoke
1½ teaspoons barbecue spice
    seasoning
1 teaspoon pepper

Serves 12
● Trim beef and brown in fat. Cook with onions, salt, pepper, and water in a tightly covered pan until meat shreds. Cool several hours or overnight.
● Shred meat and add remaining ingredients. Cook slowly about 3 hours, stirring frequently.
    Note: This will serve many more as an appetizer with small party rolls.

JoAnn Hixon Mills

Heritage Beef Stew

4 pounds beef chuck, cut in 1½"
    cubes
2 tablespoons oil
2½ cups boiling water
1 teaspoon lemon juice
1 teaspoon worcestershire sauce
1 garlic clove
3 onions, quartered
2 bay leaves
1 tablespoon salt
½ teaspoon freshly ground pepper
½ teaspoon paprika
¼ teaspoon allspice
¼ teaspoon ground cloves
1 teaspoon sugar
10 carrots, peeled and cut in
    1" lengths
6 potatoes, peeled and quartered
¼ pound mushrooms
4 tablespoons cornstarch
1½ cups red wine

Serves 8
● Thoroughly brown meat on all sides in hot oil. Add water, lemon juice, worcestershire, garlic, onions, and all seasonings. Cover and simmer for 2 hours.
● Add vegetables and cook another 25 minutes.
● Stir constarch with ½ cup wine, mixing until smooth. Add to stew with remaining 1 cup wine. Simmer uncovered until thickened.

Linda Grant Sharp

171

Entrees

Sauerbraten

Serves 12-14

1 pint claret
1 pint water
1 cup vinegar
1½ teaspoons salt
1 tablespoon ginger
1 tablespoon allspice
1 tablespoon whole cloves
1 tablespoon whole black
   peppercorns
1 cup brown sugar, packed
1 onion
1 boneless pot roast, 4-6 pounds
4-5 tablespoons flour

● Mix claret, water, vinegar, salt, ginger, allspice, cloves, peppercorns, brown sugar, and onion in dutch oven. Bring to a boil. Cool completely, then add meat. Marinate meat in liquid for 3 days in refrigerator.

● Cover tightly and cook slowly in marinade for 3 hours or until tender. Remove meat from pot. Mix flour with a little strained marinade until smooth, then stir into half the marinade. Bring to a boil and serve with sliced meat.

Judith Torrisi Wintermuth

Spicy New England Pot Roast

Serves 8

3 tablespoons flour
2 teaspoons salt
¼ teaspoon freshly ground pepper
1 boned and rolled bottom round
   roast, about 4 pounds
3 tablespoons bacon drippings or oil
½ cup grated horseradish, drained
1 cup whole cranberry sauce
1 cinnamon stick, broken
4 whole cloves
1 cup beef broth
16 small white onions
1 bunch carrots, cut in 3″ lengths

● Mix flour, salt, and pepper. Dredge meat in this mixture. Heat drippings or oil in a heavy dutch oven or casserole and brown meat very well on all sides over high heat. Pour off and reserve drippings.

● Mix horseradish, cranberry sauce, cinnamon, cloves, and broth. Add to meat. Bring mixture to boil, cover tightly, and simmer gently about 2½ hours until beef is barely tender.

● Brown onions in reserved drippings in skillet. Add carrots and cook 2 minutes longer. Drain fat and add vegetables to meat. Cover and cook about 45 minutes longer until vegetables and meat are tender.

Nancy Gould Pinkernell

Entrees

Daube Provençale

1 pound lean bacon
4 pounds stewing beef
Salt and freshly ground pepper
4 large onions, quartered
2 whole heads of garlic, peeled
1 strip orange peel, diced
1 bay leaf
1 teaspoon thyme
Red wine
Celery, carrots, mushrooms, and
    small white onions, if desired

Serves 8

● Cook bacon in a heavy, deep casserole until it has rendered its fat and is crisp. Remove bacon, crumble, and set aside.

● Cut meat in 1½"-2" cubes, trimming fat. Cook meat cubes in the bacon fat until browned.

● Place meat in a large casserole. Sprinkle with salt and pepper. Add onion quarters, crumbled bacon, garlic cloves, orange peel, bay leaf, thyme, and enough red wine to cover.

● Cover and simmer over very low heat for 3 hours until meat is tender. Add vegetables during last 30 minutes of cooking. Cool and refrigerate overnight.

● When chilled, skim fat from the surface. Heat to the boiling point before serving.

Barbara Smith Suval

Calves Liver Sauté with Vinegar Glaze

1 pound calves liver, sliced very thin
    and cut in 4-8 pieces
½ cup flour
Salt and freshly ground pepper
½ cup butter
¼ cup chopped fresh parsley
¼ cup red wine vinegar

Serves 4

● Dredge liver with a mixture of flour, salt, and pepper.

● Heat *half* the butter in a heavy skillet until bubbling. Add liver. Sauté on one side for 2-3 minutes. Turn and cook 2 minutes more. Transfer to a heated platter and sprinkle with chopped parsley. Keep warm.

● Add remaining butter to skillet and let it brown. Pour over liver on serving platter. Add vinegar to skillet. Bring to a boil and swirl around in skillet. Pour over liver.

Nancy Beck Hoggson

173

Entrees

Pastitsio

7 tablespoons butter
2 teaspoons oil
1½ cups finely chopped onion
2 garlic cloves, minced
2 pounds ground beef
Salt and freshly ground pepper
½ teaspoon oregano
½ teaspoon cinnamon
Freshly grated nutmeg to taste
¼ cup finely chopped parsley
1½ cups Italian plum tomatoes, well
    drained
½ cup dry red wine
3 cups light cream
1 cup milk
¾ cup flour
5 egg yolks
½ cup heavy cream
1 cup ricotta cheese
¾ pound pasticcio macaroni, or #2
    long macaroni or ziti
½ cup finely crumbled feta cheese
½ cup grated parmesan or romano
    cheese

Serves 10-12

● Melt *1 tablespoon* butter with oil in a large skillet. Sauté onion until golden and soft. Add garlic and beef and cook until meat is browned. Season with salt and pepper to taste. Add oregano, cinnamon, nutmeg, parsley, tomatoes, and wine. Adjust seasonings. Cook over medium-high heat until liquid evaporates, about 30 minutes.

● Scald light cream and milk together in a saucepan. Melt remaining 6 tablespoons butter in a 4-quart saucepan. Stir in flour. Cook, stirring, until smooth and bubbly. Mix in scalded cream and milk, stirring constantly. Season to taste with salt and pepper. Cook and stir until thick. Remove from heat.

● Beat egg yolks with heavy cream. Gradually blend in some of the hot sauce. Stir egg yolk mixture into cream sauce in pan. Beat in ricotta, and remove from heat.

● Boil macaroni rapidly in a large pot of boiling, salted water until cooked but still firm, about 10 minutes. Drain well.

● Preheat oven to 400°. Butter an 18" x 13" baking dish. Set aside half the cream sauce. Layer ingredients beginning with macaroni, then use ⅓ the feta cheese and ¼ the grated parmesan. Spread with a thin layer of cream sauce, then ⅓ the meat mixture. Continue these layers, ending with macaroni. Pour reserved sauce over top and sprinkle with remaining grated parmesan, if serving immediately. If preparing ahead, save the final sprinkling of cheese until ready to reheat.

Entrees

continued

• Bake 50-60 minutes until very hot and bubbly. This can be prepared ahead and frozen. Reheat, covered, in a 300° oven.

Betsy Gimpel Mena

Peach-Glazed Corn Beef

Serves 6-8

1 corned beef brisket, about 3 pounds
2 medium acorn squash, quartered and seeded
4 small apples, cored and quartered
½ cup peach preserves
½ teaspoon ground ginger

• Rinse meat in cold water to remove pickling juices. Place meat fat side up on a rack in a shallow roasting pan. Add 2 cups water and cover pan tightly. Bake 2-2¼ hours at 350°.
• Drain liquid from pan and discard. Place squash and apple pieces, skin side down, around meat. Sprinkle squash with a little salt and add ½ cup hot water. Cover and bake 20 minutes.
• Mix preserves and ginger. Spoon over apples and squash, reserving some of the glaze. Cover and bake 25 minutes more. Remove lid or foil cover and spread remaining glaze over meat and vegetables. Bake uncovered for 10 minutes.

Madeleine Galanek Egan

Beanless Chili

Serves 6

2½ pounds ground beef
4 onions, chopped
3 garlic cloves, minced
2 sweet green peppers, chopped
1 can (28 ounces) tomato purée
1 cup red wine
2 tablespoons chili powder
1 tablespoon salt
2 teaspoons cumin
2 teaspoons oregano
1 tablespoon worcestershire sauce
2 tablespoons red wine vinegar
Chopped onion

• Brown beef in a large skillet over medium heat. Drain fat. Add chopped onions, garlic, and green peppers. Cook until softened. Stir in tomato purée, wine, seasonings, worcestershire, and vinegar.
• Cover skillet and cook slowly for 1½-2 hours. Stir occasionally. Serve with chopped onion.

Barbara Smith Suval

175

Entrees

Stuffed Cucumbers

6 cucumbers, about ½ pound each
3 tablespoons salt
5 ripe tomatoes
6 tablespoons olive oil
1 tablespoon basil
1 teaspoon thyme
1 tablespoon chopped parsley
¼ cup coarsely chopped shallots or
    small white onions
1½ pounds ground lean beef
Freshly ground pepper
1 tablespoon tomato purée, or 1
    teaspoon tomato paste
¼ cup grated parmesan cheese
2 tablespoons fine, dry breadcrumbs
¾ cup dry white wine or tomato juice

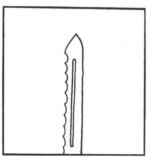

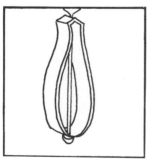

Serves 6

• To prepare cucumbers, trim ends and peel. Halve each lengthwise. Hollow out halves with a teaspoon, removing all seeds. Place in a large bowl with *2 tablespoons* of salt and cover with water. Let stand about 20 minutes.

• Drop tomatoes into a large pot of boiling water for 10 seconds. Quickly drain in a colander and run under cold water. Skin and core tomatoes. Cut them in half crosswise. Squeeze out seeds and chop flesh.

• Heat *3 tablespoons* oil in a skillet. Add basil, thyme, and parsley. Cook 1 minute. Add shallots and cook, stirring, until they are translucent. Add ground beef, remaining 1 tablespoon salt, and pepper to taste. Cook beef for 3 minutes, stirring to break up meat. Add chopped tomatoes and tomato purée. Simmer 3-4 minutes until mixture thickens. Stir in parmesan.

• Preheat oven to 400°. Drain and rinse cucumbers and blot dry with paper towels. Spoon meat filling into cucumbers, pressing in firmly. Sprinkle with bread crumbs.

• Place filled cucumbers in a greased shallow baking dish. Bake 15 minutes. Loosely cover dish with foil and bake 10 minutes more. Pour in wine or tomato juice, re-cover cucumbers and bake 10 minutes more, basting with sauce.

   Variations: This filling also works well as a stuffing for green peppers and zucchini.

Mary Vance Watson

Entrees

East Indian Lamb Curry

10 tablespoons butter
4 pounds cubed raw lamb
2 garlic cloves, minced
1 large onion, chopped
3 celery ribs, chopped
2 apples, cored and chopped
2 carrots, chopped
¼ cup chopped parsley
2 green peppers, chopped
2 tomatoes, peeled and chopped
3 cloves
2 bay leaves, crushed
1 teaspoon fresh mint leaves (or ¼ teaspoon dried)
¼ teaspoon marjoram
2 sprigs thyme
½ teaspoon basil
2-3 tablespoons curry powder
3 tablespoons flour
½ teaspoon cayenne pepper
¾ teaspoon salt
½ teaspoon freshly ground pepper
½ teaspoon grated nutmeg
1½ cups dry white wine
1 can (13¾ ounces) chicken broth
2 cups raisins
2 cups drained pineapple cubes
6 tablespoons coconut
1½ cups walnuts, coarsely chopped

Serves 8-10

● Melt 5 *tablespoons* butter in a large, heavy skillet. Brown meat on all sides. Remove to a dutch oven. Add remaining butter. Sauté garlic, onion, celery, apples, and carrots until tender. Add 2 *tablespoons* chopped parsley, green peppers, tomatoes, cloves, bay leaves, mint, marjoram, thyme, and basil. Cook for 2 minutes.

● Mix together curry powder, flour, cayenne, salt, pepper, and nutmeg. Stir into vegetables and cook 2 minutes more. Add wine and broth. Bring to a boil, stirring until smooth and thickened. Cover and simmer for 30 minutes.

● Add to lamb in dutch oven. Stir in raisins and pineapple. Simmer gently over low heat until lamb is tender, about 2 hours. Stir frequently to prevent sticking.

● Add coconut and walnuts during last 10 minutes of cooking.

● Serve over cooked rice, garnished with remaining 2 tablespoons chopped parsley and additional coconut, chopped nuts, and raisins. Chutney is the traditional accompaniment.

Stephanie Fay Arpajian

181

Entrees

Moussaka-in-Minutes

1 large eggplant (1½-2 pounds)
1 cup chopped onion
Olive or peanut oil
2 cups ground lamb, raw or cooked
1-2 garlic cloves, minced
Rosemary and thyme
Salt and freshly ground pepper to
    taste
1½-2 cups tomato sauce, or 1 fresh
    tomato, seeded, juiced, and
    chopped
¾ cup diced mozzarella cheese
⅓ cup freshly grated parmesan
    cheese

Serves 4-6

- Cut off green top, but do not peel the eggplant. Cut in lengthwise slices about ⅜" thick. Halve each slice. Blanch slices 3-4 minutes in boiling, salted water. Drain and dry on paper towels. Set aside outside slices to use on top layer.
- Arrange *half the remaining* eggplant slices in a lightly greased 9" x 12" casserole.
- Sauté chopped onion in a little oil until tender. If lamb is raw, add and sauté for several minutes. If lamb is cooked, stir into sautéed onions to heat. Blend in garlic, herbs, salt, and pepper.
- Spread half the lamb mixture over eggplant in casserole. Spread ¼ the tomato sauce over lamb, then ⅓ of each kind of cheese.
- Arrange other half of eggplant on top of cheeses. Add remaining lamb, and ⅓ the remaining sauce and cheeses.
- Cover with reserved eggplant, skin side up. Sprinkle with a little oil. Cover with foil. Reserve remaining sauce and cheeses. Refrigerate.
- Preheat oven to 375°. Bake foil-covered moussaka for 25-30 minutes. Remove foil. Spread moussaka with remaining tomato sauce. Sprinkle with remaining cheese. Bake uncovered about 15 minutes.

Ann Dodds Costello

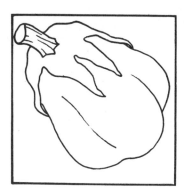

Entrees

Deviled Chicken Breasts

3 tablespoons Dijon or Dusseldorf mustard
3 tablespoons dry white wine, lemon juice, or apple juice
1 teaspoon worcestershire sauce
4 chicken breasts, halved and boned
Salt and freshly ground pepper
2½ cups fine fresh breadcrumbs
4 tablespoons butter
4 tablespoons oil

Serves 8

● At least 40 minutes before serving time, combine mustard, wine, and worcestershire, stirring to blend.
● Place chicken pieces between two sheets of wax paper and pound with a mallet. Sprinkle chicken with salt and pepper to taste. Brush generously on all sides with mustard mixture. Dip pieces in breadcrumbs to coat, patting with the flat side of a heavy knife to help crumbs adhere. Place on a rack and refrigerate until 15 minutes before serving.
● To sauté, heat equal portions of butter and oil in two skillets, or one large skillet. Add chicken pieces and brown on both sides, about 5 minutes per side.

Nancy Gould Pinkernell

Stock-Basted Chicken

4 whole chicken breasts, halved and skinned
1 cup boiling water
2 chicken bouillon cubes
6 tablespoons melted butter
4 tablespoons sherry
1 teaspoon minced garlic
½ teaspoon rosemary
1 bay leaf, crumbled
¼ teaspoon freshly ground pepper

Serves 4-6

● Preheat oven to 400°.
● Mix all ingredients except chicken in baking pan. Place chicken in mixture, meat side down. Bake 45-50 minutes.

Marcia Petersen Sandner

Entrees

Stuffed Chicken Breasts with Tarragon

2 chicken breasts, halved and boned
Salt and pepper
Nutmeg
½ teaspoon tarragon
6 tablespoons cold butter
½ cup flour
1 egg
2 tablespoons water
½ cup fine dry breadcrumbs
Lemon Tarragon Sauce (recipe
   follows)

Serves 4

● Flatten chicken pieces. Season lightly with salt, pepper, and nutmeg. Crush tarragon into 3 tablespoons butter. Chill briefly. Shape tarragon butter into 4 small fingers, each 2" long. Freeze a few minutes to harden.

● Center each finger of tarragon butter in a piece of chicken breast, folding sides in slightly. Roll up to enclose butter completely. Press edges to secure. Dip pieces lightly in flour. Beat egg with water. Dip floured chicken pieces in beaten egg first, then in breadcrumbs.

● Heat remaining 3 tablespoons butter in heavy skillet. Sauté chicken gently, turning until golden brown on all sides. Place pieces in warm serving dish. Keep warm in moderate oven while preparing Lemon Tarragon Sauce.

Alice Van Nuys Sessa

Lemon Tarragon Sauce

3 tablespoons butter
1½ tablespoons flour
½ teaspoon dry mustard
½ teaspoon crushed tarragon
1¼ cups hot chicken broth
Salt
2 egg yolks
1 tablespoon fresh lemon juice

2 cups

● Melt butter over low heat. Blend in flour without browning. When smooth, stir in mustard, tarragon, and chicken broth. Cook, stirring until smooth and slightly thickened, about 5 minutes. Add salt to taste.

● Beat egg yolks with lemon juice. Slowly whisk them into hot sauce. Cook a few seconds longer. Serve with chicken or fish.

Alice Van Nuys Sessa

Entrees

Chicken Enchiladas

12 flour tortillas
Oil for frying
1 quart chicken broth
6 tablespoons mild chili powder
¼ teaspoon garlic salt
¼ teaspoon cumin
Salt and freshly ground pepper to
　　taste
2 tablespoons cornstarch
1 tablespoon cold water
3 cups shredded cooked chicken
¾ cup ripe olives, sliced
¾ cup blanched sliced almonds
1½ cups grated cheddar cheese
2 tablespoons butter
2 cups sour cream
6 green onions, chopped, tops
　　included

Serves 4-6

● Fry tortillas quickly in hot oil, turning to brown both sides. Keep warm in a covered casserole.

● In a saucepan, combine chicken broth, chili powder, garlic, cumin, salt, and pepper to taste. Heat to the boiling point. Stir cornstarch with water until smooth. Gradually stir into boiling broth, and cook until mixture thickens. Reduce heat and simmer for 3-5 minutes.

● To prepare filling, combine chicken, olives, blanched almonds, and ½ cup grated cheese with ½ cup of the sauce just prepared. Melt all the butter in a skillet. Toss these ingredients in the hot butter, stirring to mix well.

● Dip each tortilla in the remaining hot sauce. Put a strip of chicken filling across each one and roll lightly. Place enchiladas side by side in a lightly greased pan. Sprinkle with remaining 1 cup grated cheese.

● Bake in a 350° oven for 10 minutes. Reheat any remaining chicken-chili sauce in the saucepan and pour over enchiladas. Garnish with sour cream and chopped green onions.

Susan Don Lubin

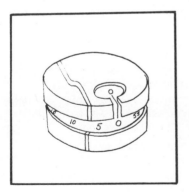

Entrees

Chicken and Mushroom Crêpes Florentine

1 chicken breast
2½ cups chicken broth
1 pound fresh spinach
½ pound mushrooms
2 shallots, finely chopped
7 tablespoons butter
5 tablespoons flour
2 cups milk
1 cup heavy cream
¼ teaspoon nutmeg
⅛ teaspoon cayenne pepper
Salt and freshly ground pepper
1½ cups grated gruyère, swiss, or
     fontina cheese
12-16 cooked crêpes (recipe follows)
Grated parmesan cheese

Serves 6

• Place chicken breast in a saucepan and cover with chicken broth. Bring to a boil and simmer, partly covered, for about 20 minutes. Cool chicken in liquid. Remove and discard skin and bones. Chop chicken and set aside.
• Wash and cook spinach. Drain well and chop.
• Rinse mushrooms and chop finely. Sauté with shallots in *2 tablespoons* butter until liquid is absorbed. Combine with chopped chicken and spinach.
• Heat remaining 5 tablespoons butter in a saucepan. Stir in flour. Add milk, stirring rapidly with a whisk. When mixture thickens, stir in cream, nutmeg, cayenne, salt, and pepper to taste.
• Add ½ cup sauce to chicken, spinach, and mushrooms, enough to hold mixture together.
• Stir cheese into remaining sauce. Spoon a thin layer of cheese sauce in the bottom of a buttered, ovenproof dish.
• Fill crêpes with chicken-mushroom-spinach mixture, and roll them up. Arrange in the baking dish. Spoon remaining sauce over the top.
• Preheat oven to 350°. Sprinkle crêpes and sauce with grated parmesan. Bake 30-40 minutes.

Constance Foti Stewart

188

Entrees

Crêpes for Savory Fillings

¾ cup flour
1 egg, beaten
1¼ cups milk
Salt
3 tablespoons melted butter

12-16 crepes

● Place flour in a bowl, blender, or food processor. Add egg, milk, and a dash of salt. Add melted butter, and mix.
● Brush a hot 7″ skillet with butter before cooking each crêpe. Set cooked crêpes aside with wax paper between each one until it is time to fill them. These stacked, unfilled crêpes freeze well. Defrost to room temperature before filling and baking.

Constance Foti Stewart

Sunshine Chicken

2 chickens, cut up
1 teaspoon salt
1 teaspoon basil
¼ teaspoon pepper
½ cup soy sauce
½ cup catsup
¼ cup honey
¼ cup corn oil
2 garlic cloves, minced
Poached Oranges (recipe follows)
Watercress for garnish

Serves 6-8

● Preheat oven to 350°.
● Sprinkle chicken with salt, basil, and pepper. In a lightly greased large, shallow pan, mix soy sauce, catsup, honey, oil, and garlic. Place chicken in single layer in sauce, turning once to coat on both sides.
● Bake uncovered for 1 hour, until fork-tender. Serve with Poached Oranges. Garnish with watercress, if desired. Mix remaining basting sauce with syrup from oranges. Heat and serve in separate bowl.

Patricia Farnsworth Kuntz

189

Entrees

Chilled Poached Oranges

½ cup sugar
¼ cup water
3 tablespoons slivered orange rind
5 navel oranges
2 tablespoons orange liqueur

● Mix sugar, water, and orange rind in large pan over medium heat. Cook until slightly thickened, about 8 minutes.
● Peel oranges, removing white membrane. Cut flesh into large wedges.
● Place orange wedges in syrup. Reduce heat and cook over low heat 3 minutes. Remove from heat. Add liqueur and chill.

Patricia Farnsworth Kuntz

Roast Stuffed Chicken

12 tablespoons butter
1 medium onion, chopped
2 celery ribs, chopped with leaves
1 roasting chicken (5½-7 pounds),
    with giblets and liver
1 teaspoon sage
½ teaspoon basil
¼ teaspoon thyme
1 teaspoon salt
¼ teaspoon freshly ground pepper
5 slices whole grain bread, cubed
Tarragon
2½-3 cups chicken broth
1 cup heavy cream
1 tablespoon lemon juice

Serves 8-10

● Melt butter. Add onion and celery. Cook to soften. Add chopped chicken liver. Cook 5 minutes. Add sage, basil, thyme, salt, and pepper. Mix well. Remove from heat and add bread cubes. Toss to moisten bread. Let mixture cool.
● Wash and dry chicken, inside and out. Stuff and truss. Place on rack in shallow pan. Sprinkle tarragon over chicken. Place giblets in roasting pan. Pour 2 cups chicken broth over the top.
● Roast in 375° oven for 1¼-1½ hours, checking occasionally and adding more broth as needed. When done, place on platter. Keep warm.
● Remove giblets from pan. Bring juices to boil on top of stove. Boil 5 minutes, scraping brown bits from bottom of pan. Add ½ cup more chicken broth. Lower heat. Add cream and lemon juice. Taste for seasoning, and serve with chicken.

Mary Hegarty Seaman

Entrees

Roast Cornish Hens

6 Rock Cornish hens (1 pound
    each), thawed
6 bacon slices, cooked and crumbled
1 cup chopped onion
1 cup chopped green pepper
3 cups small soft bread cubes
1 cup coarsely chopped walnuts
3 teaspoons salt
1 teaspoon sage
½ teaspoon thyme
½ cup butter
½ cup white wine
1 garlic clove, minced
Wine Gravy (recipe follows)

Serves 6

● Sauté bacon; drain and crumble. In hot bacon drippings, sauté chopped onion and green pepper until tender. Mix with bread cubes, walnuts, *1½ teaspoons* salt, *½ teaspoon* sage, and thyme. Toss lightly with a fork and stuff into hens. Close openings in hens with wooden picks and tie legs together.

● Arrange hens breast side up in a shallow baking pan. Preheat oven to 400°.

● Melt butter. Add wine, minced garlic, and remaining 1½ teaspoons salt and ½ teaspoon sage. Brush this basting sauce over hens, and roast 1 hour. Brush occasionally with remaining sauce.

● When hens are golden brown, arrange on a serving platter. Keep warm while you prepare Wine Gravy.

Mary Vance Watson

Wine Gravy

⅔ cup drippings from roasting Rock
    Cornish hens
3 tablespoons flour
1 cup white wine
1 cup currant jelly
1 teaspoon dry mustard
1 teaspoon salt

2 cups

● Pour off excess drippings after removing Rock Cornish hens to serving platter, leaving about ⅔ cup drippings in roasting pan. Add flour and stir to make a smooth roux. Add wine, jelly, mustard, and salt. Bring mixture to a boil. stirring to mix well. Loosen brown bits in roasting pan.

● Reduce heat and simmer gravy, stirring occasionally, as it thickens and cooks.

Mary Vance Watson

191

Entrees

Roast Duckling with Apple-Raisin Sauce

Serves 6-8

⅓ cup raisins
⅓ cup brandy
2 ducklings (5 pounds each)
Salt and freshly ground pepper
6 Delicious apples, peeled and cored
4 tablespoons butter
½ cup madeira wine
1½ cups chicken or giblet broth
1 tablespoon arrowroot or 2
   teaspoons cornstarch

- Soak raisins in brandy overnight.
- Preheat oven to 425°. Trim ducklings of all loose fat. Dry and truss them. Prick fatty parts with a skewer. Sprinkle skin and cavities with salt and pepper. Place in a large roasting pan with ½ cup water. Roast 1 hour in preheated oven.
- Remove ducklings from pan and pour off fat. Return pan to oven and roast for 1 hour longer until brown.
- Cut each apple into thin slices. Sauté in a skillet with the butter. Add more butter as needed and turn apples until tender and lightly caramelized.
- Transfer ducklings to heated serving platter to keep warm. Skim fat from pan juices.
- Drain brandy from raisins and add it to the pan juices. Ignite brandy and deglaze the pan over high heat. Scrape up brown bits clinging to bottom and sides. Add madeira to broth. Simmer 10 minutes.
- Mix arrowroot or cornstarch with 2 tablespoons cold water. Stir into pan slowly until sauce is thickened. Add raisins.
- Serve duck surrounded with sautéed apples and covered with raisin sauce.

Judith Torrisi Wintermuth

192

Entrees

Turkey and Broccoli au Gratin

1 bunch fresh broccoli
Salt
5 tablespoons butter
3 tablespoons flour
2 cups milk
Freshly ground pepper
Tabasco sauce to taste
1 egg yolk, lightly beaten
4 cups turkey meat, cut in large
    cubes
½ cup heavy cream
¼ teaspoon grated nutmeg
½ cup grated parmesan cheese

Serves 6-8

• Trim broccoli. Cut stems and flowerets into slightly larger than bite-size pieces. Drop into a pan of boiling, salted water. Return water to a boil and simmer until crisp. Drain and run under cold water. Drain again.

• Melt *2 tablespoons* of the butter in a saucepan and add flour. Stir to blend. Add milk gradually. Salt and pepper to taste. Cook and stir until sauce thickens, adding tabasco as desired. Remove from heat and rapidly mix in egg yolk.

• In another pan, melt *1 tablespoon* butter until sizzling. Toss turkey in this butter to heat through. Add cream, nutmeg, salt, and pepper. Spread turkey in the bottom of greased 9″ x 13″ casserole.

• Heat remaining 2 tablespoons butter in same skillet. Toss broccoli pieces in it to heat through. Spoon broccoli over turkey in baking dish. Cover with sauce and sprinkle with grated cheese.

• Bake in a 400° oven until bubbling and hot throughout, about 15-20 minutes.

Nancy Beck Hoggson

Entrees

Chicken Livers with Garlic

1¼ pounds chicken livers
Salt and freshly ground pepper to
    taste
Flour
½ pound mushrooms
6 tablespoons olive oil
¾ cup flour
2 tablespoons butter
2 garlic cloves, minced
3 tablespoons chopped parsley

Serves 4-6

- Cut away and discard any tough connecting membranes from chicken livers. Cut the livers into quarters. Place these quarters on a large board, flat surface, or a sheet of wax paper. Sprinkle with salt, pepper, and flour. Turn chicken liver pieces to coat on all sides.
- If mushrooms are large, cut them in halves or quarters. Sauté in *2 tablespoons* of the oil over high heat. Shake until mushrooms are browned on all sides. Remove with slotted spoon.
- Add 2 tablespoons oil to juices in skillet, and heat. Cook half the chicken livers in this hot oil. Turn to brown on all sides and cook 4-5 minutes longer. Remove from pan.
- Add remaining 2 tablespoons oil to skillet and cook other half of the chicken livers as above. Remove from skillet and add to reserved mixture. Drain skillet and wipe with a paper towel.
- Melt butter in skillet. Reheat mushrooms and chicken livers. When mixture is quite hot, add minced garlic and toss. Sprinkle with chopped parsley.

Anne Ruthrauff Seltzer

Entrees

Hazelnut Stuffing

1 loaf Italian bread
1 cup butter, melted
2 cups chopped celery
2 cups chopped onion (or a
    combination of green onions and
    shallots)
2 teaspoons salt
Freshly ground pepper to taste
1 cup chopped hazelnuts
¾ cup chopped parsley
1 teaspoon thyme
1 teaspoon tarragon
1 teaspoon sage

● Cut Italian bread into cubes. Leave uncovered at room temperature to dry out, or place in a 250° oven for 30 minutes.
● Mix all ingredients. Stuff into poultry and roast as usual. Enough for a 10-12 pound bird.

Penelope Johnson Wartels

Wild Rice Stuffing

1 cup wild rice
Turkey, duck, or chicken giblets,
    cooked and chopped
½ cup giblet broth
¼ cup finely chopped onion
1 cup finely chopped celery
½ cup finely chopped mushrooms
¼ cup butter
4 cups toasted bread cubes
1½ teaspoons salt
½ teaspoon sage
¼ teaspoon freshly ground pepper
1 egg, lightly beaten

● Spread wild rice in a large, flat pan. Pour boiling water to cover rice. Cover pan tightly and let stand 20 minutes. Drain and pour boiling water over rice again. Repeat soaking and draining 3 times until grains of rice split open. After final draining. combine rice with chopped giblets and giblet broth.
● Cook onion. celery. and mushrooms in butter until tender. Add to rice mixture. Add remaining ingredients and toss lightly. Cool. Stuff poultry. Roast as usual. Makes enough stuffing for a 12 pound turkey.

Marjorie Lister Beck

Entrees

Roast Loin of Pork Dijon

1 pork loin, about 4 pounds
   (preferably center cut)
2 garlic cloves, minced
Salt and freshly ground pepper
3 tablespoons Dijon mustard
4 tablespoons butter
1 onion, chopped
1 large carrot, chopped
3 tablespoons caraway seeds
Pinch thyme

Serves 4-6

● Wipe meat with a damp cloth. Rub with minced garlic. Rub salt and pepper into fat side of meat. Spread all sides with mustard. Arrange meat in roasting pan, fat side up.
● Melt butter, and sauté onion and carrot. Spread over roast. Sprinkle top with caraway seeds and thyme.
● Roast uncovered in a 350° oven for about 30-35 minutes per pound, basting several times. Remove from oven and let stand 10-15 minutes before carving.

Joan Schaeffer Sawyer

Pork Roast with Herbs

½ teaspoon thyme
½ teaspoon marjoram
½ teaspoon oregano
½ teaspoon minced garlic
1 pork roast, about 3 pounds
1 tablespoon salt
¼ teaspoon freshly ground pepper
4-5 whole cloves

Serves 6-8

● Mix thyme, marjoram, oregano, and garlic. Using the tip of a sharp knife, make ½" long slits 1" apart in the roast. Push herbs into openings and pinch closed. Sprinkle with salt and pepper. Stud with cloves.
● Roast in a shallow pan at 350°, 30-35 minutes per pound.

Anne Ruthrauff Seltzer

Entrees

Pork Chops with Apples

2 tablespoons oil
2 cooking apples, cored and thickly
    sliced
4 pork chops
2 green onions, diced with stems
1 teaspoon salt
⅛ teaspoon freshly ground pepper
1½ cups apple juice or cider
Chopped parsley for garnish
1 tablespoon cornstarch
¼ cup heavy cream

Serves 4

● Heat oil in skillet. Sauté apple slices about 5 minutes, turning once. Remove apples to a heated serving platter and keep warm. Sauté chops in same skillet until browned on both sides, about 10 minutes over medium-high heat.

● Add onions, salt, pepper, and *1¼ cups* apple juice or cider. Cover, turn heat low, and simmer 10 minutes, until chops are tender. Arrange on platter with cooked apples. Sprinkle with parsley.

● Blend cornstarch and remaining ¼ cup juice or cider until smooth. Add to liquid in skillet. Stir in cream and cook, stirring constantly, until mixture thickens slightly. Serve with pork chops and apples.

Janet Galley Peckham

Pork Chops Ligeoise

4 loin pork chops, about 1½ pounds
Salt and freshly ground pepper to
    taste
1 tablespoon oil
1 cup grated gruyère or swiss
    cheese (about ¼ pound)
1 tablespoon Dijon or Dusseldorf
    mustard
1 tablespoon heavy cream
1 garlic clove, minced
1 tablespoon finely chopped chives
1 egg yolk
2 tablespoons dry white wine
2 tablespoons water

Serves 4

● Sprinkle chops with salt and pepper. Heat oil in heavy skillet. Add chops. Cook about 10 minutes. Turn and brown on the other side.

● Meanwhile, blend cheese, mustard, cream, garlic, chives, and egg yolk. Smear one side of each pork chop with ¼ of this mixture, using it all.

● Broil chops until topping is browned and nicely glazed.

● Pour off fat from skillet. Add wine and water, stirring to dissolve brown particles in skillet. Pour this hot sauce over the chops.

Nancy Gould Pinkernell

197

Entrees

Oven-Barbecued Pork Chops

8 center cut pork chops
1 cup catsup
½ cup red wine vinegar
½ cup red wine
2 teaspoons salt
2 teaspoons celery seed
1 teaspoon nutmeg
2 bay leaves

Serves 8
- Brown chops. Mix remaining ingredients for sauce. Place chops in a baking pan. Pour sauce over them.
- Bake in a 325° oven for 1½ hours.

Mary Hegarty Seaman

Pork and Apple Casserole

¼ cup flour
1½ teaspoons salt
½ teaspoon freshly ground black
    pepper
½ teaspoon sweet paprika
2 pounds fresh pork shoulder, cut in
    2" cubes
3 tablespoons oil
1 large onion, thinly sliced
1 bay leaf, crumbled
1 teaspoon rubbed leaf sage
1 garlic clove, minced
1¼ cups apple cider
¼ cup Calvados (apple brandy)
4 carrots, sliced
2 tart apples, peeled, cored, and
    thinly sliced
1 cup celery, diagonally sliced
1 small yellow turnip, cut in 2" x ½"
    sticks
Chicken broth

Serves 4-6
- Mix flour with *1 teaspoon* salt, *¼ teaspoon* pepper, and the paprika. Coat pork pieces in this mixture.
- Heat oil in a heavy dutch oven or casserole. Brown meat on all sides. Remove meat from pan and reserve. Add onion slices to casserole. Cook slowly until golden. Return meat to pan along with bay leaf, sage, garlic, cider, and Calvados. Bring to boil. Cover and bake for 1 hour in a 325° oven.
- Add carrots, apples, celery, turnip sticks, and remaining salt and pepper to taste. Bring to a boil on top of the range. Add enough chicken broth to barely cover vegetables. Cover and bake 30 minutes longer, or until vegetables are tender.

Nancy Beck Hoggson

Entrees

Easy Glazed Spareribs

3-3½ pounds country style or regular
   spareribs
¾ cup catsup
¾ cup honey
½ cup light soy sauce
2-3 garlic cloves, minced
½ teaspoon tabasco sauce

Serves 4

● Sprinkle ribs with salt and pepper. Roast in a 350° oven for 45 minutes. Cool and cut into individual portions. This can be done ahead and the ribs can be refrigerated until about 30 minutes before serving time.

● Combine remaining ingredients to make basting sauce. Arrange partially cooked ribs in a shallow baking pan lined with foil. Brush ribs well with glaze. Roast in a 425° oven about 30 minutes, basting several times.

   Note: Serves 8 as an appetizer.

Betsy Gimpel Mena

Pork de Brazilia

1 cup minced onion
¼ cup soy sauce
¼ cup lemon juice
¼ cup olive oil
8 Brazil nuts, grated
2 tablespoons brown sugar
3 garlic cloves, minced
1½ tablespoons crushed coriander
   seeds
¼ teaspoon crushed red pepper
3 pounds lean pork, cut in cubes
Kumquats

Serves 8

● Make a marinade of all ingredients except pork and kumquats. Marinate meat for at least 30 minutes.

● Put pork on skewers. Place in a lightly greased shallow pan. Pour marinade over. Bake in a 450° oven for 30 minutes. Or cook on grill, basting with marinade.

● Garnish with kumquats. Serve with rice and remaining sauce.

Carol Kruse Long

Entrees

Sausage Pie

2-3 large potatoes
1 pound sausage, bulk or link
3 tablespoons butter
3 large onions, thinly sliced
2 tablespoons flour
⅔ cup milk
1 tablespoon prepared horseradish
Salt and freshly ground pepper to
    taste

Serves 4

● Peel potatoes, cut in quarters, and cover with cold water. Add salt and cook until potatoes are soft, then mash with a little milk, salt, and pepper.

● Brown sausage in a skillet. Drain.

● Pour off all fat from skillet and add butter. When melted, add onions and sauté until they are limp. Blend in flour, then add milk. Stir until very thick and smooth, then add horseradish. Season with salt and pepper.

● Preheat oven to 400°. Spread mashed potatoes evenly in bottom of a buttered 6½" by 10½" baking dish. Cover potatoes with onion sauce and place sausage on top, cutting each in half if you use link sausage. Bake 20-25 minutes and let stand 5 minutes before serving.

Anne Ruthrauff Seltzer

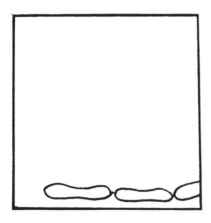
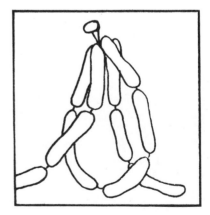

Entrees

Sausage Milanese

2 pounds sweet Italian sausage
1 tablespoon oil
1 large onion, diced
1 pound mushrooms, sliced
½ cup dry sherry
4½-5 cups chicken broth
2-3 pinches saffron
2 cups uncooked rice
¾ cup diced mozzarella cheese
Salt and freshly ground pepper
Grated parmesan cheese

Serves 6-8

● Remove sausage meat from casings. Cook over medium heat until browned. Remove sausage. Cook onions in oil in the same pan until soft. Add onions to reserved sausage meat. Sauté mushrooms over medium-high heat until browned. Stir together with sausage, onions, and sherry. Mix well.

● Bring chicken broth and saffron to a boil. Add rice and cover pot. Simmer until rice is cooked.

● Stir sausage mixture and diced mozzarella into rice. Blend over low heat. stirring to melt cheese. Season to taste with salt and pepper. Serve immediately with grated parmesan.

Alice Van Nuys Sessa

Ham and Noodle Casserole

3 tablespoons butter
¼ cup finely chopped onion
¼ pound mushrooms, sliced or
    chopped
3 tablespoons flour
3 cups milk
Salt and pepper to taste
⅛ teaspoon nutmeg
⅛ teaspoon cayenne pepper
2 cups grated cheddar cheese
    (about ½ pound)
1 cup heavy cream
2 tablespoons port wine
½ pound cooked ham, cubed
¾ pound broad noodles, cooked and
    drained
¼ cup grated parmesan cheese

Serves 6-8

● Melt butter and sauté onions and mushrooms. Remove vegetables with slotted spoon. Stir in flour until smooth. Gradually add milk, stirring constantly. Cook, stirring, over medium-low heat until sauce thickens. Add seasonings. Stir in cheese until it melts. Add cream and wine. Bring to a boil and remove from heat.

● Stir in ham and cooked noodles. Put in a large, lightly greased 9" x 13" casserole. Sprinkle with grated parmesan and bake at 450° until heated through.

Mildred McElvein Cooley

Entrees

Ham Croquettes with Mustard Sauce

3 tablespoons butter
5 tablespoons flour
1 cup milk
¼ teaspoon salt
⅛ teaspoon freshly ground pepper
¼ teaspoon lemon juice
½ teaspoon worcestershire sauce
1 teaspoon finely minced onion
2 cups diced or chopped ham
¼ cup minced green pepper
1 teaspoon chopped onion
2 eggs
2 cups coarse breadcrumbs
Peanut oil for frying
Mustard Sauce (recipe follows)

Serves 4-6

● Melt butter, stir in flour, and rub hard with a wooden spoon to make a smooth paste. Stirring constantly, gradually add the next 6 ingredients. Cook over low heat, stirring, until sauce is very thick. Remove from heat and allow to cool.

● When sauce is cool, add it to ham, green pepper, and onion. Mix well with your hands. Chill to stiffen the mixture. Form it into flat patties.

● Beat the eggs. Roll patties in breadcrumbs, then beaten eggs and breadcrumbs again. Chill patties until time to fry.

● Heat peanut oil to cover the bottom of a heavy iron skillet. Sauté croquettes until heated through and lightly browned. Serve with Mustard Sauce.

Susan Kross Cowan

Mustard Sauce

1 tablespoon butter
1 tablespoon flour
1 cup milk
3 tablespoons mayonnaise
2 tablespoons Dijon mustard
1 tablespoon lemon juice
¼ teaspoon salt
Dash freshly ground pepper

1 cup

● Melt butter over low heat or in top of double boiler. Add flour and stir to make a smooth paste. Add milk gradually and stir constantly until thickened. Add mayonnaise, mustard, and lemon juice. Stir until very thick. Season with salt and pepper. Serve warm.

   Note: Keeps well in refrigerator or freezer. Good with fish and cauliflower. Always reheat over hot water.

Susan Kross Cowan

Entrees

Ham-Broccoli Casserole

Serves 10-12

1 large bunch fresh broccoli, or 2 packages (10 ounces) frozen broccoli spears
¾ pound thin egg noodles
2½ pounds baked ham
½ cup butter, melted
¼ cup flour
2¾ cups evaporated milk
1¾ cups water
½ cup chicken broth
1 cup grated cheddar cheese
½ cup grated parmesan cheese
Juice of 1 lemon
1½ tablespoons finely chopped onion
1 tablespoon Dijon mustard
1 tablespoon minced parsley
2½ teaspoons salt
⅛ teaspoon rosemary
1 cup mayonnaise

• Cook broccoli in a little salted water until half cooked. Remove from hot water while still crisp. Cook noodles and drain. Cube ham.
• To prepare sauce, melt butter and blend in flour. Slowly add evaporated milk, water, and chicken broth. Cook, stirring until thickened. Add remaining ingredients except mayonnaise. Continue to cook, stirring constantly until cheese melts and flavors blend. Taste and adjust seasonings. Remove from heat and add 1 cup mayonnaise. Cool. Add a little sauce to the noodles to prevent them sticking together.
• Layer noodles, broccoli, ham, and sauce in a large greased casserole. Repeat layers, ending with sauce on top. Bake uncovered at 350° for 30-40 minutes.

Suzanne Rich Beatty

Ham Steak au Poivre Vert

Serves 4

1 jar (2 ounces) green peppercorns in vinegar
1 fully cooked smoked ham center slice, 1" thick
2 tablespoons butter

• About 1½ hours before serving time, crush peppercorns with their liquid in blender or food processor.
• Spread both sides of ham with crushed peppercorns. Let stand at least an hour, to allow pepper flavor to permeate meat.
• Melt butter in a skillet. Sauté ham, turning after 5 minutes.

Penelope Johnson Wartels

203

Entrees

Stuffed Striped Bass

¼ cup butter
½ cup finely chopped onion
½ cup finely chopped celery
4 mushrooms, chopped
2 cups sea scallops or shucked
　　oysters, drained
2-2½ cups soft breadcrumbs
2 tablespoons chopped parsley
Salt and freshly ground pepper to
　　taste
½ teaspoon thyme
¼ teaspoon marjoram
¼ cup white wine
1 striped bass (about 4 pounds),
　　cleaned, with head and tail left
　　on
Lemon juice
4 slices bacon

Serves 6

● Heat butter in a skillet. Sauté onion and celery until tender. Add mushrooms and cook 2 minutes.
● Chop scallops or oysters. Add to mushroom mixture along with breadcrumbs, parsley, salt, pepper, thyme, and marjoram. Mix well. Add enough reserved oyster liquor and white wine to moisten.
● Wash and dry the bass. Sprinkle cavity with salt, pepper, and lemon juice. Stuff loosely and secure with toothpicks. Place fish in lightly greased shallow baking pan. Arrange bacon strips over top. Refrigerate until an hour before serving time.
● Bake at 350° for 40 minutes until fish flakes.

Betsy Gimpel Mena

Bluefish Chanticleer

½ cup olive oil
2 tablespoons lemon juice
¼ cup chopped green onions and
　　stems
2 tablespoons chopped parsley
Salt and freshly ground pepper
2 pounds bluefish fillets, boned and
　　skinned
3-4 tablespoons Dijon mustard
1 tablespoon mayonnaise
1 teaspoon tarragon
1 teaspoon thyme
1 teaspoon crumbled rosemary
2 tablespoons butter, melted
¼ cup grated gruyère cheese

Serves 6

● Mix olive oil, lemon juice, chopped green onion, parsley, salt, and pepper in a shallow glass or earthenware dish. Marinate bluefish in this mixture for 4-5 hours.
● Remove fish from marinade and blot lightly with paper towels. Mix mustard, mayonnaise, and herbs. Spread on bluefish. Arrange in a lightly greased shallow baking dish. Pour melted butter over fish. Sprinkle with grated cheese.
● Broil 5-7 minutes, then bake at 425° for 10 minutes.

Christine Church Gimpel

Entrees

Crabmeat-Broccoli Bake

10 ounces broccoli, fresh or frozen
4 tablespoons butter
2 tablespoons minced onion
2 tablespoons flour
⅛ teaspoon curry powder
½ teaspoon salt
Sugar to taste
1 cup milk
1 cup grated sharp cheddar cheese
1 tablespoon lemon juice
1 package (6 ounces) frozen
   crabmeat, thawed and drained
2 tablespoons melted butter
½ cup soft breadcrumbs

Serves 4

● Pour boiling salted water over broccoli and cook 5 minutes. Drain and arrange broccoli in a greased 1-quart casserole.
● Melt butter in a saucepan. Add onion and sauté until golden. Stir in flour, curry powder, salt, and sugar. Gradually stir in milk and cook over medium-low heat until thickened. Add grated cheese and continue to stir over low heat until cheese melts. Stir in lemon juice and crabmeat. Pour over broccoli.
● Mix melted butter with breadcrumbs and sprinkle over top. Bake 30 minutes in a 350° oven.

Suzanne Rich Beatty

Crab Imperial

¼ green pepper, chopped
3 green onions, chopped
3 tablespoons butter
1 can (1 pound) fresh crabmeat
1 heaping tablespoon mayonnaise
¼ teaspoon dry mustard
⅛ teaspoon cayenne pepper
2 tablespoons chopped parsley
Dash paprika
Salt and freshly ground pepper

Serves 4

● Sauté green pepper and green onions in butter.
● Pick over crabmeat, keeping chunks as large as possible. Place in a mixing bowl. Add remaining ingredients, including sautéed mixture. Toss gently with hands.
● Place mixture in a small, buttered baking dish or 4 individual ramekins. Dot top with butter and bake for 20 minutes in a 350° oven. Brown under broiler before serving.

Adrienne Wheeler Rudge

205

Entrees

Fish in Beer Batter

1 cup flour
½ teaspoon salt
1 tablespoon paprika
2 eggs, separated
⅔ cup beer
2 tablespoons melted butter

2 cups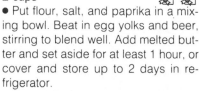

● Put flour, salt, and paprika in a mixing bowl. Beat in egg yolks and beer, stirring to blend well. Add melted butter and set aside for at least 1 hour, or cover and store up to 2 days in refrigerator.

● Just before using batter, beat egg whites until stiff but not dry. Fold into batter. Dip fish in batter. Fry in hot, deep fat until golden brown, turning once. Use on fish fillets, shrimp, or clams. Makes enough batter for 2 pounds of seafood.

Madeleine Galanek Egan

Broiled Scallops

2¼ pounds scallops
½ cup butter, melted
2 tablespoons fine dry breadcrumbs
Pinch salt
2-3 garlic cloves, minced
Sherry

Serves 6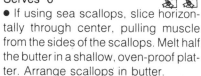

● If using sea scallops, slice horizontally through center, pulling muscle from the sides of the scallops. Melt half the butter in a shallow, oven-proof platter. Arrange scallops in butter.

● Mix breadcrumbs, salt, and minced garlic. Sprinkle over scallops. Pour on remaining melted butter. Refrigerate until 20 minutes before serving time.

● Broil 10 minutes, then turn off broiler. Let scallops remain in closed oven 5 minutes more. Drizzle a few drops of sherry over scallops. Serve hot with fresh lemon wedges.

Lucie Ling Campbell

Entrees

Salmon Steaks Teriyaki

4 salmon steaks, approximately ½"
    thick
½ teaspoon sesame oil
4 teaspoons soy sauce
2 teaspoons lemon juice
1 garlic clove, minced
1 tablespoon butter, melted.

Serves 4

● Place steaks in a shallow pan. Mix sesame oil, soy sauce, lemon juice, and garlic. ·Pour over salmon. Let stand 20 minutes at room temperature, turning occasionally.

● Remove salmon steaks from marinade. Brush on both sides with melted butter. Broil 5-7 minutes on each side until browned and easily flaked.

Karin Best Garson

Coquilles St. Jacques

3 tablespoons butter
2 pounds scallops
Salt and freshly ground pepper
2 tablespoons finely chopped
    shallots
2 cups quartered or sliced fresh
    mushrooms
12 cherry tomatoes
¼ cup dry white wine
1 cup heavy cream
1 tablespoon finely chopped parsley

Serves 4-6

● Heat *2 tablespoons* butter in a large skillet. If using sea scallops, cut in quarters to approximate the size of bay scallops. Blot scallops with paper towels. Add to sizzling butter. Cook 1-2 minutes over high heat, shaking skillet and stirring. Add salt and pepper. When scallops are lightly browned, remove with a slotted spoon.

● Add chopped shallots to pan juices and cook 1-2 minutes. Add mushrooms and cherry tomatoes. Stir about 1 minute over medium heat. Add wine, and simmer until liquid is reduced by half.

● Add cream, and more salt and pepper to taste. Cook 3 minutes longer over medium-high heat. Add scallops and swirl in remaining 1 tablespoon butter. Sprinkle with chopped parsley.

Nancy Beck Hoggson

Entrees

Hot Scallop Mousse with Sauce Duglère

4 cups fresh scallops
2 tablespoons butter
1 tablespoon chopped shallots
Salt and pepper
½ cup dry white wine
Nutmeg
2 egg yolks
2 cups heavy cream
Sauce Duglère (recipe follows)
Chopped parsley

Serves 8

● If using sea scallops, quarter them to approximate the size of bay scallops. Set aside 1 cup scallops.

● Heat *1 tablespoon* butter in a skillet. Add shallots and cook briefly. Add reserved cup of scallops, and salt and pepper to taste. Cook about 1 minute over high heat. Add wine and cook a minute more. Remove scallops with a slotted spoon. Reserve liquid in skillet along with liquid that collects around drained scallops.

● Put *half* the uncooked scallops in blender or food processor, with salt, pepper, and a touch of nutmeg. Add *1 egg yolk*. Blend to chop scallops finely, scraping down sides of blender or food processor container as necessary. Gradually add *1 cup* cream. Process until very smooth. Scrape mixture into a mixing bowl, and reserve.

● Repeat above step with remaining scallops, seasonings, egg yolk, and cream. Mix the two batches of purée. Fold in cooked whole or quartered scallops.

● Preheat oven to 375°. Cut a piece of wax paper to fit the top of a 2-quart mold. Lightly grease mold and fill it with mousse mixture. Spread butter on wax paper to coat one side, and cover mousse with buttered side of paper facing down.

Entrees

continued

- Place mold in a large pan of hot water and bring to a boil on top of stove. Place in oven and bake 45 minutes. Meanwhile prepare Duglère Sauce.
- Remove mousse from oven. It will be puffed and brown on top. Remove the wax paper and pull off the brown "skin" from the surface. Unmold the mousse. Add liquid that has accumulated around the base to the Sauce Duglère.
- Spoon sauce over the mousse and sprinkle with chopped parsley. Slice and serve immediately.

Barbara Smith Suval

Sauce Duglère

2 tablespoons butter
2 tablespoons chopped shallots
2 tablespoons chopped onion
1 pound fresh tomatoes, cored,
    peeled, and cubed (about 2
    cups)
Salt and freshly ground pepper
Pan liquid from cooking scallops
1½ cups heavy cream

2 cups
- Melt butter. Add shallots and chopped onion. Cook to wilt. Add tomatoes, salt, and pepper to taste. Cook to evaporate most of the liquid.
- Meanwhile, cook liquid from scallops down to about 2 tablespoons. Add cream. Let this mixture simmer about 5 minutes over medium heat. Add to tomato mixture and blend. Serve hot.

Barbara Smith Suval

Entrees

Fruits de Mer au Gratin

1 pound shrimp, shelled and
   deveined
1 pound scallops or 2 cans (7½
   ounces each) king crabmeat
3 green onions, tops included
⅔-1 cup dry white wine
1 package (9 ounces) frozen
   artichoke hearts, or 1 can (14
   ounces) artichoke hearts
¼ cup butter
2 tablespoons chopped shallots
1 garlic clove, minced
½ pound fresh mushrooms, sliced
¼ cup flour
¾ cup milk or cream
1 tablespoon snipped fresh dill weed
½ teaspoon freshly ground pepper
Grated parmesan cheese
Breadcrumbs
Chopped parsley

Serves 6

● Place shrimp and scallops in a small pan with green onions. Add white wine to cover and poach for about 3 minutes. Strain, reserving wine for sauce. If using crabmeat, remove cartilage and flake.

● If using frozen artichokes, cook as package directs. If canned, drain and rinse under cold water.

● Melt butter in a skillet. Add shallots, garlic, and sliced mushrooms. Sauté 5 minutes. Remove from heat and stir in flour. Gradually stir in milk, dill, and pepper. Bring to boiling point, stirring constantly. Stir in wine.

● Combine all ingredients in a lightly greased 2-quart casserole. Sprinkle with grated parmesan, breadcrumbs, and chopped parsley.

● Bake at 375° for about 30 minutes until bubbling.

Joan Keach Magrauth

Scallop or Mussel Stew

2 tablespoons olive oil
2 garlic cloves, minced
1 large onion, chopped
1 green pepper, chopped
¼ pound fresh mushrooms, or 1 can
   (4 ounces), drained
1 can (28 ounces) tomatoes
¼ cup dry white wine
Salt, freshly ground pepper, sweet
   basil, and parsley to taste
½ pound bay scallops or 2 pounds
   mussels, well-scrubbed and
   debearded

Serves 2-4

● Heat oil in a large skillet. Sauté garlic, onion, green pepper, and mushrooms until onions are golden.

● Add tomatoes and wine. Bring to a boil, breaking tomatoes into pieces. Add seasonings to taste, and scallops or mussels.

● Simmer uncovered for 15 minutes. Serve over rice or noodles, or in soup plates.

Carole Kruse Long

Entrees

Shrimp with Tarragon Sauce

4 tablespoons butter
2 tablespoons finely chopped onion
1 tablespoon finely chopped shallots
1 teaspoon finely minced garlic
1 can (28 ounces) peeled tomatoes, chopped, or 2½ cups chopped peeled fresh tomatoes
Salt and freshly ground pepper to taste
1 tablespoon chopped fresh tarragon, or 1½ teaspoons dried
1 tablespoon chopped parsley
⅓ cup dry white wine
2 pounds shrimp, peeled and deveined
2 tablespoons cognac

Serves 4-6

● Melt *2 tablespoons* butter in a skillet and add onion, shallots, and garlic. Cook briefly, stirring until wilted. Add tomatoes, salt, and pepper to taste. Add tarragon and parsley. Cook 5 minutes.

● Add wine and simmer 15 minutes more. In the meantime, peel and devein shrimp. At this point, you can set the sauce aside until a few minutes before serving and refrigerate the shrimp.

● To serve, heat remaining 2 tablespoons butter in a skillet large enough to hold the shrimp in one layer. Arrange shrimp in the sizzling butter. Cook about 45 seconds over medium-high heat, turning shrimp until they turn pink. Add cognac.

● Add tomato mixture, salt, and pepper to taste. Remove pan from heat as soon as mixture comes to a simmering point.

Robin Collins Vermylen

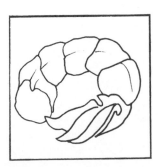

Entrees

Garlic-Broiled Shrimp with Basil Mayonnaise

1½-2 pounds shrimp
1 tablespoon chopped shallots
2 garlic cloves, minced
1 tablespoon minced parsley
½ cup olive oil
¼ cup butter, melted
¼ cup white wine
1-2 tablespoons lemon juice
1 teaspoon salt
½ teaspoon oregano
Pepper
Basil Mayonnaise (recipe follows)

Serves 4-6
● Shell and devein shrimp. Chop shallots, garlic, and parsley by hand or in food processor. Add olive oil, melted butter, wine, lemon juice, and seasonings. Marinate shrimp in this mixture at least 2 hours.
● Prepare Basil Mayonnaise. Chill.
● Skewer shrimp and broil 3 minutes on each side. Serve with Basil Mayonnaise.

Susan Sample Marx

Basil Mayonnaise

2 egg yolks
1 tablespoon capers, drained and rinsed
2 teaspoons Dijon mustard
2 teaspoons wine vinegar
1 teaspoon salt
½ cup fresh basil leaves
1 small garlic clove
Pepper
½ cup oil

1⅓ cups
● Combine all ingredients except oil in blender or food processor. Turn on and off until basil is chopped. Slowly and constantly trickle in oil, continuing until all oil is added and mayonnaise is thick.

Susan Sample Marx

212

Entrees

Shrimp Tetrazzini

½ pound thin spaghetti
2 tablespoons butter
1 medium onion, chopped
½-¾ pound cleaned and deveined
  shrimp
8 ounces mushrooms, sliced
¼ cup mayonnaise
¼ cup flour
1 teaspoon salt, or more to taste
⅛ teaspoon freshly ground pepper
2 cups milk
¼ cup sherry
¼ cup grated parmesan cheese

Serves 4
● Cook spaghetti according to package directions. Drain.
● In a large skillet, melt butter over low heat. Add onion and sauté until tender. Stir in shrimp and mushrooms. Cook 5 minutes, stirring frequently. Remove from skillet.
● Mix mayonnaise, flour, salt and pepper in the skillet. Gradually stir in milk and sherry. Bring to a boil, stirring constantly. Cook 1 minute. Toss with drained spaghetti.
● Layer spaghetti mixture with mushroom mixture in a lightly greased 1½-quart casserole. Sprinkle top with grated parmesan.
● Bake 30 minutes in a 350° oven until heated through and bubbling.

Lucie Ling Campbell

Oven-Fried Sole Amandine

⅓ cup toasted almonds
¼ cup fine dry breadcrumbs
½ teaspoon salt
¼ teaspoon paprika
¼ cup butter
1 egg
1 tablespoon water
¼ cup flour
1 pound fillet of sole

Serves 4
● Chop almonds quite finely. Mix with breadcrumbs, salt, and paprika on a sheet of wax paper.
● Melt butter in a shallow baking pan.
● Beat egg with water in a pie plate. Spread flour on a second sheet of wax paper.
● Preheat oven to 375°. Dip sole pieces one at a time in flour to coat both sides, shaking off excess. Dip in egg, then dip both sides in almond-crumb mixture. Place in pan with melted butter, turning once to coat both sides.
● Bake at 375° for 25 minutes, until fish flakes easily. Serve with lemon wedges and tartare sauce.

Lucie Ling Campbell

Entrees

Sole Florentine

3 packages (10 ounces each) frozen, chopped spinach
2 cups sour cream
3 tablespoons flour
½ cup chopped green onions and stems
2 tablespoons lemon juice
2 teaspoons salt
1½-2 pounds fresh sole fillets
½ pound small shrimp
2 tablespoons butter
Paprika

Serves 6-8

● Cook and drain spinach. Blend sour cream with flour, green onions, lemon juice, and salt. Combine *half* the sour cream mixture with spinach. Spread over bottom of a lightly greased shallow baking dish.
● Arrange sole fillets on spinach. Sprinkle *half* the shrimp on top. Spread remaining sour cream mixture over sole. Dot with butter and sprinkle remaining shrimp on top. Dust with paprika.
● Bake at 375° for 25 minutes.

Suzanne Rich Beatty

Mustard-Baked Fish Fillets

1 egg white
¼ cup mayonnaise
1 tablespoon Dijon mustard
¼ teaspoon salt
Freshly ground pepper
4 fresh fish fillets

Serves 4

● Beat egg white until stiff. Fold in remaining ingredients except fish.
● Preheat oven to 400°. Place fish in a lightly greased shallow baking dish. Spread with meringue mixture. Bake 20 minutes until puffed and golden brown.

Mary Lewis

Entrees

Sole Sauté with Lemon and Capers

4 sole fillets
¼ cup milk
Salt and freshly ground pepper to
  taste
½ cup vegetable oil
¼ cup sweet butter
½ cup flour
1 small lemon, peeled, seeded, and
  cubed
2 tablespoons capers, drained
1 tablespoon finely chopped parsley

Serves 4
● Soak sole fillets at least 1 hour in milk. Sprinkle with salt and pepper. Turn occasionally.
● Heat oil and *1 tablespoon* butter in a large skillet. Coat fish on all sides with flour. Cook in sizzling oil-butter until slightly browned. Turn and brown on the other side. Total time to sauté should be 4-5 minutes. Transfer to a warm platter.
● Heat remaining 3 tablespoons butter in a small skillet. Cook until butter foams up and turns hazelnut-brown in color. Remove from heat and add lemon and capers. Pour over fillets. Sprinkle with chopped parsley.

Barbara Smith Suval

Veal Polonnaise

4 loin veal chops or veal cutlets
Salt and freshly ground pepper to
  taste
¼ cup flour
1 tablespoon oil
1 large onion, sliced in rings
3 tablespoons chopped parsley
¼ pound fresh mushrooms, sliced or
  quartered
1 can (8 ounces) tomato sauce, or 3
  tablespoons tomato paste
1 beef bouillon cube
½ cup boiling water or beef broth
½ cup sour cream
2 tablespoons sherry

Serves 4
● Sprinkle veal on both sides with salt, pepper, and flour. Heat oil in a large skillet. Brown chops over medium heat. Remove chops from skillet.
● Add onion and parsley to skillet. Cook briefly to wilt onion rings. Stir in mushrooms, cook briefly, then add tomato sauce or paste.
● Dissolve bouillon cube in boiling water or broth and stir into pan. Add chops, cover, and simmer until chops are tender, about 30 minutes. Arrange chops on a heated platter.
● Stir sour cream and sherry into gravy and bring just to the boiling point. Pour over chops. Garnish with fresh parsley and serve with rice.

Lucie Ling Campbell

215

Entrees

Blanquette de Veau

2 pounds stewing veal
1 onion, studded with 4 cloves
¼ cup chopped carrots
1 bay leaf
1 sprig thyme
2 sprigs parsley
5 peppercorns
2 teaspoons salt
12 small white onions
5 tablespoons butter
¼ pound whole mushrooms
¼ cup flour
2 tablespoons lemon juice
2 egg yolks, slightly beaten
1 tablespoon chopped parsley

Serves 6-8

● Cut veal in 2″ pieces and wipe with a cloth.

● Tie onion, carrots, herbs, and peppercorns in a piece of cheesecloth. Bring 1 quart of water to a boil, and add the bouquet garni just prepared. Add salt and veal. Simmer 1 hour until tender. Strain, reserving stock.

● Drop white onions into a pan of boiling water for 1 minute. Drain and run under cold water to cool. Cut off ends and the skins will come right off. Dry onions well.

● Sauté onions in *2 tablespoons* butter until golden. Add mushrooms and sauté briefly.

● Melt remaining 3 tablespoons butter. Stir in flour and blend well. Cook several minutes over low heat. Add 3 cups of the strained veal stock. Stir constantly over medium heat until mixture thickens and boils.

● Add lemon juice to slightly beaten egg yolks. Stir in a little hot sauce. Gradually blend egg yolks into hot mixture. stirring constantly. Add veal and chopped parsley. Reheat.

● Serve on a hot platter with the warm sautéed onions and mushrooms. surrounded with rice.

Nancy Beck Hoggson

Veal Provençale

2 tablespoons butter
2 pounds veal, cubed
4 carrots, sliced
2 celery ribs, diced
1-2 white onions, sliced
¼ cup chopped parsley
2 teaspoons salt
½ teaspoon thyme
¼ teaspoon mace
Dash white pepper
12 ounces beer
12 ounces mushrooms, sliced
1 cup sour cream
2 tablespoons flour

Serves 4

● Heat butter in a large casserole or dutch oven. Add meat and brown on all sides. Add carrots, celery, onions, parsley, and seasonings. Stir to mix. Add beer. Cover and simmer for 2 hours. Add sliced mushrooms and cook 15 minutes.

● To serve: Turn off heat under stew, mix sour cream and flour, and stir into sauce. Stir over low heat for 3 minutes. Taste for seasonings.Serve with rice.

Karin Rahm Carlson

Classic Veal Scallopini

1½ pounds veal steak for scallopini
⅓ cup flour, seasoned with salt and
   pepper
¼ cup salad oil
¼ cup butter
Minced garlic to taste
½ cup white wine
¼ cup water or bouillon
1 tablespoon lemon juice
1 onion, sliced
1 bay leaf
1 teaspoon salt
¼ teaspoon pepper
3 whole cloves
Chopped parsley for garnish

Serves 4-6

● Wipe veal. Pound with a meat mallet until thin. Dust with seasoned flour.

● Heat oil and butter together in a skillet. Add minced garlic. Brown veal slices on both sides.

● Combine remaining ingredients except parsley. Pour over veal in skillet. Cover and simmer 45 minutes. Serve meat with sauce remaining in skillet, adding more wine or bouillon to increase amount of sauce. Remove bay leaf and cloves before serving. Garnish with chopped parsley.

Margo Dineen Muccia

desserts

For Perfect Desserts

Use only sweet butter for baking. It does make a difference.

Measure liquids in glass measuring cups, dry ingredients in aluminum or plastic cups that can be leveled with a knife.

Beat egg whites after bringing them to room temperature first. They will hold their volume better than whites from chilled eggs.

Strictly fresh eggs do not whip as well as older ones. To tell an older egg from a rotten one, put them in a pan of cool, salted water. A rotten egg will come up to the top.

Egg whites are best beaten with a balloon whisk in a large copper bowl. Both should be perfectly clean without a trace of grease.

When folding in egg whites, your hands are the best instruments. Do not be afraid to use them.

Heavy cream whips better if both the bowl and the beaters are refrigerated before whipping.

Grate cold butter by hand or in the food processor if a recipe calls for softened butter.

Store cooking chocolate air tight. If a dusty-looking powder forms on the surface, do not discard the chocolate. This is due to exposure to air and will not affect the taste.

Line cake pans with greased cooking parchment paper and the pan will release the cake neatly and perfectly every time.

If a recipe for cake batter calls for addings eggs one at a time, do so. If eggs are added all at once, the batter will not absorb the eggs properly.

Bake cookies in middle of oven. Remove from baking sheet as soon as they come out of the oven, then let the sheet cool thoroughly before using again.

Cool cakes, cookies, and pies on a rack, not a plate, or they will become soggy.

To soften rock-hard brown sugar, process it in a food processor or blender. An unpeeled apple slice will keep brown sugar soft when stored air tight.

Desserts

Brandied Carrot Cake

Serves 8

1 slice white bread
1 cup flour
¾ teaspoon baking powder
½ teaspoon cinnamon
¼ teaspoon salt
⅔ cup walnuts
3 eggs, at room temperature
¾ cup sugar
½ cup butter, at room temperature
⅓ cup plus 1 tablespoon cognac or
    brandy
1 teaspoon vanilla extract
1 cup finely shredded carrots

Garnish:
Fresh strawberries or raspberries
1 cup heavy cream, whipped

- Toast bread until it is just dry but not brown. Break into quarters and put in blender or food processor to make fine crumbs. Butter the inside of a 4-cup tube pan. Coat bottom and sides with breadcrumbs.
- Sift together flour, baking powder, cinnamon, and salt. Combine 2 tablespoons of this mixture with walnuts in blender or food processor. Chop to a fine texture.
- Beat eggs with clean beaters in a deep, narrow bowl until pale and thick. Gradually add sugar and beat for 15 minutes.
- Preheat oven to 350°. Cream butter until soft. Add ⅓ cup cognac gradually until well incorporated. Add vanilla. Beat in remaining flour mixture about ⅓ at a time at lowest speed on electric mixer.
- Mix *half* the egg mixture into the creamed butter and cognac, folding in well with a rubber spatula. Stir in carrots and gently fold in *half* the remaining egg mixture. Sprinkle a handful of reserved nut mixture over cake batter. Fold in gently. Alternately fold in the rest of the nut and egg mixtures, taking care not to deflate batter.
- Pour batter into prepared pan and bake in the center of the oven for 45 minutes.
- Cool on a rack in the pan for 10 minutes. Invert on rack and cool completely. Cover and let stand for about a day before serving.
- Serve at room temperature with berries in the center. Fold remaining 1 tablespoon cognac into whipped cream and serve on top.

Nancy Beck Hoggson

221

Desserts

West Side Cheesecake

Crumb crust or Paté Sucrée (see
   Index)
2½ pounds cream cheese, at room
   temperature
1¾ cups sugar
3 tablespoons flour
1½ teaspoons grated orange rind
1½ teaspoons grated lemon rind
¼ teaspoon vanilla extract
5 eggs
2 egg yolks
¼ cup heavy cream
Strawberry Glaze (recipe follows)

Serves 12

● Prepare crumb crust or Paté Sucrée. Butter bottom and sides of a 9″ spring-form pan. If using crumb crust, dust bottom and sides of pan with crumb mixture, patting excess onto bottom.
● If using Paté Sucrée, preheat oven to 400°. Remove bottom from springform pan. Roll out ⅓ of the chilled pastry and place it over the pan bottom. Chill remaining dough. Trim excess dough by running a rolling pin over the sharp edge. Bake 10 minutes until golden. Remove from oven and cool. Butter sides of pan and snap in place over pastry-covered base. Roll remaining dough ⅛″ thick and cut it to fit sides of pan. Fit strips in, joining ends to line the inside completely. Trim dough so it comes only ¾ of the way up the sides.
● Preheat oven to 500°. Beat together cream cheese, sugar, flour, grated orange and lemon rind, and vanilla. Add eggs and egg yolks one at a time, stirring after each addition. Stir in cream.
● Pour into prepared pan and bake 12 minutes. Reduce oven temperature to 200° and continue baking 1 hour longer.
● Remove from oven and cool completely. Top with Strawberry Glaze. Chill until serving time.
● Remove sides from springform pan and place cheesecake on a serving plate.

Marcia Petersen Sandner

Desserts

Strawberry Glaze

1 quart strawberries
¾ cup sugar
¼ cup cold water
Salt
1½ tablespoons cornstarch
1 teaspoon butter

1½ cups

● Wash berries. Crush about 1 cup berries and put in a saucepan. Add sugar, water, a dash of salt, and cornstarch. Boil gently, for 2 minutes, stirring constantly. Stir in butter. Cool slightly.
● Arrange uncooked strawberries on top of cake, and spoon glaze over them. Chill at least 3 hours.

Marcia Petersen Sandner

Bavarian Cheesecake

1¾ cups graham cracker crumbs
¼ cup finely chopped walnuts or
    pecans
½ teaspoon cinnamon
½ cup butter, melted
2 eggs, well beaten
1 pound cream cheese, at room
    temperature
1 cup sugar
¼ teaspoon salt
2 teaspoons vanilla extract
½ teaspoon almond extract
2 cups sour cream

Serves 6-8

● To prepare crust, mix graham cracker crumbs, walnuts, cinnamon, and butter. Reserve 3 tablespoons of the mixture. Press the rest in the bottom and 2½" up the sides of a 9" springform pan.
● Preheat oven to 375°. Combine eggs, cream cheese, sugar, salt, and vanilla and almond extracts. Beat until smooth. Blend in sour cream and pour mixture into crust. Sprinkle with reserved crumb mixture.
● Bake for 35 minutes until set. Cool and chill well at least 4 to 5 hours before serving.

Joyce Verhalen Pandolfi

223

Desserts

Almond Blackbottom Cheesecake

1½ cups chocolate wafer crumbs
(about 30 wafers)
1 cup blanched almonds, lightly
toasted and chopped
1⅓ cups plus 1 tablespoon sugar
6 tablespoons butter, at room
temperature
1½ pounds cream cheese, at room
temperature
4 eggs
⅓ cup heavy cream
¼ cup Amaretto or almond-based
liqueur
2 teaspoons vanilla extract
2 cups sour cream
Blanched, slivered, toasted almonds
for garnish

Serves 10-12

● Preheat oven to 375°. Combine chocolate wafer crumbs, chopped almonds, ⅓ cup sugar, and softened butter. Pat mixture on the bottom and sides of a buttered 9½" or 10" spring-form pan.

● Cream together softened cream cheese and 1 cup sugar. Beat in eggs one at a time, beating well after each addition. Add heavy cream, almond liqueur, and 1 teaspoon vanilla. Beat mixture until light.

● Pour into blackbottom shell. Bake 30 minutes and cool on a rack for 5 minutes. It will not be firm yet.

● Combine sour cream and remaining vanilla with 1 tablespoon sugar. Spread mixture evenly on cake. Return to oven and bake 5 minutes more. Cool completely on rack in the pan.

● Cover lightly and chill at least 5 hours, then remove sides of pan. Transfer cake to a cake stand or plate. Press some blanched, slivered, toasted almonds around top edge for garnish.

Ellen Parry Pinkernell

Desserts

Chocolate Mousse Torte

8 ounces semi-sweet chocolate
1 tablespoon instant coffee powder
¼ cup boiling water
Fine dry breadcrumbs
8 eggs, separated
⅛ teaspoon salt
⅔ cup sugar
2½ teaspoons vanilla extract
1½ cups heavy cream
3 tablespoons sifted confectioners
    sugar

Serves 8

• Preheat oven to 350°.

• Place chocolate in top of double boiler over simmering water. Dissolve instant coffee powder in boiling water. Add to chocolate. Cover and let stand over low heat, stirring occasionally. When chocolate is almost melted, whisk mixture until smooth.

• Dust well-buttered 9″ pie plate with dry breadcrumbs. Beat egg whites and salt until stiff but not dry.

• Beat egg yolks until thick. Gradually beat in sugar until mixture is thick and lemon-colored. Slowly beat in melted chocolate and *1 teaspoon* vanilla. Stir in ¼ of the beaten egg whites. Fold in remaining whites.

• Fill prepared pie plate with enough mousse to reach top edge. Cover the remaining mousse and refrigerate. Bake 25 minutes. Turn off oven but leave mousse in warm oven 5 minutes longer.

• Remove mousse from oven. Cool for 2 hours on wire rack at room temperature. The mousse will sink in the middle to form the shape of a pie shell.

• Fill cooled shell with the chilled, uncooked mousse. Chill for 2-3 hours.

• Whip cream with confectioners sugar and remaining 1½ teaspoons vanilla. Spread over pie. Serve now, or chill until serving time.

Adrienne Wheeler Rudge

Desserts

Wellesley Fudge Cake

⅔ cup butter
2⅔ cups dark brown sugar, well packed
1 egg and 3 egg yolks
⅔ cup boiling water
4 squares (4 ounces) unsweetened chocolate
1 teaspoon vanilla extract
2⅔ cups sifted cake flour
1½ teaspoons baking powder
1 teaspoon salt
1¼ teaspoons baking soda
1 cup sour cream
Fudge Frosting (recipe follows)

Serves 12-16
● Preheat oven to 350°. Grease and flour a 13″ x 9″ pan or two 9″ round pans.
● Cream butter and brown sugar until very light. Add egg and beat well. Add egg yolks one at a time, beating well after each addition.
● Add boiling water to chocolate. Stir until melted and smooth. Add to butter mixture and beat until blended. Beat in vanilla.
● Sift together flour, baking powder, and salt. Stir baking soda into sour cream and use a wooden spoon to blend in dry ingredients alternately with sour cream.
● Turn batter into prepared pan and bake for 45 minutes.
● Cool and remove from pan. Ice with Fudge Frosting and sprinkle with chopped nuts.

Keene Harrill Rees

Fudge Frosting

2 squares (2 ounces) unsweetened chocolate
2 cups sugar
2 tablespoons light corn syrup
⅔ cup milk
Dash salt
2 tablespoons butter
1 teaspoon vanilla extract

2 cups
● Cut chocolate squares. Place in saucepan with sugar, corn syrup, milk, and salt. Bring slowly to a boil, stirring until the sugar is dissolved. Cook to 232° on a candy thermometer or until a very soft ball forms in ice water. Stir occasionally while cooking.
● Remove from heat. Beat in butter and add vanilla. Beat 5-10 minutes, until frosting is of spreading consistency. Frost cake quickly, before fudge sets.

Keene Harrill Rees

Desserts

A Small Chocolate Cake

¼ cup butter, at room temperature
1¼ cups brown sugar
1 egg
½ cup strong coffee
½ cup buttermilk, sour cream, or
    sour milk
½ teaspoon salt
1 cup flour
1 teaspoon baking powder
1 teaspoon baking soda
4 heaping tablespoons unsweetened
    dry cocoa
1 teaspoon vanilla extract

Serves 6-8

● Preheat oven to 375°. Grease and flour an 8" square pan.
● Cream butter and brown sugar. Add egg and beat well. Mix in coffee and buttermilk.
● Sift together all dry ingredients. Add to batter. Mix well and add vanilla.
● Pour batter into prepared pan. It will be runny. Bake 30-35 minutes until a cake tester comes out clean. Sprinkle with confectioners sugar or frost as desired.

Marion Black Beck

Wonderful Chocolate Cake

12 tablespoons butter
6 ounces semi-sweet chocolate
5 ounces sugar
6 eggs, separated
1 cup heavy cream, whipped
Candied Orange Peel (see Index)

Serves 6-8

● Preheat oven to 325°. Melt butter, chocolate, and sugar in a double boiler. Remove from heat. Add yolks and beat to form a thick paste.
● Beat egg whites until stiff peaks form. Fold into chocolate mixture.
● Butter a 9" cake pan. Line bottom with a round of wax paper cut to fit. Butter paper and dust with flour. Turn cake into prepared pan.
● Bake 35-40 minutes until cake is high and firm but still quivers when shaken. Serve warm or cool. topped with whipped cream and slivers of Candied Orange Peel.

Karin Lawrence Siegfried

227

Desderts

Chocolate Roll

8 ounces sweet chocolate, broken in
    small pieces
⅓ cup strong coffee
1 teaspoon vanilla extract
7 egg yolks
1 cup sugar
8 egg whites
3 tablespoons unsweetened dry
    cocoa, sifted
2 cups heavy cream
Flavoring for filling: ¼ cup Grand
    Marnier plus 1 tablespoon grated
    orange rind; or chopped
    hazelnuts; or ¼ cup cognac and
    2 teaspoons powdered espresso

Serves 10-12

• Melt chocolate with coffee in the top of a double boiler over simmering water. Remove from heat. Stir in the vanilla and cool.

• Preheat oven to 350°. Beat egg yolks at low speed on electric mixer. Gradually beat in ¾ cup sugar. Continue to beat until fluffy and lemon-colored. Stir into lukewarm or nearly cool chocolate mixture, blending well.

• Beat egg whites until stiff but not dry. Stir ⅓ of beaten egg whites into chocolate mixture. Fold in the rest of the whites until no white patches show.

• Lightly butter an 11" x 17" jelly roll pan. Line it with wax paper with a little paper extending at each end of the pan. Butter wax paper. Pour in batter, spreading evenly and smoothing top.

• Bake 10 minutes. Lower oven temperature to 300° and bake 5 minutes more. Remove pan from oven and cover with a damp cloth. Refrigerate 1 hour.

• When chilled, remove cloth and loosen roll from sides of pan. Dust heavily with sifted cocoa. Cover with a sheet of wax paper. Turn over on a large tea towel by grasping both ends of the wax paper and flipping quickly. The cake should rest upside down on the towel and wax paper covering. Carefully remove wax paper from roll.

• Beat heavy cream until slightly thickened. Beat in remaining ¼ cup sugar and the flavoring you have selected.

• Spread filling evenly over cake leaving a small border along the sides.

Desserts

continued

Gently roll from one long side to the other, pulling the cloth and wax paper away as you go. On the last turn, roll cake onto a serving board, seam down. Gently shape the roll with your hands. Trim ends so filling is flush with end of cake. Cover any cracks with another sifting of cocoa. Cover lightly and refrigerate 2-3 hours.

Nancy Beck Hoggson

Grandma Alice's Jelly Roll

4 eggs, separated
1 cup sugar
1½ tablespoons lemon juice
1½ tablespoons water
1 teaspoon vanilla extract
1 cup flour
1¼ teaspoons baking powder
¼ teaspoon salt
1 cup jelly or jam

Serves 8-10

● Preheat oven to 350°. Grease an 11" x 15" baking sheet with sides.
● Beat egg whites to soft peaks, adding ¼ cup sugar a little at a time. Without washing beater, beat egg yolks in another bowl until thick and lemon-colored. Beat in lemon juice, water, vanilla, and remaining ¾ cup sugar. Pour over beaten egg whites and fold in until blended.
● Sift flour, baking powder, and salt onto the batter. Fold in gently. Pour onto baking sheet. Spread and bake for 12 minutes.
● Spread a tea towel and sprinkle it with sifted confectioners sugar. Turn cake from pan onto towel.
● Warm jam or jelly slightly over very low heat to make it more spreadable. Spread immediately on the warm cake and roll it up, using the cloth to push so the cake will not break. Wrap in the cloth until cool and set.

Variation: Fill with Lemon or Orange Curd (see Index).

Betsy Gimpel Mena

229

Desserts

Gênoise

6 large eggs
1 cup sugar
1 cup sifted flour
½ cup butter, melted and clarified
　(see Index)
1 teaspoon vanilla extract

2-3 layers

● Combine eggs and sugar in a large bowl. Stir 1 minute until combined. Set bowl over a saucepan containing 1"-2" of hot water. Water should not touch bottom of bowl. Place saucepan with bowl over low heat for 5-10 minutes until eggs are lukewarm. Do not let water boil. Stir eggs lightly 3 or 4 times to prevent them from cooking at the bottom.

● When eggs feel lukewarm to your fingertip, remove bowl from heat. Beat 10-15 minutes with electric mixer. Scrape sides of bowl with rubber spatula until eggs become light, fluffy, and cool. They will triple in bulk and look like whipped cream.

● Preheat oven to 350°. Grease and lightly flour cake pans: 2 layer pans (9" or 10" each), 3 layer pans (8" each), or 1 jelly roll pan (11" x 16").

● Sprinkle flour on the whipped eggs a little at a time. Fold in gently. Beat a little egg batter into the slightly cooled and clarified butter. Pour all back over the batter and fold in with vanilla.

● Pour batter gently into prepared pans. Bake 25-30 minutes until cakes pull away from sides of pans. Top will be golden brown and springy to the touch. Remove from pans immediately and cool on a cake rack.

　　Note: This versatile, buttery French spongecake can be made in one bowl and is leavened entirely with air incorporated by beating.

Nancy Beck Hoggson

Desserts

Gênoise with Orange Curd

1 cup sugar
Zest (outer rind) of 4 large lemons
Zest of 3 large oranges
⅔ cup freshly squeezed lemon juice
    (use 3 lemons)
⅓ cup freshly squeezed orange juice
    (use 1 orange)
4 eggs
5 egg yolks
1 cup cold butter, sliced
Gênoise, split in 3 layers
Candied Orange Peel (see Index)

Serves 6-8

● Mix sugar with lemon and orange zest in a large saucepan, crushing zest into sugar with the back of a wooden spoon. Add lemon and orange juice, eggs, and egg yolks. Whisk over moderate heat until sugar is dissolved. Add butter and continue to cook, whisking constantly just until mixture comes to a boil.
● Scrape into a bowl. Chill overnight.
● The next day, strain curd through a fine mesh and spread on each cake layer. Sift confectioners sugar over cake and decorate with Candied Orange Peel. Chill until serving time.

Nancy Beck Hoggson

Bourbon-Glazed Orange Cake

1¼ cups butter
2½ cups sugar
5 eggs
½ teaspoon vanilla extract
2 tablespoons grated orange rind
3 cups flour
Pinch salt
1 tablespoon baking powder
¾ cup fresh orange juice
⅓ cup bourbon

Serves 12-16

● Preheat oven to 350°. Grease and flour a 10″ springform or tube pan.
● Cream *1 cup* butter and *2 cups* sugar until light and fluffy. Beat in eggs one at a time, beating well after each addition. Add vanilla and grated orange rind.
● Sift together the flour, salt, and baking powder. Add to batter alternately with orange juice.
● Pour into prepared pan and bake 1 hour.
● Prepare bourbon glaze by bringing to a boil the remaining ¼ cup butter, ½ cup sugar, and bourbon.
● Remove cake from the oven when done. Pour glaze over hot cake. Let cool in pan, then turn out.

Barbara Isaac O'Donnell

231

Desserts

Frozen Lemon Meringue Cake

2 eggs
2 egg yolks
1⅓ cups sugar
6 tablespoons butter, cut in chunks
1½ tablespoons grated lemon rind
⅓ cup fresh lemon juice
⅓ teaspoon salt
3 egg whites
⅜ teaspoon cream of tartar
¾ teaspoon vanilla extract
3 cups vanilla ice cream

Serves 10-12

• Combine eggs and egg yolks in a heavy pan with 1 cup sugar and butter, lemon rind, juice, and salt. Cook over medium-low heat, stirring until butter melts and mixture thickens enough to coat a spoon. Do not let it boil. Cover and chill.

• Invert an 8″ cake pan and trace 2 circles onto sheets of parchment paper. Set paper circles on a large baking sheet.

• Preheat oven to 350°. Beat egg whites with cream of tartar until they hold soft peaks. Gradually beat in remaining ⅓ cup sugar and vanilla. Beat until shiny and stiff. Spread half the meringue on each paper circle, smoothing it with a spatula. Bake 1 hour. Turn off heat and let meringue dry for 2 hours in oven as it cools.

• When meringues are ready, let the ice cream soften slightly. Peel off the paper. Put one meringue on a serving plate and spread it with 1 cup ice cream. Freeze until firm. Spread half the lemon butter on the ice cream and freeze again.

• Now spread with second cup of ice cream. Freeze solid. Spread with remaining lemon butter. Freeze again. Top with remaining 1 cup ice cream and the other meringue. Cover with plastic wrap. Freeze until serving time.

Patricia Farnsworth Kuntz

Desserts

Gâteau d'Helène

¾ cup butter, at room temperature
1 cup sugar
1 orange
3 eggs
1 cup cake flour
1½ teaspoons baking powder
⅛ teaspoon salt
Apricot-Coconut Cream (recipe
    follows)

Serves 8

• Preheat oven to 375°. Heavily butter an 8½" or 9" cake pan. Line bottom with buttered wax paper, buttered side up. Sprinkle pan with flour, and shake off excess.

• Cream butter and sugar. Beat until smooth and pale yellow. Grate orange peel. Squeeze orange. Add peel to butter and reserve juice for apricot filling.

• Beat eggs into creamed butter, one at a time. Sift flour with baking powder and salt. Add to batter. Beat smooth.

• Pour batter into cake pan. Bake 35-40 minutes.

• Cool cake on a rack. Turn out after about 20 minutes. Fill and frost with Apricot-Coconut Cream.

Apricot-Coconut Cream

2 cups grated unsweetened coconut
½ cup fresh orange juice
¼ cup dark rum
½ cup apricot jam, strained
1½ cups heavy cream, chilled
1 teaspoon vanilla extract
⅓ cup sugar

2 cups

• The day before making Gâteau d'Helène, spread coconut to dry, uncovered, at room temperature.

• Mix orange juice and rum. Slice cake in 3 layers, pricking each with a fork. Sprinkle each layer with ⅓ of the rum-juice mixture. Spread 2 layers with apricot jam, reserving a little jam.

• Whip cream and add vanilla. Beat in sugar until quite stiff.

• Mix 5 *tablespoons* dried coconut with ¼ *cup* whipped cream.

• To assemble cake, spread coconut cream on first and second layers. Cover top layer with remaining apricot jam. Coat top and sides with remaining whipped cream. Sprinkle entire cake with remaining coconut and chill.

Nancy Beck Hoggson

Desserts

Broiled Frosting

1 cup evaporated milk
1 cup sugar
3 egg yolks
½ cup butter
1 teaspoon vanilla extract
⅓ cup flaked coconut
1 cup chopped pecans

2 cups
● Combine evaporated milk, sugar, egg yolks, butter, and vanilla in saucepan. Cook and stir for 12 minutes until thickened. Stir in coconut and pecans. Spread on a cooled cake.
● Brown under broiler until bubbly. Good warm or cool.

Anne Ruthrauff Seltzer

Chocolate Frosting

2 squares (2 ounces) unsweetened chocolate
3 tablespoons butter
1 pound confectioners sugar
1 teaspoon vanilla extract
3-4 tablespoons milk or cream

2 cups
● Melt chocolate with butter. Beat in confectioners sugar and vanilla. Add a little milk or cream to thin to spreading consistency.

Anne Ruthrauff Seltzer

Maple Syrup Frosting

½ cup pure maple syrup
⅛ teaspoon salt
¾ cup lightly packed brown sugar
1 egg white
½ teaspoon vanilla extract

1½ cups
● Measure syrup, salt, brown sugar, and egg white into top of double boiler. Place over simmering water. Beat constantly with electric mixer at high speed until frosting is stiff enough to stand in peaks. Remove from heat and beat in vanilla.

Marjorie Lister Beck

Desserts

Greek Butter Cookies

1 cup unsalted butter
½ cup confectioners sugar
1 egg yolk
2¼ cups sifted flour
½ teaspoon baking powder

5 dozen

● Cream butter and *6 tablespoons* sugar. Add egg yolk and beat well. Blend flour and baking powder. Stir dry ingredients into butter mixture. Roll into a ball. Chill for several hours.

● Preheat oven to 350°. Roll dough ½" thick. Cut with round 2" cookie cutter. Bake on ungreased cookie sheet for 10 minutes until browned.

● Loosen from baking sheet while still warm. Let cool. Dust with remaining confectioners sugar. Store in cupcake liners, because the baked cookies break easily.

Kathryn Kirchmaier Mack

Cheesecake Cookies

⅓ cup butter, at room temperature
⅓ cup firmly packed brown sugar
1 cup flour
½ cup finely chopped walnuts
¼ cup sugar
8 ounces cream cheese, at room temperature
1 egg
2 tablespoons milk
1 tablespoon fresh lemon juice
½ teaspoon vanilla extract

16 squares

● Preheat oven to 350°. Cream butter with brown sugar in small bowl. Add flour and walnuts. Make a crumb mixture. Reserve 1 cup for topping. Press remainder in bottom of 8" square pan.

● Bake 12-15 minutes until lightly browned.

● Blend sugar with cream cheese until quite smooth. Add egg, milk, lemon juice, and vanilla. Beat well and spread over baked crust. Sprinkle with reserved crumb mixture. Bake 25 minutes more.

● Cool and cut in squares to serve. Store in refrigerator.

Joyce Thom Alfieri

235

Desserts

Chocolate Meringue Macaroons

1 package (6 ounces) semi-sweet
  chocolate chips
2 egg whites
½ cup sugar
¼ teaspoon salt
½ teaspoon vanilla extract
1½ cups shredded coconut

2½ dozen
● Melt chocolate chips over hot water. Cool slightly.
● Beat egg whites until foamy. Gradually sift sugar into whites, beating until mixture stands in peaks. Add salt, vanilla, and coconut. Fold in melted chocolate and mix well.
● Preheat oven to 325°. Drop batter in small mounds on parchment paper spread on baking sheets. Bake 20 minutes. Cool before removing from paper.

Susan Don Lubin

Cinnamon Almond Crisps

1 cup sugar
1 cup butter, at room temperature
1 egg, separated
2 cups flour
1 tablespoon cinnamon
⅛ teaspoon salt
½ cup chopped or slivered almonds

7 dozen
● Preheat oven to 300°. Cream sugar, butter, and egg yolk in mixing bowl or food processor. Add dry ingredients except for almonds. Mix well.
● Spread mixture on 2 ungreased baking sheets with sides. Mixture will barely cover bottoms. Cookies should be quite thin.
● Beat egg white until foamy. Spread on top of dough with pastry brush. Sprinkle nuts evenly over tops.
● Bake 25 minutes until golden brown. Cut into squares after removing from oven.

Jeanne Ditzler Dodds

Desserts

Coconut Bars

½ cup butter
1 cup plus 2 tablespoons flour
1½ cups packed brown sugar
2 eggs
1 cup unsweetened shredded
    coconut
1 cup chopped nuts
1 teaspoon vanilla extract
1 teaspoon baking powder
½ teaspoon salt

2 dozen
● Preheat oven to 350°. Cream together butter, flour, and ½ cup brown sugar. Pat mixture in ungreased 9" x 13" pan. Bake 10 minutes.
● Beat remaining 1 cup brown sugar with rest of ingredients. Spread on baked first layer. Return to oven and bake 20 minutes longer. Cool and cut into bars.

Ellen Zox Wedeles

Fudge Brownies

4 squares (1 ounce each)
    unsweetened chocolate, or ⅔
    cup unsweetened dry cocoa
1 cup butter
4 eggs
2 cups sugar
1½ cups flour
1 teaspoon baking powder
½ teaspoon salt
1 package (6 ounces) semi-sweet
    chocolate chips
1 cup chopped nuts
2 teaspoons vanilla extract

16-20 bars
● Preheat oven to 350°. Melt butter over very low heat with chocolate or cocoa. Cool slightly.
● Beat eggs and add sugar gradually. Add chocolate/butter mixture and beat well. Add flour, baking powder, and salt. Fold in chocolate chips, nuts, and vanilla. Pour into greased 13" x 9" pan.
● Bake 30 minutes. Cool before cutting.

Anne Ruthrauff Seltzer

237

Desserts

Granola Cookies

2 cups sifted flour
1 teaspoon baking powder
1 teaspoon baking soda
½ teaspoon salt
1 cup butter, at room temperature
1 cup sugar
1 cup brown sugar, packed to
    measure
2 eggs
2 teaspoons vanilla extract
3 cups granola (see Index)

8 dozen
● Sift or mix together dry ingredients. Set aside.
● Preheat oven to 375°. Grease baking sheets.
● Cream butter and sugars until light and fluffy. Add eggs and beat again. Gradually add blended dry ingredients and vanilla. Mix thoroughly. Stir in granola.
● Drop by well-rounded teaspoonfuls onto prepared baking sheets.
● Bake for 8-12 minutes until browned. Loosen from baking sheets while still warm, then cool on wire racks.

Betsy Gimpel Mena

Jamaican Squares

1 cup plus 2 tablespoons sugar
¾ cup flour
1 teaspoon baking powder
1 teaspoon cinnamon
½ teaspoon freshly grated nutmeg
¼ teaspoon ground cloves
1 cup chopped dry dates
1 cup chopped pecans or walnuts
2 eggs
1 tablespoon rum
Confectioners sugar

18 squares
● Preheat oven to 350°. Butter and flour 9″ square cake pan.
● Blend *1 cup* sugar with flour, baking powder, and spices. Toss chopped dates with remaining 2 tablespoons sugar. Stir into flour mixture along with chopped nuts.
● Beat eggs with rum and stir in. Scrape batter into prepared pan. Smooth top with spatula. Bake 25-30 minutes until top is lightly browned.
● Remove pan from oven. Sprinkle with confectioners sugar. Cut in squares or rectangles while still warm.

Thea Nielsen Pitassy

Desserts

Lemon Bars

1 cup butter, at room temperature
¼ teaspoon salt
2¼ cups sifted flour
½ cup confectioners sugar
2 cups sugar
Grated zest of 1 lemon
6 tablespoons lemon juice
4 eggs, beaten

5 dozen

● Preheat oven to 350°. Mix butter, salt, *2 cups* flour, and confectioners sugar. Press firmly into a 9″ x 13″ pan. Bake 15-20 minutes until golden brown at the edges.

● Gradually add sugar, grated lemon zest, and lemon juice to beaten eggs. Sift remaining ¼ cup flour and fold in gently. Pour onto slightly cooled crust. Return to 350° oven and bake 20-25 minutes longer.

● Remove from oven. Sprinkle with confectioners sugar. Cool, cut into bars, and serve.

Ann Evans Gum

Melting Moments

1 cup butter, at room temperature
1 cup flour, sifted
½ cup cornstarch
½ cup confectioners sugar
1 teaspoon vanilla extract
½ teaspoon almond extract

3 dozen

● Preheat oven to 375°.

● Cream butter and flour. Sift cornstarch with confectioners sugar. Add to butter mixture. Add flavorings. Drop by teaspoonfuls onto ungreased baking sheets.

● Bake for 8-12 minutes. Loosen while warm, and cool on wire racks. Store in airtight containers, stacked in paper muffin cups to prevent crumbling.

Marcia Mead Thomas

Desserts

Mincemeat Squares

1½ cups flour
1¼ cups oatmeal
1 cup brown sugar
¾ cup butter
½ teaspoon salt
1½-2 cups mincemeat (see Index)
1 egg yolk
1 tablespoon water

16-20 squares
• Preheat oven to 400°. Grease an 8" or 9" square pan.
• Combine flour. oatmeal. brown sugar. butter. and salt. Spread half this crumb mixture in the prepared pan. Spread mincemeat over crumbs to make second layer.
• Spread other half of crumbs over mincemeat. Beat egg yolk with water. Brush over top.
• Bake 20-25 minutes. Cool and cut.

Christine Church Gimpel

Oatmeal Carmelitas

1 cup plus 3 tablespoons flour
1 cup quick-cooking oats
¾ cup firmly packed brown sugar
½ teaspoon baking soda
¼ teaspoon salt
¾ cup butter, melted
1 package (6 ounces) semi-sweet chocolate chips
½ cup chopped pecans
¾ cup caramel ice cream topping

12-16 bars
• Preheat oven to 350°. Combine 1 cup flour. oats. brown sugar. baking soda. and salt with melted butter to form crumbs. Press half this crumb mixture into bottom of 9" square pan. Bake 10 minutes.
• Combine chocolate chips and nuts. Sprinkle over baked crust.
• Mix caramel topping with remaining 3 tablespoons flour. Drizzle on chocolate and nuts in pan. Sprinkle remaining crumbs over all.
• Return to oven and continue to bake at 350° 15-20 minutes until golden brown. Chill for easy cutting.

Marion Young

Desserts

Raspberry or Apricot Squares

¾ cup butter
1½ cups flour
1 teaspoon baking powder
¼ teaspoon salt
¼ cup sugar
¼ cup lightly packed brown sugar
1½ cups quick-cooking oatmeal
1 cup raspberry or apricot preserves
¼ cup chopped nuts

2 dozen

● Preheat oven to 375°. Melt butter over medium heat in saucepan. Stir in flour, baking powder, salt, and sugars. Stir in oatmeal. Press about ⅔ of this mixture in greased 9″ square baking pan.
● Heat and stir preserves over very low heat. Spread over crust. Toss nuts with remaining oat mixture. Sprinkle over top and pat down lightly.
● Bake 30-35 minutes until golden brown. Cool 30 minutes on a wire cake rack before serving.
    Note: Use pecans or walnuts with raspberry preserves or almonds with apricot preserves.

Nancy Beck Hoggson

Raspberry Meringue Kisses

3 egg whites
⅛ teaspoon salt
3½ tablespoons raspberry flavored gelatin
¾ cup sugar
1 teaspoon vinegar
1 package (6 ounces) semi-sweet chocolate chips

5 dozen

● Beat egg whites with salt until foamy. Gradually beat in raspberry gelatin and sugar. Continue to beat until stiff peaks form and sugar is completely dissolved. Mix in vinegar. Fold in chocolate chips.
● Preheat oven to 250°. Drop raspberry meringues onto greased baking sheets covered with parchment paper.
● Bake 25 minutes. Turn off oven and leave cookies in the oven for 20 minutes longer. Cool before removing from paper.

Mary Dorothy Hubbard

Desserts

Southern Pecan Bars

¼ cup butter, at room temperature
⅓ cup plus ¼ cup packed brown
  sugar
1 cup plus 2 tablespoons flour
¼ teaspoon baking powder
1 cup chopped pecans
2 eggs, beaten
¾ cup light corn syrup
½ teaspoon salt
1 teaspoon vanilla extract

25 bars

● Preheat oven to 350°. Cream butter and ⅓ cup brown sugar. Beat in 1 cup flour and baking powder until mixture resembles corn meal. Add ¼ cup pecans. Pat into 12″ x 8″ pan. Bake 10 minutes.

● Beat eggs until foamy. Add corn syrup, remaining ¼ cup brown sugar, 2 tablespoons flour, salt, and vanilla. Mix well. Pour over baked crust. Sprinkle with remaining ¾ cup chopped pecans. Bake 25-30 minutes more. When cool, cut into bars.

Dorothy McClanahan Watson

Spicy Oatmeal Wafers

1 cup butter, at room temperature
2 teaspoons vanilla extract
½ cup sugar
1 cup firmly packed brown sugar
2 eggs
2 cups old-fashioned oatmeal
½ cup flour
1 teaspoon salt
¼ teaspoon baking soda
1 teaspoon cinnamon
1 teaspoon ground cloves
1 teaspoon allspice
1 teaspoon ginger
1 teaspoon nutmeg
1 cup walnuts, chopped medium-fine

5 dozen

● Preheat oven to 350°. Adjust oven racks ⅓ down from top of oven. Cut foil to fit baking sheets.

● Cream butter. Add vanilla and sugars and beat well. Beat in eggs, then oatmeal. Add dry ingredients, then the nuts. Beat until well mixed.

● Drop batter from small teaspoons, placing them 3″ apart. Bake 15 minutes until completely browned.

● Cool cookies 10 minutes by inverting foil so that bottom-side is up and cookies are facing down. Then peel foil away from backs of cookies. Store in an airtight container or freeze.

Barbara Smith Suval

Desserts

Svinges

Oil
1 pound ricotta cheese, drained
4 eggs, slightly beaten
1 cup self rising flour
2 tablespoons sugar
½ teaspoon salt
Cinnamon and sugar

3 dozen

● Fill deep saucepan or electric frying pan with oil 2"-3" deep. Heat to 375°.
● Combine ricotta, eggs, flour, sugar, and salt.
● Drop cheese mixture by teaspoonfuls into hot oil. Doughnuts will brown on one side, and flip over on their own to brown on the other. Remove from oil and drain. Roll in cinnamon and sugar. Serve immediately.

Note: Any leftover batter can be stored in the refrigerator for several days.

Judith Torrisi Wintermuth

Vamino Bars

First layer
½ cup butter
1 egg
¼ cup sugar
1 teaspoon vanilla extract
5 tablespoons unsweetened dry cocoa
1 cup flaked coconut
½ cup chopped nuts
2 cups graham cracker crumbs

Second layer
½ cup butter, at room temperature
6 tablespoons milk
4 tablespoons instant vanilla pudding powder
4 cups confectioners sugar

18 bars

● Place butter, egg, sugar, vanilla, and cocoa in bowl. Set bowl in pan of boiling water. Stir and cook until mixture resembles custard. .
● Blend coconut, nuts, and crumbs. Stir into custard mixture. Press into 9" x 13" pan. Refrigerate 15 minutes.

● Cream butter. Add milk, pudding powder, and sugar. Blend well. Spread over first layer. Refrigerate 15 minutes longer until set.

243

Desserts

continued

Third layer
4 squares semi-sweet chocolate
4 tablespoons butter

● Melt chocolate with butter over very low heat. Spread over vanilla layer. Refrigerate at least 30-45 minutes.
● Remove from refrigerator 30 minutes before serving. Cut and serve.

Marcia Mead Thomas

Almond Fruit Gel

3 envelopes (3 tablespoons)
    unflavored gelatin
¾ cup cold water
1¼ cups boiling water
7 tablespoons sugar
1¾ cups milk
2 tablespoons almond extract
Canned fruit cocktail or chunky fruit
    pieces in syrup, chilled

Serves 6-8
● Soften gelatin by sprinkling it in cold water. Stir to dissolve. Add boiling water. Stir thoroughly until mixture is clear and gelatin is dissolved.
● Add sugar, milk, and almond extract. Stir well. Pour into 12" x 7½" pan. Chill until set.
● To serve, cut gelatin in diamond-shaped pieces. Mix with fruit and its syrup.

Lucie Ling Campbell

Hot Apricot Soufflé

4 egg whites
⅛ teaspoon cream of tartar
¼ teaspoon salt
½ cup sugar
2 jars (7¾ ounces each) baby-food
    apricots
¼ teaspoon almond extract
2 cups heavy cream

Serves 6-8
● Preheat oven to 325°. Butter a 1½-quart soufflé dish.
● Beat egg whites until foamy. Add cream of tartar and salt. Continue to beat until soft peaks form. Gradually add sugar and beat until stiff peaks form. Fold in apricots and almond extract. Pour into soufflé dish.
● Set dish in a pan of warm water. Bake for 45-50 minutes, until firm. Serve at once, topped with whipped cream.

Kathryn Kirchmaier Mack

Desserts

Christmas Charlotte

1 envelope (1 tablespoon) unflavored
   gelatin
¼ teaspoon salt
½ cup sugar
½ cup cold water
1 teaspoon grated orange rind
1 cup orange juice
½ teaspoon vanilla extract
1 cup heavy cream
Lady fingers or gênoise, split to line
   serving bowl
1-2 tablespoons sherry

Serves 6

- Combine gelatin, salt, sugar, and water in saucepan. Heat to boiling point, stirring constantly until gelatin is dissolved. Remove from heat and stir in orange rind, orange juice, and vanilla.
- Chill, stirring occasionally until softly set. Beat until foamy.
- Whip cream until stiff. Fold into orange mixture.
- Split lady fingers and sprinkle with sherry. Line bowl with cut side of lady fingers. Turn whipped mixture into bowl. Chill overnight. Garnish with a holly sprig.

Marjorie Lister Beck

Cherries Jubilee

2 cans (1 pound each) pitted dark
   sweet cherries
½ cup red currant jelly
⅓ cup kirsch
⅔ cup cognac
1 quart vanilla ice cream

Serves 6

- Drain cherries. reserving ¼ cup liquid. Set both aside.
- Melt jelly over low heat. Add cherries, reserved liquid. and kirsch. Thoroughly heat cherry mixture. stirring gently. Transfer mixture to chafing dish to keep warm.
- Rapidly heat cognac in small saucepan. Do not boil. Ignite cognac and pour over cherries. After flames die down, immediately spoon cherries over individual servings of ice cream.

Victoria Eastman Ohlandt

Desserts

Old-Fashioned Bread Pudding

8-10 slices firm white bread
4 tablespoons melted butter
½ cup raisins, light or dark
¾ cup sugar
1 teaspoon cinnamon
4 eggs
¼ teaspoon salt
4 cups milk
1 teaspoon vanilla extract
¼ cup apple jelly

Serves 6-8

● Brush one side of each bread slice with melted butter. Cut in quarters. Arrange overlapping quarter-slices in lightly greased, shallow 2-quart casserole. Sprinkle with raisins.
● Mix sugar and cinnamon. Sprinkle *half* the mixture over bread.
● In large bowl, beat eggs with salt and remaining cinnamon sugar. Stir in milk and vanilla. Pour over bread.
● Set baking dish in shallow pan. Pour 1″ of boiling water into pan surrounding pudding.
● Bake in 350° oven for 50 minutes, until center is set but still soft. Cool.
● To serve, melt apple jelly and brush on bread pudding. Serve with cream.

Anne Ruthrauff Seltzer

Crème Brulée

3 cups heavy cream
6 tablespoons sugar
6 egg yolks
2 teaspoons vanilla extract
½ cup light brown sugar

Serves 6-8

● Preheat oven to 300°. Heat cream over boiling water and stir in sugar. Beat egg yolks in a bowl until light. Gradually pour hot cream over them, stirring vigorously. Stir in vanilla. Strain mixture into a lightly greased 1-quart baking dish or individual ramekins.
● Place dish or ramekins in a pan containing 1″ of hot water and bake 1 hour until firm. Chill.
● Before serving, cover surface with brown sugar. Set dish on a bed of cracked ice. Broil until sugar is brown and melted. Serve immediately.

Nancy Gould Pinkernell

Desserts

Coeur de Crème

8 ounces cream cheese, at room
    temperature
½ cup confectioners sugar
1 teaspoon vanilla extract
2 cups heavy cream
1 package (10 ounces) frozen
    strawberries, at room
    temperature
½ cup red currant jelly
1 tablespoon Framboise liqueur or
    Cassis
2 cups fresh strawberries

Serves 6-8

● Beat cream cheese until fluffy. Add sugar and vanilla and mix well. Whip cream in another bowl. Mix with cream cheese.

● Cut a large square of cheesecloth to line a coeur de crème mold. Soak it with cold water and wring it out well. Place in mold, overlapping slightly at edges. Pour in cream cheese mixture. Fold in cheesecloth edges to cover top.

● Place mold right-side-up on a plate to drain. Refrigerate at least 6 hours or overnight. The excess moisture will seep through cheesecloth out onto the plate.

● Prepare strawberry sauce by whirling the frozen strawberries until smooth in blender or food processor. Add currant jelly and liqueur and blend well. Refrigerate in glass dish or pitcher.

● To unmold, remove cloth and turn the coeur de crème onto a serving plate. Decorate with fresh berries.

Judith Freyermuth Rex

Desserts

Cream Puffs Supreme

1 cup water
½ cup cold butter
¼ teaspoon salt
1 teaspoon sugar
1 cup flour
4 eggs
Chocolate Cream Filling (recipe
    follows)
Chocolate Glaze (recipe follows)

Serves 12-16

● To make cream puffs or pâté a choux, bring water to boil slowly with cold butter, salt, and sugar. Add flour all at once. Stir vigorously until mixture forms a ball and no longer clings to sides of pan.

● If using food processor, process flour mixture a few seconds. Add eggs and beat 30 seconds longer. By hand, mix well and add eggs one at a time. Beat 2 minutes after each addition.

● Preheat oven to 400°. Drop choux paste by spoonfuls on buttered baking sheet, using 1 tablespoon for large puffs or 1 teaspoon for small ones. Bake about 20 minutes for small puffs, about 45 minutes for large. Prick or slit while warm to release steam.

● Cool on rack. Make Chocolate Cream Filling. Make Chocolate Glaze.

● Slice puffs and spoon in Chocolate Cream Filling. Top with lids. Refrigerate or freeze.

● If frozen, defrost cream puffs at room temperature for 2 hours before serving. If refrigerated, bring to room temperature for 1 hour before serving.

● Spread with Chocolate Glaze.

Chocolate Cream Filling

1 package (6 ounces) semi-sweet
    chocolate chips
⅓ cup hot coffee
4 egg yolks
2 tablespoons Grand Marnier, or 1
    tablespoon vanilla extract
½ cup butter, at room temperature

1 cup

● Place chocolate chips in blender or food processor. Add hot coffee and blend until smooth. Add egg yolks and Grand Marnier or vanilla. Mix until smooth. Add butter a little at a time, creaming well. Chill until mixture has consistency of whipped cream.

Desserts

Chocolate Glaze

3 ounces sweet chocolate
2 tablespoons water
2 tablespoons butter
3 tablespoons confectioners sugar
1 tablespoon Grand Marnier
Sliced almonds (optional)

⅓ cup
● Mix all ingredients except Grand Marnier in top of double boiler. Heat slowly and add Grand Marnier. Let cool a few minutes to spreading consistency. Spread a little on each cream puff. Sprinkle with almonds.

Susan Sample Marx

Mourêmes au Chocolat

1 cup heavy cream, well chilled
½ cup sugar
¼ cup water
2 eggs
1 package (6 ounces) semi-sweet chocolate chips
½ teaspoon instant coffee powder
Pinch salt
2 tablespoons Grand Marnier

Serves 6
● Whip cream until it stands in soft peaks. Set aside.
● Heat sugar and water in a saucepan until sugar dissolves and mixture comes to a boil. Simmer sugar syrup for 2 minutes.
● Place eggs, chocolate chips, instant coffee powder, and salt in blender or food processor. Process for 20 seconds. With machine running, add syrup to chocolate mixture. Blend thoroughly. Add liqueur and process 20 seconds more.
● Fold in whipped cream until it disappears. Transfer this liquid mixture to a serving bowl or individual dishes. Cover and refrigerate overnight. Mourêmes will set to a perfect consistency when chilled.

Nancy Beck Hoggson

Desserts

Coffee Buttercream Porcupine

½ cup blanched almonds
1 cup unsalted butter
Pinch salt
¼ cup sugar
6 egg yolks
2 teaspoons vanilla extract
2 tablespoons instant coffee or
    espresso powder
1 tablespoon hot water
9″ Gênoise (see Index)
2 cups (8 ounces) slivered almonds
1½ cups heavy cream
Chocolate chips for "eyes"

Serves 12

• Toast blanched almonds 8-10 minutes and slivered almonds 10-12 minutes in a 350° oven until lightly browned. Set both aside to cool.

• Cream butter until fluffy. Add salt and gradually add sugar. Beat 3-4 minutes until mixture is very light.

• Grind toasted almonds in food processor or blender until powdered. Save 6 tablespoons of ground nuts. Set aside any extra to use another time.

• Add 1 egg yolk at a time to creamed butter and sugar. Beat well after each addition. Add 6 tablespoons ground almonds and vanilla. Stir instant coffee with hot water to dissolve. Beat into buttercream until smooth. Set aside.

• Lightly coat the inside of a 2-quart bowl with soft butter. Cut gênoise into pieces the size of half a ladyfinger. Arrange in bowl to line the bottom and rise about ¾ up the sides.

• Gently pour in about half the buttercream. Arrange a layer of gênoise over this and top with the rest of the buttercream. Smooth surface and cover with plastic wrap pressed onto the buttercream. Refrigerate overnight.

• To serve, remove plastic wrap and quickly turn dessert onto an oval platter. Carefully press two sides with your hands to form a long, rounded shape—the body of the porcupine. Near one end, make an indentation for the neck. This end will be the rounded head. Return platter to refrigerator.

Desserts

continued

● Whip cream until stiff. Use it to frost the porcupine, forming a well-defined shape. Make a face with chocolate chips. Stick in slivered, toasted almonds in close-set lengthwise rows over the body of the porcupine. Start at the neck and arrange so they stand straight.
● Chill until serving time. Keeps well overnight.

Barbara Smith Suval

Coffee Parfait

¾ cup sugar
⅓ cup water
4 egg yolks
Dash salt
2 cups heavy cream
2 tablespoons instant coffee
2 teaspoons vanilla extract
1 square (1 ounce) unsweetened
    chocolate, frozen

Serves 6-8
● Boil sugar and water in a saucepan until syrup will spin a thread, 230° on a candy thermometer.
● Beat egg yolks and salt thoroughly. Beat hot syrup into egg yolks in a thin, gradual stream. Continue to beat until cool.
● Beat heavy cream, instant coffee, and vanilla until cream holds definite peaks. Fold in yolk mixture along with thin shavings of the frozen square of chocolate. Reserve some chocolate shavings for garnish.
● Spoon mixture into ramekins. Freeze until firm. Remove from freezer to refrigerator 1 hour before serving.

Nancy Beck Hoggson

Desderts

Flan

1 cup sugar
5 eggs
¼ teaspoon salt
1 teaspoon vanilla extract
3½ cups milk

Garnish:
1 cup strawberries
1 cup seedless grapes

Serves 6-8
● Preheat oven to 325°. Sprinkle *½ cup* sugar in a heavy skillet. Stir frequently over low heat until sugar melts to a golden syrup. Pour syrup immediately into a 5-cup ring mold. Tilt mold quickly to coat bottom and sides. Let cool.
● Beat eggs well with remaining ½ cup sugar, salt, and vanilla. Gradually add milk, beating until smooth.
● Place prepared ring mold in a shallow baking pan. Set aside 1 cup of egg mixture. Pour remainder into mold. Place baking pan on the middle oven rack. Fill mold with reserved custard. Pour 1″ of hot water into baking pan around the mold. Bake for 55-60 minutes until set.
● Remove mold from pan. Cool and refrigerate at least an hour.
● To unmold, loosen edges with a spatula and invert on a serving plate. Shake flan loose. The caramel will run down the sides. Fill center with fruit.

Betsy Gimpel Mena

Cream Cheese Flan

1 cup sugar
2 eggs
9 ounces cream cheese, at room
    temperature
1 can (14 ounces) condensed milk
1 can (14 ounces) evaporated milk
1¾ cups milk
1 teaspoon vanilla extract

Serves 10-12
● Preheat oven to 375°.
● Place sugar in heavy pan. Melt over low heat until golden-brown. Pour syrup into 6-8 cup ring mold or 2-quart soufflé dish. Swirl to cover bottom and sides.
● Blend remaining ingredients until smooth, half at a time.
● Pour into mold. Place mold in larger pan. Pour boiling water in outer pan to depth of 1½″-2″. Bake 1¼ hours.
● Cool and chill overnight. Turn onto platter to serve.

Susan Necarsulmer Dallin

Desserts

Coconut Flan

2 tablespoons plus 2 cups sugar
1 tablespoon water
1 cup grated coconut
6 eggs, separated
2 cans (13 ounces each) evaporated
   milk
2 tablespoons coconut extract

Serves 12-14

● Place *2 tablespoons* sugar and the water in a mold over high heat. Stir and melt until caramel forms. Quickly tilt the mold to cover the sides and the bottom. Remove from heat and sprinkle grated coconut over caramel coating.

● Beat egg whites until stiff. Gradually add remaining 2 cups sugar, egg yolks, evaporated milk, and coconut extract. Beat all together.

● Pour mixture into mold and cover with foil. Place in a pan of boiling water and bake 45 minutes in a 350° oven. Remove foil and bake 30 minutes more. When custard is set, a toothpick inserted in the center should come out dry.

● Cool at room temperature and refrigerate. Unmold to serve.

Ann Keyser Griffin

253

Desserts

Lemon Fluff

7 eggs, separated
1¼ cups sugar
Grated rind of 2 lemons
Juice of 3 lemons
1 envelope (1 tablespoon) unflavored
    gelatin
¼ cup cold water
12 ladyfingers, or gênoise
1 cup heavy cream, whipped

Serves 8-10

● Beat egg yolks in a double boiler with
1 cup sugar until they are light. Add
lemon rind and juice. Cook over boiling water, stirring until thickened.
● Soften gelatin in cold water. Add to
hot mixture, stirring to dissolve. Remove from heat.
● Beat egg whites until frothy. Add remaining ¼ cup sugar gradually. Beat
until stiff and fold into yolk mixture.
● Line bottom of a 2-quart springform
pan with ladyfingers or gênoise.
Spoon lemon mixture over ladyfingers.
Chill several hours.
● Unmold. Spread with whipped
cream.

Peggy Swanson Smith

Mousse au Citron

3 eggs, separated, at room
    temperature
½ cup plus 1 tablespoon sugar
⅓ teaspoon salt
¼ cup fresh lemon juice
1 teaspoon grated lemon zest (outer
    yellow rind only)
1 cup heavy cream
Candied violets or fresh raspberries
    for garnish

Serves 4

● Beat egg yolks with sugar, salt, and
lemon juice. Cook over simmering water in a double boiler. Stir constantly
until custard thickens and coats a metal spoon. If custard threatens to cur-
dle, remove from heat immediately.
Add few drops of cream and beat.
● Add lemon zest to custard. Cool.
● Whip cream and set aside. Beat egg
whites until stiff. Fold whipped cream
and egg whites into cooled custard.
Pour into serving bowl or 4 individual
serving dishes. Freeze until firm.
● Remove from freezer about 15 minutes before serving. Garnish with candied violets or berries.

Sheilah Plenke Gallagher

Desserts

Lemon Ice

1 cup sugar
1 cup milk
1 cup heavy cream
Juice and grated rind of 1 large or 2
    small lemons

3 cups

- Combine sugar, milk, and heavy cream. Stir until sugar is dissolved. Freeze until mixture is almost solid, about 2 hours.
- Add lemon juice and rind. Return to freezer until firm.
- Remove 10-15 minutes before serving.

Carole Kruse Long

Frozen Orange Soufflé

2 egg yolks
1¼ cups sugar
3 tablespoons flour
Salt
1 cup milk, scalded
¼ teaspoon vanilla extract
2 tablespoons grated orange rind
½ cup orange juice
¼ cup Grand Marnier
7 egg whites, at room temperature
⅛ teaspoon cream of tartar
2 cups heavy cream, whipped
Candied Orange Peel (see Index)

Serves 12

- Beat egg yolks with ¼ cup sugar until thick and pale. Beat in flour and salt.
- Gradually beat in hot scalded milk until mixture is smooth. Heat, stirring, until it thickens. Stir in vanilla. Cool mixture. Cover and chill.
- When pastry cream is cold, fold in grated orange rind, orange juice, and Grand Marnier.
- Beat egg whites until foamy. Add cream of tartar and a pinch of salt. Continue beating, gradually adding remaining 1 cup sugar. Beat until meringue is shiny and stiff. Fold in pastry cream and whipped cream.
- Freeze large soufflé at least 4 hours, smaller ones at least 2 hours. Garnish with Candied Orange Peel.

    Variations: Freeze mixture in 12 large scooped-out orange shells which have been frozen in advance.

Nancy Beck Hoggson

255

Desserts

Peaches and Cream Cobbler

1¼ cups sugar
¾ teaspoon salt
¼ teaspoon mace
1 teaspoon grated lemon rind
2 tablespoons lemon juice
⅓ cup plus 1½ cups flour
1 cup sour cream
6 cups sliced peaches
2 teaspoons baking powder
½ cup butter
½ cup milk
½ teaspoon cinnamon

Serves 6-8

● Combine *1 cup* sugar, *¼ teaspoon* salt, mace, lemon rind, lemon juice, *⅓ cup* flour, and sour cream in a large bowl. Mix well. Add peaches and spoon mixture into a lightly greased 2-quart baking dish or pan.

● Preheat oven to 425°. In a mixing bowl, combine remaining 1½ cups flour, baking powder, *2 tablespoons* sugar, and remaining ½ teaspoon salt. Cut in butter. Add milk and stir with fork until flour is damp. Turn out on a floured board and knead lightly 20 times. Roll out dough and place over peach mixture.

● Combine remaining 2 tablespoons sugar with cinnamon, and sprinkle over dough. Bake 25 minutes, until top is brown.

Pamela Sullivan Livingston

Baked Pears à la Crème

4 ripe Bosc pears, peeled
Juice of 1 lemon
3 tablespoons sugar
1 cup heavy cream

Serves 4

● Preheat oven to 400°. Paint pears with lemon juice. Cut in half lengthwise and remove stems. Arrange pear halves cut-side-up in a buttered baking dish.

● Fill the well of each pear with a heaping teaspoon of sugar. Bake for 25 minutes until the sugar has caramelized. Turn off oven. Add cream to bottom of dish. Leave pears in oven with door closed for 20 minutes.

● Allow pears to stand for 10 minutes before serving.

Marie Donovan

Desserts

Chocolate Covered Pears

Serves 4

1 cup sugar
4 cups water
Juice of 1 lemon
2 cinnamon sticks
4 whole cloves
4 *firm* comice pears with stems intact
3 squares (3 ounces) semi-sweet
   chocolate
1 square (1 ounce) unsweetened
   chocolate
4 tablespoons unsalted butter
8-10 whole strawberries, stems intact

● Combine sugar, water, lemon juice, cinnamon, and cloves. Bring to a boil in a large pot. Simmer 5-10 minutes. Peel pears carefully, leaving stems intact. Remove a thin slice from bottom of each pear so it will stand upright.
● Put pears in the simmering sugar syrup. Cook about 15 minutes until they feel tender when tested with a toothpick. Do *not* overcook or pears will become mushy. Chill pears overnight in syrup.
● The next day, melt chocolate with butter in top of double boiler.
● Remove pears from syrup and dry with paper towels. Holding each pear by the stem, dip it into the melted chocolate. Allow to drain. Keep chocolate liquid by placing over hot water occasionally. When all the pears are dipped, trim each with a mint sprig or a pretty leaf. Press the leaf lightly into the chocolate.
● Use any remaining chocolate to dip the berries. Serve as a garnish for the pears.
● Chill dipped fruits on wax paper until chocolate hardens.

Phyllis Heller Wharton

257

Desserts

Steamed Cranberry Pudding

1 egg
1 heaping tablespoon sugar
¼ cup light corn syrup
¼ cup molasses
1 teaspoon baking soda
⅓ cup hot water
1½ cups flour
½ teaspoon salt
1 heaping cup halved or quartered
    cranberries
½ cup chopped walnuts
Vanilla Cream Sauce (recipe follows)

Serves 8

- Beat egg well. Add sugar, corn syrup, and molasses. Stir baking soda into hot water and beat into sugar mixture. Stir in flour, salt, cranberries, and walnuts.
- Pour into a buttered 1-pound coffee can, or a 1-quart decorative mold. Cover top with foil.
- Simmer in a large, covered kettle of simmering water for 1½ hours. Turn pudding upside-down in mold and remove when cool. Wrap in foil and refrigerate until serving time. Reheat in oven before serving if desired. Serve with Vanilla Cream Sauce (recipe follows).

Sheila Plenke Gallagher

Vanilla Cream Sauce

½ cup butter
½ cup heavy cream
1 cup sugar
1 teaspoon vanilla extract
2 tablespoons rum or brandy
    (optional)

1 cup

- Melt butter in a saucepan. Add heavy cream and sugar. When hot, add vanilla and optional rum or brandy. Serve warm over hot pudding, which has been sliced ½" thick.

Sheila Plenke Gallagher

Desserts

Fig Pudding

1 pound dried figs, stemmed and
    chopped
1¾ cups milk
1½ cups flour
2½ teaspoons baking powder
1 teaspoon grated nutmeg
1 teaspoon cinnamon
¾ teaspoon salt
¾ pound suet, ground
1 cup sugar
3 eggs
1½ cups fresh fine breadcrumbs
3 tablespoons grated orange rind
Rum Butter (recipe follows)

Serves 10-12

● Combine figs with milk in a heavy saucepan. Bring just to boiling point over low heat, stirring with a wooden spoon to prevent scorching. Simmer 15-20 minutes stirring often. Let mixture cool.

● Sift together flour, baking powder, spices, and salt.

● Cream suet with sugar in a large bowl. Add eggs one at a time, beating well after each addition. Stir in breadcrumbs and orange rind. Add flour mixture alternately with fig mixture, beating well after each addition.

● Turn batter into a well-buttered 2-quart decorative pudding mold fitted with a tight lid or 2 coffee cans, 1 pound each. If using coffee cans, cover tightly with foil.

● Place mold or coffee cans in a heavy kettle. Add enough hot water to reach halfway up sides of mold. Cover kettle and steam pudding for 2 hours over moderately low heat.

● Remove mold from hot water and cool pudding for 20 minutes. Remove lid. Place a serving plate over mold and invert pudding. Serve warm with Rum Butter.

Betsy Gimpel Mena

Rum Butter

1 cup butter, at room temperature
1 cup brown sugar
¼ cup dark rum
2 tablespoons grated lemon or
    orange rind
Freshly grated nutmeg

2 cups

● Cream butter and sugar in a warm bowl. Beat in 1 tablespoon rum at a time, then lemon or orange rind and nutmeg to taste. Beat until light and fluffy and transfer to a small serving bowl.

Betsy Gimpel Mena

Desfserts

Pineapple Delight

1¼ cups graham cracker crumbs
¼ cup sugar
¾ cup softened butter, at room
    temperature
1½ cups sifted confectioners sugar
1 egg, beaten
1 can (1 pound, 4 ounces)
    unsweetened crushed pineapple
⅔ cup coarsely chopped pecans
1 cup heavy cream, whipped

Serves 8-12

- Preheat oven to 375°. Blend graham cracker crumbs, granulated sugar, and ¼ cup softened butter. Press half of crumb mixture firmly into a lightly greased 8″ square pan with a spatula. Bake 8 minutes and cool. Reserve extra crumbs for topping.
- Cream remaining ½ cup butter and confectioners sugar until fluffy. Beat in the egg.
- Drain the pineapple. Fold pineapple and pecans into creamed mixture. Fold in whipped cream until well combined. Turn into prepared pan, spreading evenly. Sprinkle with the rest of the crumbs.
- Cover with plastic wrap and refrigerate 24 hours. Cut in squares to serve.

Madeleine Galanek Egan

Cold Pumpkin Soufflé

2 envelopes (2 tablespoons)
    unflavored gelatin
½ cup dark rum
8 eggs
1⅓ cups sugar
2 cups cooked or canned pumpkin
1 teaspoon cinnamon
1 teaspoon ginger
½ teaspoon mace
½ teaspoon ground cloves
1 cup heavy cream, whipped
Chocolate shavings and chopped
    pecans for garnish

Serves 8-10

- Sprinkle gelatin on rum to soften. Set in top of a double boiler over simmering water until gelatin is dissolved.
- Beat eggs and gradually add sugar. Continue to beat until smooth and thick. Stir in pumpkin, seasonings, and gelatin-rum combination.
- Whip cream. Fold into pumpkin mixture. Pile lightly in a 2-quart soufflé dish or individual ramekins. Garnish with thin chocolate shavings and chopped pecans. Chill to set.

Nancy Beck Hoggson

Desserts

Marbled Strawberry Mousse

3 pints strawberries, hulled
3 envelopes (3 tablespoons)
    unflavored gelatin
¾ cup sugar
⅛ teaspoon salt
¾ cup water
2 tablespoons lemon juice
1 teaspoon vanilla extract
4 egg whites
2 cups heavy cream

Serves 10

● A day before serving, wrap a 1½-quart soufflé dish with a 2″ foil collar. Oil collar lightly.
● Purée berries in blender or food processor. Pour 1 cup purée into a small bowl and the rest into a large bowl.
● Mix gelatin, sugar, and salt in a saucepan. Add water and place over low heat until gelatin is dissolved, stirring often. Stir 2 tablespoons of gelatin mixture into purée in small bowl.
● Add lemon juice, vanilla, and remaining gelatin mixture to purée in large bowl.
● Refrigerate both mixtures stirring often until gelatin mounds on a spoon.
● Beat egg whites until stiff. Beat cream until soft peaks form. Fold beaten egg whites and cream into strawberry mixture in large bowl.
● Alternate layers of each mixture in the soufflé dish. Cut through with a knife to make a swirling design. Refrigerate overnight.

Lee Macioce Beach

Strawberries Romanoff

2 quarts washed strawberries
Sugar
1 cup heavy cream, whipped
1 pint ice cream, slightly softened
    and whipped
6 tablespoons Cointreau

Serves 6-8

● Wash berries. Hull and sprinkle lightly with sugar. Chill for several hours.
● Fold whipped cream and ice cream together. Add Cointreau. Pour over berries and serve immediately.

Frances Matko Bartlett

261

Desserts

Tangerine Granité

10-12 tangerines, or 9-10 oranges
1 tablespoon honey
1½ ounces Cointreau or another
    orange flavored liqueur
Fresh tangerine or orange sections
    (optional)

Serves 6

● Grate ¼ teaspoon of the peel of a tangerine or orange, and set aside.
● Slice and squeeze the tangerines or oranges measuring 2 cups of juice.
● Stir honey with 2 tablespoons of the fruit juice until it is dissolved. Stir in remaining juice, grated zest, and liqueur.
● Pour into a 13" x 9" baking dish. Cover with foil and freeze until solid, about 3 hours. Do not stir.
● To serve, scrape surface with a fork to break up ice crystals into a granular consistency. Mound in sherbet dishes and garnish with fresh tangerine or orange sections.

Madeleine Galanek Egan

Tortoni

1 cup heavy cream
¼ cup confectioners sugar
1 egg white
6 Italian macaroons
2 teaspoons marsala wine

Serves 6

● Whip cream until stiff. Fold in sugar.
● Beat egg white until stiff. Fold into sweetened whipped cream.
● Crush macaroons in a blender or food processor. Fold cookie crumbs and wine into whipped cream mixture. Spoon into 6 small dishes or one larger mold. Cover and freeze.
● Remove from freezer. Place in refrigerator 15 minutes before serving. Garnish with a fresh berry. macaroon crumbs. or whipped cream.

Ann Dodds Costello

Coffee Tortoni

1 cup heavy cream
6 tablespoons sugar
1 teaspoon vanilla extract
¼ teaspoon almond extract
2 eggs
⅛ teaspoon salt
1 tablespoon powdered coffee
   (overgrind in blender)
⅓ cup chopped toasted almonds or
   walnuts

Serves 6

● Beat heavy cream. Beat *2 tablespoons* sugar into cream until stiff. Fold in vanilla and almond extracts.
● Beat eggs and salt with remaining ¼ cup sugar until light and fluffy. Add powdered coffee.
● Fold two mixtures together. Stir in toasted almonds. Pour into parfait glasses. Garnish with additional chopped nuts. Cover and freeze.
● Remove from freezer to refrigerator for 10-15 minutes before serving.

Ann Keyser Griffin

Chilled Zabaglione

7 egg yolks
¾ cup superfine sugar
1 tablespoon warm water
1 cup marsala wine
½ teaspoon vanilla extract
Grated peel of half a lemon
Pinch cinnamon
1 cup heavy cream

Serves 4-6

● Place egg yolks, sugar, and warm water in top of double boiler over simmering water. Beat with a wire whisk scraping sides and bottom of pan constantly until mixture begins to foam.
● Gradually add the marsala in a steady stream. Continue beating until mixture forms very soft mounds. Remove from heat. Continue to beat until cool, using an electric mixer.
● When cooled to room temperature, add vanilla, lemon peel, and cinnamon. Place mixing bowl in a larger bowl filled with cracked ice. Continue beating until mixture is chilled.
● Beat heavy cream until stiff. Fold into the cold zabaglione. Fill champagne glasses and chill until ready to serve.

Alice Van Nuys Sessa

263

Desserts

Lemon Curd

½ cup butter, melted
Zest of 2 lemons
Juice of 3 lemons
1 pound (2 cups) superfine sugar
6 eggs, lightly beaten

2 cups
● Combine melted butter with lemon zest and juice in medium bowl. Slowly whisk in sugar, until dissolved. Whisk in eggs thoroughly.
● Transfer mixture to a saucepan. Cook over low heat for 15 minutes, stirring constantly with a wooden spoon until thickened to the consistency of honey. Do not boil. Cool, then cover, and chill until serving.

> Note: This will keep for several weeks in the refrigerator or indefinitely in the freezer. Serve on English muffins, French toast, jelly rolls, or layer cakes.

Nancy Beck Hoggson

Curried Fruit

6-8 cups assorted cut fresh fruits
1 cup brown sugar
½ cup butter, melted
1 tablespoon curry powder
½ teaspoon ground cloves
½ teaspoon cinnamon

Serves 8-10
● Preheat oven to 350°. Mix fruits with other ingredients in a large bowl and toss lightly. Fruits may include pears. peaches. cherries. apricots. plums. apples. grapes. and pineapple.
● Pour fruits into buttered casserole. Cover and bake 30 minutes. Refrigerate overnight.
● To serve. drain mixture and bake again for 45 minutes. Serve warm over ice cream or topped with a tablespoon of sour cream.

Susan Necarsulmer Dallin

Desserts

Broiled Grapefruit Caribbean

3 large grapefruits
Brown sugar to taste
6 tablespoons shredded coconut
½ cup dark rum

Serves 6

● Halve grapefruits and loosen flesh around sides and bottom of each shell. Free each section from membranes and remove center pith.
● Sprinkle each grapefruit half with brown sugar, coconut, and rum. Place in a shallow baking dish or pan. Set aside until shortly before mealtime.
● To serve, broil 4-5″ from heat until golden brown. Serve warm.

Nancy Reese Corbett

Green Grapes with Sour Cream

1 large bunch seedless green grapes
1 cup sour cream
½ cup brown sugar

Serves 4

● Preheat oven to 325°. Remove stems from grapes. Combine all ingredients. Place in oven long enough to melt sugar, 7-8 minutes. Do not overheat or sour cream will separate.

Kathryn Kirchmaier Mack

Yogurt Honey Dip

1 cup plain yogurt
2 tablespoons honey, or more to taste
¼ teaspoon cinnamon
¼ teaspoon grated nutmeg

1 cup

● Combine all ingredients. Serve with assorted fresh fruits.

Carole Kruse Long

265

Desserts

One-Step Fudge Sauce

1 package (6 ounces) semi-sweet chocolate chips
¼ cup water, milk, or heavy cream

⅔ cup

● Heat ingredients in a small saucepan over low heat, stirring constantly until bubbling.

● The longer the sauce cooks. the thicker it will get. Do not let it boil.

Note: Made with water this sauce will harden on ice cream. It will stay creamy when made with milk or cream.

W. Curtis Livingston. III

Port Wine Blueberry Sauce

½ cup sugar
1 tablespoon cornstarch
¾ cup port wine
3 thin lemon slices
1½ cups fresh blueberries
6 scoops vanilla ice cream
3 ripe cantaloupes, halved

1 cup

● Mix sugar and cornstarch with port. Add lemon slices and bring to boil. stirring. Stir and simmer 5 minutes. until transparent and slightly thickened. Remove lemon slices. Stir in blueberries. Chill thoroughly.

● Place ice cream in cantaloupe halves. Top with sauce.

Barbara Byrne Esau

Sauce Sabayon

2 tablespoons sugar
2 eggs, separated
1 teaspoon vanilla extract
Grated rind of 1 lemon
2 tablespoons medium dry sherry

1 cup

● Mix sugar. egg yolks. vanilla. and grated lemon rind in bowl. Stand bowl over hot water. Beat until mixture is smooth and lemon-colored.

● Add sherry and again place bowl over saucepan of hot water. Beat until fluffy.

● Beat egg whites until stiff. Fold into hot mixture. Serve immediately with soufflés and fruit desserts.

Donna Chisholm Clark

Desserts

Viennese Apple Tart

1¾ cups flour
¾ cup sugar
6 ounces swiss cheese, finely grated
¾ cup butter
2 egg yolks
6-8 tablespoons lemon juice
3½ pounds tart cooking apples
3 tablespoons water
1 tablespoon rum
½ cup strained apricot preserves
½ cup heavy cream, whipped
¼ cup sliced almonds

Serves 6-8

● Mix flour, ¼ *cup* sugar, and cheese in a bowl or food processor. Cut in ½ *cup* butter until particles are very fine. Stir in egg yolks and ¼ *cup* lemon juice. Process or knead until dough forms a smooth ball.

● Preheat oven to 375°. Line a 9″ or 10″ layer cake pan with a square of heavy-duty foil, allowing corners to extend over edges of the pan. Place dough in lined pan. With floured fingers press it evenly over bottom and sides.

● Bake for 15 minutes. Cool in pan.

● Peel and core apples. Cut 2 of the largest apples into very thin slices. Sprinkle well with remaining 2-4 tablespoons lemon juice and set aside. Chop the other apples and place in a saucepan. Add water. Cover and simmer about 5 minutes. Stir in remaining ¼ cup butter and ½ cup sugar. Cook 15 minutes longer, stirring occasionally. Stir in rum and cool.

● Preheat oven again to 375°. Spread cooled apple mixture evenly on tart shell. Top with reserved apple slices arranged in overlapping circles. Bake 20 minutes. Spread apricot preserves over the apple slices to glaze. Chill.

● To serve, use extending edges of foil to lift tart from pan to a serving plate. Foil will slide out. Chill.

● Serve cold. Garnish with rosettes of whipped cream. Sprinkle with sliced almonds.

Madeleine Galanek Egan

267

Desserts

Brandy Alexander Pie

1 envelope (1 tablespoon) unflavored
    gelatin
½ cup cold water
⅔ cups sugar
⅛ teaspoon salt
3 eggs, separated
¼ cup cognac
¼ cup crème de cocao
2 cups heavy cream, whipped
9″ graham cracker crust, baked and
    cooled
Semi-sweet chocolate curls

Serves 6-8

● Sprinkle gelatin in cold water in a small pan. Add ⅓ cup sugar, salt, and egg yolks. Stir to blend. Cook over very low heat. Stir until gelatin dissolves and mixture thickens. Do not boil.
● Remove from heat. Stir in cognac and crème de cocao. Chill, stirring occasionally. When mixture will mound on a spoon, beat egg whites until stiff. Gradually beat remaining ⅓ cup sugar into whites to form a glossy meringue. Fold into gelatin mixture, along with 1 cup whipped cream.
● Turn into cooled graham cracker crust. Chill. Garnish with remaining whipped cream and chocolate curls.

Eugenia McCuen Thomason

Butter Tarts

Unbaked pastry for 2-crust pie (see
    Index)
1 cup raisins
2 eggs
1 cup brown sugar
½ cup chopped walnuts
1 tablespoon melted butter
1 tablespoon milk

30 small tarts
10 large tarts

● Make tart shells with pastry. Set aside, unbaked.
● Preheat oven to 425°. Soak raisins in warm water for about 15 minutes.
● Beat eggs. Add sugar and beat again until fluffy and lemon-colored. Add remaining ingredients, including well-drained raisins.
● Spoon mixture into unbaked tart shells. Bake 10 minutes. Cool and serve.
● These can be baked ahead and frozen. Before serving, bring to room temperature. Warm slightly in a low oven. Serve with whipped cream.

Mary Jean Borden Potter

Desserts

Castle Pie

4 eggs, separated
¼ teaspoon cream of tartar
1½ cups sugar
1 tablespoon grated lemon rind
3 tablespoons fresh lemon juice
⅛ teaspoon salt
2 cups heavy cream
1 teaspoon confectioners sugar
1 teaspoon vanilla extract
Chocolate shavings and chopped nuts
    for garnish

Serves 8-10
● Preheat oven to 275°. Beat egg whites until stiff. Add cream of tartar. Gradually beat in *1 cup* sugar. Spread meringue in buttered 10″ pie plate.
● Bake 1 hour. Cool.
● To make filling, beat egg yolks until smooth in double boiler. Add remaining ½ cup sugar, lemon rind and juice, and salt. Cook and stir until thick. Cool.
● Whip *1 cup* cream. Fold into egg yolk mixture. Spoon into meringue shell. Cover gently. Refrigerate for 24 hours.
● An hour before serving, whip remaining 1 cup heavy cream. Add confectioners sugar and vanilla. Spread on pie. Garnish with chocolate shavings and chopped nuts. Chill.

Anne Hollingbery Corper

Grasshopper Pie

1¼ cups chocolate wafer crumbs
    (about 25 wafers)
⅓ cup melted butter
24 marshmallows
⅔ cup scalded milk
1 cup heavy cream
¼ cup green crème de menthe
2 tablespoons crème de cocao

Serves 6-8
● Combine crumbs with melted butter. Pat into buttered 9″ pie plate. Freeze about 2 hours.
● Add marshmallows to scalded milk in top of a double boiler. Melt very slowly over simmering water, stirring often. Cool to room temperature.
● Whip cream. Fold into above mixture. Add liqueurs. Pour into the frozen crust. Freeze until firm.
● Garnish with cookie crumbs, whipped cream, or chocolate curls. Serve frozen.

Bettina Blake Girdwood

Desserts

Chocolate Mousse Pie

½ cup butter, at room temperature
¾ cup sugar
2 squares (2 ounces) unsweetened
    chocolate, melted and cooled
1 teaspoon vanilla extract
2 eggs
8″ pastry shell, baked and cooled
Whipped cream and chocolate
    shavings for garnish

Serves 6

● Cream butter. Gradually beat in sugar. Beat until light. Blend in chocolate and vanilla. Add eggs one at a time. Beat 3 minutes after each addition on medium speed of electric mixer.
● Turn into cooled pastry shell. Chill several hours.
● Serve with whipped cream and garnish with chocolate shavings.
    Variation: This may also be served in ramekins or demitasse cups topped with whipped cream and chocolate shavings.

Marcia Petersen Sandner

Chocolate Velvet Pie

½ teaspoon baking powder
3 egg whites
1 cup sugar
1½ teaspoons vanilla extract
14 Ritz crackers, crushed
⅔ cup chopped walnuts
1 package (4 ounces) German sweet
    chocolate
3 tablespoons water
1 cup heavy cream

Serves 8-10

● Preheat oven to 350°. Butter a 9″ pie plate.
● Add baking powder to egg whites. Beat until stiff. Gradually beat in sugar. Add ½ *teaspoon* vanilla. Fold in cracker crumbs and nuts. Spread in pie plate to form a meringue-like crust. Bake for 25 minutes. Cool, cover lightly, and let stand overnight at room temperature.
● The next morning, stir chocolate and water together over very low heat until chocolate melts. Cool until thickened. Add remaining 1 teaspoon vanilla.
● Whip cream and fold into chocolate mixture. Turn into meringue crust. Chill until firm.

Judith Lawson Florence

270

Desserts

Coconut Pie

4 eggs
1½ teaspoons vanilla extract
2 cups milk
¼ cup sugar
½ cup flour
1 teaspoon baking powder
4 tablespoons butter, melted
1 cup shredded coconut

Serves 8

● Preheat oven to 350°. Beat eggs with a wire whisk. Blend in vanilla, milk, and sugar. Mix in flour, baking powder, and melted butter. Stir in coconut.
● Place this mixture in a greased 9" pie plate. Bake 50-60 minutes.

Leslie May Marra

Cranberry Apple Pie

Pastry for 2-crust pie (see Index)
¾ cup water
6 cups tart apple slices (unpeeled)
1½ cups raw cranberries
2 cups sugar
¼ cup cornstarch
¼ teaspoon cinnamon
1 cup chopped walnuts
4 tablespoons butter
Milk
Sugar
Nutmeg

Serves 6-8

● Roll out half the dough. Shape to line a 10" pie plate.
● Combine water, apples, and cranberries in a large saucepan. Bring to a boil. Simmer 5 minutes. Stir sugar with cornstarch. Add to pan with cinnamon and walnuts. Cook and stir until mixture boils. Pile into pastry shell. Dot with butter.
● Preheat oven to 400°. Roll out remaining dough. Cut in strips. Arrange strips in lattice design over the filling. Seal at edges, crimping all around. Brush with milk. Sprinkle lightly with sugar and nutmeg.
● Bake for 50 minutes.
> Note: 1½ cups whole-berry cranberry sauce may be substituted if fresh cranberries are not available. If using cranberry sauce, decrease the amount of sugar by ½ to ¾ cup.

Elizabeth Boote

271

Desserts

Japanese Fruit Pie

2 eggs, separated
1 cup sugar
½ cup butter, melted
1 tablespoon vinegar
½ cup coconut
½ cup pecans
½ cup raisins
1 unbaked 8″ pastry shell
Unsweetened whipped cream

Serves 8

● Preheat oven to 325°. Beat together egg yolks, sugar, butter, and vinegar. Add coconut, pecans, and raisins.
● Beat egg whites and fold in. Pour mixture into unbaked pastry shell. Bake 50-60 minutes.
● Cool and serve with unsweetened whipped cream.

Madeleine Galanek Egan

Midsummer Fruit Tart

1 cup heavy cream, whipped
3 ounces cream cheese, at room temperature
⅓ cup sugar
Pinch salt
2 cups strawberries
2 cups blueberries
1-2 bananas
9″ or 10″ pastry shell, baked and cooled
1 jar (12 ounces) apricot jam
2-3 tablespoons dark rum

Serves 8

● Whip cream. Mix with softened cream cheese, sugar, and salt. Turn into baked pastry shell. Spread evenly.
● Wash and drain berries. Slice bananas. Place a circle of blueberries around edge of pastry. Place bananas in overlapping slices inside the ring of blueberries. Fill center with strawberries, pushing them into the cream so they all appear to be the same height.
● Melt jam in a small saucepan over very low heat until syrupy. Add enough rum to thin to pouring consistency. Stir until mixture is smooth. Cool slightly. Spoon jam carefully over all the fruit, making sure bananas are well covered. Chill until serving time.

Constance Foti Stewart

WHIPPING CREAM

Desserts

Peach Custard Pie

1¼ cups plus 2 tablespoons flour
½ teaspoon salt
½ cup butter
½ cup sour cream
8 fresh peaches
3 egg yolks
1 cup sugar

Serves 6-8

● Preheat oven to 425°. Sift *1¼ cups* flour and add salt. Cut in butter. Blend in *2 tablespoons* sour cream to form dough. Pat out in a 10" pie plate or a 6" x 10" baking dish. Bake for 10 minutes.
● Peel and slice peaches. Combine egg yolks, sugar, remaining 2 table-spoons flour, and remaining 6 table-spoons sour cream to make custard.
● Remove crust from oven. Arrange peaches in overlapping rows or circles on the crust. Pour the peach custard over all. Cover with foil. Reduce oven temperature to 350° and return pie to oven. Bake 20-30 minutes longer until custard is set.

Valerie Korn Luther

Pumpkin Chiffon Pie

3 eggs, separated
1½ cups canned pumpkin
1 cup brown sugar
2 teaspoons cinnamon
½ teaspoon ginger
¼ teaspoon allspice
½ teaspoon salt
1 envelope (1 tablespoon) unflavored gelatin
¼ cup cold water
1 tablespoon grated orange rind
2 tablespoons sugar
1 cup heavy cream
9" or 10" baked pastry shell (graham cracker or cream cheese pastry—see Index)

Serves 6-8

● Place egg yolks in top of a double boiler with pumpkin, brown sugar, spices, and salt. Blend, then cook over simmering water until mixture thickens slightly.
● Soften gelatin in cold water. Stir into thickened egg yolk mixture. Remove from heat.
● Chill until mixture will mound on a spoon. Remove from refrigerator. Stir in orange rind.
● Beat egg whites until stiff. Slowly beat in sugar to make a meringue. Fold into chilled pumpkin mixture. Beat *½ cup* cream and fold in.
● Mound mixture in cooled pie crust. Chill at least 2 hours. Whip remaining ½ cup cream. Spread on pie.

Keene Harrill Rees

273

Desserts

Lime Pie

1¼ cups graham cracker crumbs
1 cup superfine sugar
¼ cup butter, at room temperature
5 eggs, separated
4 teaspoons grated lime rind
⅔ cup fresh lime juice
⅛ teaspoon salt

Garnish:
1 cup heavy cream, whipped
Thin lime slices or fresh strawberries
Granulated sugar

Serves 6-8

● Preheat oven to 350°. Place graham cracker crumbs and ¼ *cup* sugar in a bowl. Blend in butter. Press mixture into a 9″ pie plate and bake 10 minutes. Cool to room temperature before filling.

● Beat egg yolks in top of double boiler until very thick. Gradually beat in ½ *cup* superfine sugar until mixture is very pale and forms a rope when dropped from the beater. Stir in lime rind and juice. Heat over simmering water, stirring until mixture coats the back of a spoon. Do not boil. Turn into a large bowl and cool to room temperature.

● When lime custard has cooled, beat egg whites with salt until soft peaks form. Gradually beat in remaining ¼ cup superfine sugar until mixture is stiff and shiny. Stir ⅓ of meringue into cooled custard. Fold in remaining meringue.

● Turn into cooled graham cracker crust. Bake 15 minutes, until lightly brown. Cool, then chill or freeze. Once frozen, cover with plastic wrap.

● If serving frozen, remove from freezer 10 minutes before serving. Cover pie with whipped cream. Garnish with sugar-dipped lime slices or fresh strawberries.

Betsy Gimpel Mena

Desserts

Brandied Mince Pie

Pastry for 2-crust pie
3 cups mincemeat (see Index)
1 cup coarsely chopped walnuts
¼ cup chopped Candied Orange
    Peel (see Index)
¼ cup brandy or sherry
2 tablespoons sliced candied
    cherries

Serves 6

● Preheat oven to 425°. Line bottom of a 9″ pie plate with pastry.
● Combine remaining ingredients in a large bowl. Mix well. Pour into pastry shell.
● Roll out remaining pastry into an 11″ circle. Place over the filling and trim. Fold edge of top crust under edge of bottom crust. Press together, trim, and flute the edge. Make slits in center of crust for steam to escape.
● Bake 40-45 minutes until crust is golden brown. Cool on a rack and serve warm.

Betsy Gimpel Mena

Mud Pie

1½ cups chocolate wafer crumbs
    (about 30 wafers)
6 tablespoons melted butter
1 teaspoon cinnamon
½ gallon coffee or butter almond ice
    cream
1 can or jar (12 ounces) chocolate
    topping
½ cup chopped walnuts
1 cup heavy cream, whipped

Serves 8

● Preheat oven to 300°. Mix chocolate wafer crumbs with melted butter and cinnamon. Pat into a 9″ pie plate. Bake for 15 minutes and cool.
● Soften ice cream slightly. Mound in the cooled pastry crust. Cover with foil or plastic wrap and freeze.
● When frozen solid, add the layer of chocolate dessert topping and nuts and re-freeze. Cover again when firm.
● To serve, spread with whipped cream.

Robin McNevin Robertson

Desserts

Pecan Pie

9" pastry shell, unbaked
1 cup light corn syrup
¾ cup sugar
½ teaspoon salt
1 tablespoon butter, melted and
    cooled
1 teaspoon vanilla extract
2 tablespoons dark rum
4 eggs, lightly beaten
1 cup pecans, halved

Serves 6-8

- Preheat oven to 400°. Roll out pastry. Line a 9" pie pan, crimping edges. Prick bottom so crust will not bubble up when pre-baking. Refrigerate 15 minutes.
- Bake chilled pastry for 10-12 minutes until lightly colored. Remove from oven. Leave oven set at 400°.
- Combine corn syrup, sugar, salt, butter, vanilla, rum, and eggs. Stir to mix thoroughly. Spread pecans in pastry shell. Pour egg mixture over.
- Place pie in oven. Reduce oven temperature immediately to 350°. Bake 50 minutes until pastry is golden and pecans have risen to the top. Cool before serving.

Barbara Smith Suval

Miniature Pecan Tarts

Crust
1 cup butter
½ cup sugar
2 egg yolks
1 teaspoon almond extract
2 cups flour

Filling
½ cup butter
⅓ cup light corn syrup
1 cup confectioners sugar
1 cup chopped pecans
36 pecan halves

3 dozen

- Preheat oven to 400°. Cream butter and sugar. Stir in egg yolks, almond extract, and flour. Form this crumbly mixture into 36 small balls. Press each to fit an ungreased miniature muffin cup. Bake for 8-10 minutes. Cool.
- To prepare filling, melt butter and bring to a boil with corn syrup and confectioners sugar. Remove from heat. Stir in chopped nuts. Let filling cool for a few minutes.
- Preheat oven to 350°. Fill tart shells about ¾ full with caramel-pecan mixture. Top each tart with a pecan half. Bake 5 minutes.

Karen Rudge Richards

Desserts

Strawberry Rhubarb Pie

1 cup cut rhubarb (1″ pieces), or ½ package frozen rhubarb
1 cup sugar
⅓ cup flour
⅛ teaspoon salt
2 cups halved strawberries
Pastry for 2-crust pie (see Index)
2 tablespoons butter
Milk
1 tablespoon sugar

Serves 6-8
● Preheat oven to 425°. Parboil rhubarb until slightly tender.
● Mix sugar, flour, and salt. Toss dry ingredients with strawberries and rhubarb, coating well.
● Line a 9″ or 10″ pie plate with a pastry crust. Heap fruit in the pastry. Dot with butter. Top with remaining pastry as a full crust or in a lattice-work design. Brush top crust with milk. Sprinkle with sugar.
● Bake 40-50 minutes.

Penelope Crabb Baylis

Frozen Strawberry Pie

1 cup flour
¼ cup brown sugar
½ cup butter, at room temperature
½ cup chopped pecans
2 egg whites
1 package (10 ounces) frozen strawberries, thawed
1 cup sugar
1 tablespoon fresh lemon juice
½ cup heavy cream

Serves 10-12
● Preheat oven to 325°. Blend flour with brown sugar, butter, and pecans. Press half this mixture into two 8″ or 9″ pie plates. Bake for 15-20 minutes and cool.
● Mix egg whites, berries, sugar, and lemon juice in a large bowl. Beat at high speed of electric mixer for 15 minutes. Whip cream and fold into mixture.
● Pour into cooled shells. Freeze immediately. When firm, cover tightly with foil or plastic wrap. Return to freezer until serving time.
● Garnish with whipped cream and fresh berries.

Suzanne Rich Beatty

potpourri

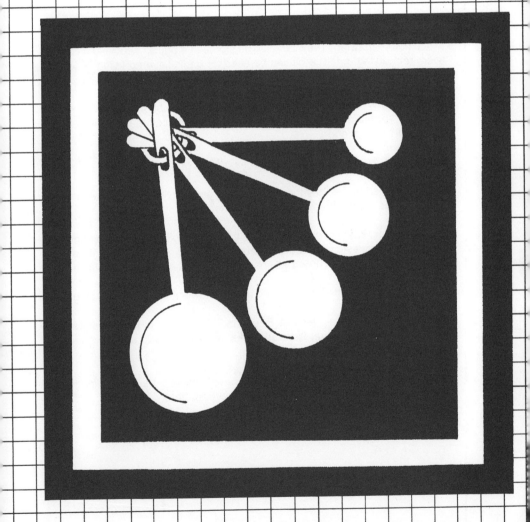

Spice Up Your Life

To freeze fresh herbs, rinse with cold water. Dry with a towel or a salad spinner. Fill plastic bag loosely with herbs and freeze. At the same time, freeze the plastic or glass container that will eventually hold the herbs. Quickly remove bag of frozen herbs and squeeze the bag to crush without letting them defrost. Quickly shake the crushed herbs into frozen container. Return to freezer until ready to use.

Never use garlic powder or garlic salt. Use cloves of fresh garlic. Buy it loose and not packaged. Keep cloves tightly wrapped in the freezer to peel and mince before thawing. They can also be stored in a bottle of cooking oil to keep from drying out. The oil can be used for garlic-flavored frying or for salad dressing.

Buy spices in small quantities. Store in a cool, dark cupboard. Try grinding your own spices for a fresher touch. A small electric coffee mill makes a wonderful spice grinder.

Use ⅓ to ½ as much of a dried herb as a fresh one.

If you buy dried herbs, buy those with the largest leaves. Avoid powders. Crush leaves between your fingers when needed.

Use coarse or "kosher" salt rather than the usual table salt which is often mixed with magnesium or sodium carbonate to make it pour easily in all weather. Kosher salt is 100% salt, coarse in texture, and less salty to taste.

Cold onions and the sharpest knife will produce fewer tears when chopping.

Buy only fresh, young ginger root. Peel it and store in a small jar of vodka in the refrigerator. The ginger flavored vodka can also be used as a flavoring ingredient.

Vanilla flavor evaporates when it is boiled. Add vanilla extract to puddings and desserts after they have been removed from heat.

Potpourri

Back To Basics

A primer of sauces, pastries, multi-purpose recipes, cooking techniques.

Clarified Butter

To clarify butter, melt sweet butter over low heat in a heavy pan. Skim off white froth that rises to top. The clear, yellow "clarified" butter can be carefully poured into a container leaving white dregs in bottom of pan.

Use clarified butter when sautéing at high heat or in very delicate cakes such as gênoise. One cup butter yields about ¾ cup clarified butter.

Ann Dodds Costello

Croutons

Always make croutons with stale bread. Fresh bread absorbs too much of the oil or butter used to sauté. If using butter, make sure it is clarified (see above).
● Remove crusts from bread and cut in whatever shape croutons you wish.
● Let croutons dry out in a 150°-175° oven for 15-20 minutes.
● Sauté briefly in clarified butter until nicely browned on all sides.

Ann Dodds Costello

Potpourri

Fort Mountain Bar B-Q Sauce

2 tablespoons butter
2 small onions, diced
4 tablespoons brown sugar
2 cups catsup
¾ cup (6 ounces) A-1 Sauce
¼ cup bottled steak sauce
1-3 tablespoons tabasco sauce
⅓ cup worcestershire sauce
2 tablespoons lemon juice
1 tablespoon freshly ground pepper

4 cups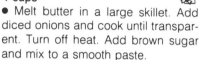
● Melt butter in a large skillet. Add diced onions and cook until transparent. Turn off heat. Add brown sugar and mix to a smooth paste.
● Add catsup, A-1, steak sauce, tabasco, and worcestershire. Mix until well blended. Continue to blend as you add lemon juice and pepper.

Ann Evans Gum

No-Cook Texas Barbeque Sauce and Marinade

1 cup claret wine
½ cup oil
½ cup catsup
2 onions, chopped
1 tablespoon worcestershire sauce
1 tablespoon salt
1 teaspoon freshly ground pepper

2 cups
● Pour wine into a bowl. Stir in oil and catsup. Add remaining ingredients and stir again.
   Note: Marinate steak or chicken in this sauce for several hours before cooking on the grill, then use the sauce to baste the meat while it cooks.

Peggy Swanson Smith

Betsy's Marinade

2 tablespoons dry English mustard
¼ cup wine vinegar
1½ cups corn oil
2 garlic cloves, minced
2 tablespoons chopped parsley
1 teaspoon freshly ground pepper
¾ cup soy sauce
¼ cup worcestershire sauce
⅓ cup fresh lemon juice

3 cups
● Combine all ingredients. Extra marinade keeps well in refrigerator.

Betsy Gimpel Mena

Potpourri

Hand-Beaten Mayonnaise

2 cups

2 large egg yolks
1 teaspoon salt
½ teaspoon Dijon mustard
1½ cups olive oil
1 tablespoon wine vinegar or lemon
 juice

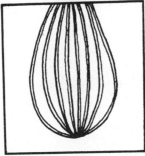

● Have all ingredients at room temperature. Warm mixing bowl in hot water and heat oil if it is cool.

● Place egg yolks, salt, and mustard in a 2½-3 quart mixing bowl. Beat with large wire whisk until yolks become thick and sticky. At this point, they are ready to absorb the oil. Add oil slowly, drop by drop, and beat mixture thoroughly as you go.

● As a thick emulsion forms and mayonnaise becomes lighter in color, you may add the rest of the oil more rapidly. Be sure to incorporate each batch of oil before adding the next. When the mixture is thick and all the oil is incorporated, beat in lemon juice or vinegar.

● Store mayonnaise covered in the refrigerator.

 Note: To correct curdled mayonnaise or hollandaise, put an egg yolk into a clean pan. Beat until thick. Gradually beat in curdled sauce until it becomes smooth again.

Ann Dodds Costello

Food Processor Mayonnaise

1 cup

1 egg
1 teaspoon vinegar or lemon juice
1 tablespoon plus 1 cup oil
¼-½ teaspoon salt
¼-½ teaspoon Dijon mustard

● Place egg, vinegar or lemon juice, and *1 tablespoon* oil in processor bowl. Turn on machine and very slowly pour in remaining 1 cup oil, beating until mixture thickens. Blend in salt and mustard to taste.

Anne Ruthrauff Seltzer

Potpourri

Never-Fail Hollandaise Sauce

2 egg yolks
3 tablespoons lemon juice
½ cup very cold butter

1 cup

● Stir egg yolks and lemon juice with a wooden spoon in a small pan. Add *half* the butter, and stir over very low heat until butter is melted. Add remaining butter. Continue to cook and stir over low heat until butter melts and sauce thickens.

● Serve immediately, or cool and serve at room temperature. Sauce can be chilled, then reheated in a double boiler.

Variations: Adapt to a Bernaise Sauce by adding 1 tablespoon minced parsley, 1 tablespoon tarragon vinegar, and ½ teaspoon tarragon.

Susan Sample Marx

Lemon Cream Sauce for Vegetables

4 tablespoons butter
¾ cup heavy cream
1 egg
Salt and freshly ground pepper
¼ cup grated parmesan cheese
¼ teaspoon grated nutmeg
1½ lemons

1 cup

● Melt butter. Stir in *all but* 2 tablespoons cream. Cook over medium heat.

● Break egg in a small bowl. Add remaining 2 tablespoons cream, salt, pepper, parmesan, and nutmeg. Stir well. Squeeze lemons and add juice to egg mixture. Beat well with a fork or small whisk to blend all ingredients. Add to saucepan with cream and butter. Cook 2-3 minutes until sauce thickens.

Nancy Gould Pinkernell

Potpourri

Sauce Chasseur

1 tablespoon butter
2 cups sliced mushrooms (about ½ pound)
1 tablespoon finely chopped shallots
Salt and freshly ground pepper
⅓ cup dry white wine
½ cup peeled, chopped tomatoes
½ cup beef broth
¼ teaspoon tarragon
1 teaspoon cornstarch or arrowroot
2 teaspoons water

1½ cups
● Melt butter in a saucepan. Add mushrooms, shallots, salt, and pepper to taste. Sauté for about 10 minutes.
● Add wine and simmer 2 minutes over high heat. Add tomatoes, beef broth, and tarragon. Cook 5 minutes longer, stirring occasionally.
● Blend arrowroot and water until smooth. Stir into sauce. Cook until thickened.

Nancy Beck Hoggson

Piquant Herb Sauce

½ cup dry white wine
½ cup chopped parsley
¼ cup white vinegar
1 small onion, quartered
2 garlic cloves
2½ teaspoons dried tarragon, crushed
¼ teaspoon dried chervil leaves, crushed
⅛ teaspoon freshly ground pepper
1 cup mayonnaise

1 cup
● Blend first 8 ingredients in blender or food processor. Transfer to a small saucepan. Stir over medium heat until reduced to ⅓ cup, about 10 minutes.
● Strain liquid and return to saucepan with 2 teaspoonfuls of unstrained herb mixture. Stir in mayonnaise and heat until warm. Serve now, or chill and serve cold. Delicious with meats, fish, or poultry.

Suzanne Rich Beatty

Grandaddy's Sauce for Lobster

½ cup butter
½ teaspoon dry mustard
½ teaspoon worcestershire sauce
1 tablespoon lemon juice

Serves 4
● Combine all ingredients over low heat. Stir with whisk or wooden spoon until butter is just melted.
● Serve as soon as possible in small bowls for dipping hot lobster or cooked clams.

Judith Freyermuth Rex

285

Potpourri

Herbal Mustard Coating

½ cup Dijon-type prepared mustard
2 teaspoons soy sauce
1 clove mashed garlic
1 teaspoon ground rosemary or thyme
1 teaspoon powdered ginger
2 teaspoons olive oil

¾ cup
● Combine all ingredients well. Brush on lamb, lamb chops, or chicken several hours before cooking.
● Cook normal amount of time, but keep food a little further from flame, if broiling.

Ellen Zox Wedeles

Mustard Sauce

⅓-½ cup dry mustard, to taste
1 cup sugar
3 eggs
⅔ cup champagne vinegar

1 cup
● Beat all ingredients together. Place in double boiler. Stir over simmering water about 10 minutes.
● Serve immediately or chill.

Suzanne Rich Beatty

Pesto

4 cups fresh basil leaves
4-5 garlic cloves
½ cup pine nuts
1 cup olive oil
Salt
⅔ cup freshly grated imported
  parmesan, romano, and/or sardo
  cheese

2 cups
● Put half the basil in blender or food processor with garlic, pine nuts, olive oil, and 1 teaspoon salt. Purée. Add remaining basil and purée. Add oil, if needed. Stir in grated cheese. Taste for seasonings.

Penelope Johnson Wartels

Potpourri

Your Own Tomato Sauce

½ cup olive oil
3 onions, peeled and chopped
4-8 garlic cloves, minced
3 celery ribs, sliced
2 carrots, peeled and sliced
1 bunch parsley, chopped coarsely
Freshly ground pepper
¼ cup chopped fresh basil leaves, or
    1 tablespoon dried basil
9 pounds fresh tomatoes (about 5½
    quarts)
2 tablespoons coarse salt
2 teaspoons sugar

3½ quarts

• Heat oil in a large, non-aluminum pot. Sauté onions until wilted, about 5 minutes. Add garlic and sauté 2 minutes longer. Add celery and carrots. Toss and cook for 5-8 minutes. Vegetables will begin to soften. Stir in parsley, pepper, and basil. Toss over medium heat for 2 minutes.

• Meanwhile, halve tomatoes crosswise and squeeze out as many seeds as possible. Cut tomatoes in quarters or coarse chunks.

• Add tomatoes, salt, and sugar to pot. Toss with sautéed vegetables. Bring to a boil and lower heat to simmering and partially cover pot. Simmer 20 minutes to 1 hour, stirring occasionally. Sauce will be thick and reduced. Cool slightly.

• Pass sauce through a food mill, using medium disc. Correct seasoning. Re-cook to reduce sauce still further.

• Cool completely, then freeze in plastic containers.

• When needed, defrost sauce and reheat slowly. Add tomato paste if necessary to thicken sauce to desired consistency. Use in any recipe calling for tomato sauce.

Nancy Beck Hoggson

Easy Tomato Sauce

2 tablespoons tomato paste
2 cups diced tomatoes
Bouquet garni: celery, thyme,
    parsley, 1-2 garlic cloves, ½ bay
    leaf
Salt and freshly ground pepper

2 cups

• Stir tomato paste into diced tomatoes. Add bouquet garni. Cook 30-40 minutes over low heat. Remove bay leaf. Purée if desired.

• Season to taste with salt and pepper.

Ann Dodds Costello

Potpourri

Duxelles

1 pound mushrooms, finely minced
6 tablespoons butter
4 shallots, finely minced
1½ tablespoons cognac or madeira
  wine
2 tablespoons minced parsley
Salt and freshly ground pepper
Nutmeg

2 cups

● Put minced mushrooms in the corner of a tea towel, a handful at a time. Extract as much liquid as possible. (Save liquid to add to soups and sauces.)

● Melt butter. Sauté shallots over low heat until soft. Add mushrooms and cook 10-15 minutes over low heat, stirring occasionally. When all liquid evaporates and mixture is very dark, season to taste with cognac or madeira, parsley, salt, pepper, and nutmeg.

● Raise heat slightly and cook 2-3 minutes more. Store in refrigerator or freezer. Use in hors d'oeuvres such as stuffed mushrooms or Duxelles Strudel (see Index).

Penelope Johnson Wartels

Fish Stock

2 pounds fish bones and heads, gills
  removed (halibut, cod, whiting,
  haddock, flounder)
3 cups water
1 cup dry white wine
½ cup sliced onions
¼ cup chopped celery
4 parsley sprigs
2 sprigs fresh thyme, or ¼ teaspoon
  dried
2 whole garlic cloves
1 bay leaf
Salt
10 peppercorns

4 cups

● Combine all ingredients in a saucepan. Simmer 15 minutes, skimming foam from top. Strain and use in any recipe requiring fish stock.

Betsy Gimpel Mena

Potpourri

Pastry Tips

To bake an empty pie shell, preheat oven to 400°. Prick bottom and sides of pastry shell with fork. Cut wax paper to fit over dough and press it down firmly onto the crust. Cover paper with a layer of rice or dried beans, scattering them evenly. Bake 25 minutes in preheated oven, then remove paper and rice or beans. Return pastry shell to hot oven until lightly browned, about 5 minutes.

Perfect Pastry

1½ cups flour
4 tablespoons butter
¼ cup solid vegetable shortening
¼ teaspoon salt
Grated rind of 1 lemon or 1 small
    orange (optional)
¼ cup cold water or orange or lemon
    juice combined with water

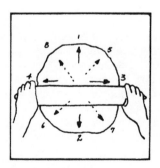

- Blend flour, butter, shortening, salt, and optional grated lemon or orange rind in food processor or electric mixer. When mixture forms pieces the size of peas, add liquid. Mix until dough comes clean from sides of bowl and forms a ball.
- Flatten ball into an 8" circle. Wrap and refrigerate 30 minutes.
- Transfer chilled dough to a lightly floured working surface. With a floured rolling pin, roll into a 12" circle. Roll from center of circle toward the outer rim.
- Again flour the rolling pin and pastry. Place rolling pin on the edge of the pastry circle and roll dough lightly around it. Gently unroll dough onto the pie plate. Press it in without forcing or stretching. Allow 1" of dough to hang over the edge of the pan, and trim excess.
- Turn dough overlap to form a narrow, rolled rim. Flute the edge. To bake, see "TIPS" at beginning of this pastry section. Makes 1 pastry shell (9" or 10"). Recipe doubles easily.

Madeleine Galanek Egan

289

Potpourri

Pâté Sucrée

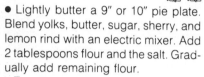

2 egg yolks
⅓ cup butter, at room temperature
¼ cup sugar
2 teaspoons sherry
½ teaspoon grated lemon rind
1 cup plus 2 tablespoons flour
⅛ teaspoon salt

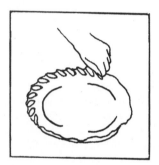

● Lightly butter a 9″ or 10″ pie plate. Blend yolks, butter, sugar, sherry, and lemon rind with an electric mixer. Add 2 tablespoons flour and the salt. Gradually add remaining flour.
● Turn pastry onto a sheet of wax paper. Flatten into an 8″ circle. Wrap in plastic and chill at least 2 hours.
● Pat chilled dough evenly onto the bottom and sides of buttered pie plate.
● To bake pastry, see "Tips" at beginning of section. Bake unfilled crust at 350°. Reduce temperature to 300° to brown after removing wax paper lined with rice or beans. Makes 1 pie shell.

Madeleine Galanek Egan

Cream Cheese Pastry

8 ounces cream cheese, at room
    temperature
1 cup butter
2¼ cups sifted flour
1 teaspoon salt
1 egg yolk (optional)
1 tablespoon water (optional)

● Beat cream cheese and butter until smooth in electric mixer or food processor. Gradually mix in flour and salt, just until dough comes together.
● Wrap dough in wax paper and chill for about 3 hours.
● Roll out pastry to make two 9″ or 10″ pastry shells. If desired, brush pastry before baking pies or turnovers with a mixture of the beaten egg yolk and the water.
   Note: This is excellent for turnovers, fruit pies, and custard pies.

Marcia Petersen Sandner

290

Potpourri

Puff Pastry

2 cups flour
Pinch salt
¾ cup butter
⅓ cup plus 2 teaspoons ice cold
    water

● Sift flour with salt into a mixing bowl.
● Rub *2 tablespoons* butter into the flour until mixture resembles fine meal. Add ice water 2 tablespoons at a time. Mix to a firm but pliable dough.
● Knead lightly until smooth. Set in a cool place for 10-15 minutes.
● Place remaining butter between 2 pieces of wax paper. Beat to a flat cake with a rolling pin.
● Roll out dough on a lightly floured surface, forming a rectangle. Place butter in the middle and fold in thirds like a parcel. Turn upside down.
● Roll into an oblong shape. Fold in thirds and give a half turn to bring the open edge toward you. Repeat this step 3-6 times, chilling 10 minutes after each rolling.
● Chill an additional 10 minutes, then use as required.

Marcia Petersen Sandner

No-Bake Crumb Crusts

1½ cups crumbs (use graham crackers, chocolate or vanilla wafers, zweiback, pretzels, cereal, soda crackers, gingersnaps, or dried cake)
*½ cup finely ground nuts (optional)
6 tablespoons butter
¼ cup sugar

*If using nuts, substitute them for half the crumbs (use only ¾ cup crumbs).

● To make in food processor, place broken crumbs in container. Grind with steel blade until fine. Add butter and sugar. Process 3-5 seconds to a fine texture. Pat into a buttered 9″ or 10″ pie plate or spring-form pan. Chill unbaked for at least 30 minutes.
● To make without a food processor, melt butter and mix with the remaining ingredients. Pat into pie plate or spring-form pan. Chill as above. Makes one 9″ or 10″ crust.

Leslie May Marra

Potpourri

Beverages

Arabella's Iced Tea

5 tea bags
2½ quarts boiling water
⅔ cup sugar
3 lemons
6 mint sprigs
1 quart chilled ginger ale

3½ quarts
● Steep tea 5 minutes in boiling water. Remove tea bags and stir in sugar to dissolve completely. Cut lemons in wedges. Squeeze into tea and drop in squeezed lemon rinds, as well. Add mint. Let mixture cool.
● Strain cooled tea. Add ginger ale and serve over ice, with lemon slices or mint leaves for garnish.

Ann Evans Gum

League Tea

2 cups powdered orange juice
1 cup instant iced tea
1 package (6 ounces) lemonade mix
1½ cups sugar
½ teaspoon cinnamon
½ teaspoon ground cloves
Chopped mint leaves (optional)

● Combine all ingredients and store in a jar.
● To make hot tea. put 2 heaping tea-spoonfuls of above mixture in a teacup. Add boiling water and stir.
● For iced tea. use about 3 teaspoon-fuls of tea mix for a 10-ounce glass. Stir with cold water. and add ice to fill the glass.
● To make iced tea for a crowd. add 3 quarts cold water to the above recipe. Add ice and mix well. Garnish with chopped mint leaves.

Suzanne Rich Beatty

Potpourri

Breakfast Nog

2 ripe bananas
1½ cups cold milk
2 eggs
1 teaspoon vanilla extract

Serves 2
● Break bananas into quarters, and place in blender or food processor. Add remaining ingredients. Blend until smooth.

Barbara Smith Suval

Café Diavalo

1 tablespoon cinnamon
6 measures strong coffee
Water for brewing
3 ounces Sabra liqueur
1½ ounces cognac
1 cup freshly whipped cream

12 demi-tasse cups
● Add cinnamon to coffee, then brew as usual to make 6 cups strong coffee.
● Pour hot coffee into a carafe. Add Sabra and cognac. Stir gently. Serve in cups, topped with a scoop of whipped cream.

Paul Cioffari

Gin Frappé

1 can (6 ounces) frozen
   lemon-limeade
1 cup gin or vodka
10-12 mint leaves

Serves 4-6
● Place frozen lemonade-limeade in blender with gin or vodka and mint leaves. Partially fill blender container with crushed ice. Blend until smooth.
● Garnish with additional mint sprigs.

Eugenia McCuen Thomason

Kahlúa

1 quart distilled water
3 cups sugar
10 teaspoons instant coffee powder
1 tablespoon vanilla
3 cups 80 or 100 proof vodka

6 cups
● Boil distilled water, sugar, and instant coffee powder in an uncovered saucepan until syrupy, about 1 hour. Cool.
● Add vanilla and vodka to cooked syrup. Mellow in glass bottles or jars for at least 2 weeks.

Georgia Moseley Adams

Potpourri

Gifts

Bake a gift. Preserve a gift. Stir a gift together.

English Toffee

1 cup butter
1 cup sugar
3 tablespoons water
1 tablespoon light corn syrup
4 squares (1 ounce each)
   semi-sweet chocolate, melted
½ cup chopped toasted almonds

¾ pound

- Butter a 9″ square baking pan.
- Heat butter, sugar, water, and corn syrup in a heavy, 3-quart saucepan over medium heat, stirring occasionally. When mixture boils, increase heat to medium-high. Cook without stirring until candy thermometer registers 250°, about 15 minutes.
- Watch closely and continue to cook, stirring constantly, until thermometer registers 300° (hard crack stage).
- Quickly turn candy onto buttered baking pan. Let it cool.
- Remove candy from pan and spread top with melted chocolate. Sprinkle immediately with chopped almonds, pressing lightly into the chocolate. Cool completely and break in pieces.
- Store in an airtight container in refrigerator.

Madeleine Galanek Egan

Potpourri

Sesame Crunch

2 cups hulled sesame seeds
1¼ cups sugar
½ cup light corn syrup
¼ cup water
¼ cup honey
2 tablespoons butter
⅛ teaspoon salt
⅛ teaspoon vanilla extract

1¾ pounds

● Preheat oven to 300°. Spread sesame seeds on a baking sheet with sides. Bake 5 minutes, or until seeds are a creamy beige color. Stir a few times while baking.
● In a large, heavy saucepan, combine toasted sesame seeds with sugar, corn syrup, water, honey, butter, and salt. Bring to a boil over medium heat, stirring constantly. Boil without stirring until a candy thermometer reads 295°.
● While candy cooks, butter a metal spatula and a baking sheet with sides.
● Remove pan from heat. Stir in vanilla. Pour quickly onto prepared baking sheet. Spread immediately with buttered spatula to a thickness of ⅛".
● Score crunch into 1" squares while still lukewarm. Cool completely. Lift sheet of candy from pan. Break in pieces.
● Store in an airtight container with wax paper between layers of candy.

Nancy Beck Hoggson

Sugared Pecans

1 cup sugar
5 tablespoons orange juice
2 teaspoons grated orange rind
½ teaspoon cinnamon
Pinch salt
1½ cups shelled pecans

2 cups

● Put all ingredients except pecans in a heavy saucepan. Cook until syrup spins a thread and becomes thick with heavy bubbles.
● Add pecans. Stir rapidly until syrup becomes cloudy and dull.
● Turn out onto a sheet of aluminum foil, and break apart when mixture is cool enough to handle. Store in an airtight container.

Barbara Smith Suval

295

Potpourri

Candied Orange Peel

2-3 oranges
1 cup sugar
½ cup water

2 cups

• Peel oranges in a spiral, starting at top and working around with very sharp knife. Cover orange peel with cold water. Bring to boil. Cook slowly until soft (15 minutes). Drain and cool. Scrape off white membrane. Cut peel in thin strips with scissors.

• Bring sugar and water to boil. Add prepared orange peel. Cook slowly until peel is almost transparent (230° on candy thermometer).

• Remove candied orange peel from syrup with slotted spoon. Spread on cookie sheet to cool. Roll in granulated sugar. Spread on wax paper to dry.

> Note: Keeps in refrigerator indefinitely and freezes well. It makes a lovely cake decoration.

Nancy Beck Hoggson

Caramel Popcorn

3 quarts freshly popped popcorn
1-3 cups unsalted peanuts
½ cup butter
1 cup firmly packed brown sugar
¼ cup honey
1 teaspoon vanilla extract

4 quarts

• Combine popcorn and nuts in a lightly greased 14" x 11" baking or roasting pan. Mix well and set aside.

• Melt butter over low heat in a medium saucepan. Add brown sugar and honey. Bring to a boil. Boil 5 minutes without stirring. Add vanilla and stir well. Pour syrup over popcorn mixture, stirring until popcorn is evenly coated.

• Bake 1 hour in a 250° oven, stirring every 15 minutes.

• Cool completely and break into pieces. Store in airtight containers.

Stephanie Fay Arpajian

Potpourri

Gingerbread Boys

4 cups sifted flour
1 teaspoon salt
2 teaspoons baking powder
1 teaspoon baking soda
2 teaspoons ginger
1 teaspoon ground cloves
1 teaspoon cinnamon
1 teaspoon grated nutmeg
1 cup shortening
1 cup sugar
1 cup molasses
2 egg yolks

2 dozen

● Sift flour again with salt, baking powder, baking soda, and spices.
● Cream shortening. Add sugar gradually and beat until fluffy. Add molasses and egg yolks. Mix well. Thoroughly mix in sifted dry ingredients.
● Chill dough at least 3 hours until it can be handled easily.
● Preheat oven to 350°. Roll out a ball of dough to ⅛" thickness on a floured board. Cut with a gingerbread boy cookie cutter. Place on ungreased baking sheets. Make a hole in the top of each cookie with a toothpick. After baking, put yarn through holes to hang cookies on the Christmas tree. Give each cookie a cinnamon candy heart and raisin or currant eyes and buttons.
● Bake 10-12 minutes. Cool 2 minutes before removing from baking sheets. Cool completely. Store in airtight containers.

Marcia Mead Thomas

Granola

6 cups rolled oats
1 cup wheat flakes
1-1½ cups chopped nuts
1 cup unsweetened coconut
1 cup wheat germ
½ cup sunflower seeds
¼ cup toasted sesame seeds
¼ cup soy nuts
Dash salt
1 cup corn oil
¾ cup honey or maple syrup

8 cups

● Preheat oven to 325°. Mix all dry ingredients in a roasting pan. Warm oil and honey together in a saucepan. Pour over dry ingredients, mixing well.
● Bake 40 minutes. stirring every 10 minutes. Baking time will determine the crunchiness. All ingredients can be varied. Dried fruits can be added after granola is cool.

Betsy Gimpel Mena

297

Potpourri

Cheese-in-a-Crock

4 tablespoons horseradish
3 tablespoons worcestershire sauce
2 tablespoons dry red wine
2 tablespoons fresh lemon juice
1 tablespoon Dijon mustard
1 garlic clove, minced
10-12 ounces cheddar cheese
    spread

1½ cups
● Blend all ingredients except cheese spread in food processor or by hand. Add cheese a little at a time. Process until mixture is smooth.
● Pack cheese in crocks and store in refrigerator. Bring to room temperature before serving.

Leslie May Marra

Apple Chutney

12 sour apples (about 4 pounds)
3 onions (½ pound), peeled and
    chopped
1 pound raisins
1 tablespoon mustard seed, crushed
Grated rind and juice of 1 lemon
1 tablespoon ground ginger
3 cups vinegar
2 pounds brown sugar

10 pints
● Peel apples and chop. Mix in a large kettle with chopped onions, raisins, and crushed mustard seed. Add lemon rind and juice, ginger, and 2 cups vinegar.
● Cook, covered, until apples and onions are tender. Pour remaining 1 cup vinegar over sugar and place in a warm spot for sugar to dissolve.
● When fruits are cooked, add sugar and vinegar to kettle. Cook, uncovered, until quite thick.
● Spoon into sterilized jars and seal to store.

Anne Ruthrauff Seltzer

298

Potpourri

Cranberry Relish

1 pound (4 cups) fresh cranberries
1 small navel orange, quartered and
   unpeeled
1 cup sugar
3 tablespoons Grand Marnier

3 cups

● With metal blade in place, add *half* the cranberries and *half* the orange pieces to food processor bowl. Turn off and on rapidly until mixture is chopped to desired texture. Transfer to a bowl.

● Repeat with remaining cranberries and orange pieces.

● Add first batch to the second in the processor bowl. Add sugar and Grand Marnier. Process to mix.

● Store in an airtight container in the refrigerator.

Nancy Beck Hoggson

Summer Relish

4 cups chopped cucumbers
4 cups whole small gherkins
4 cups chopped onions
4 cups small, peeled white onions
1 bunch celery, chopped or sliced
1 head cauliflower, in flowerets
3 green peppers, chopped
3 hot red peppers, chopped
9 cups very hot water
1 cup coarse salt
3 cups sugar
2 quarts white wine vinegar
4 ounces mustard seed
1 tablespoon celery seed
⅔ cup flour
¼ cup dry mustard
2 tablespoons powdered turmeric

8 pints

● Mix all vegetables in a large non-metal bowl. Mix hot water and coarse salt. Pour over vegetables to cover. Let stand overnight, then drain.

● Add sugar, vinegar, mustard seed, and celery seed. Bring to a boil.

● Make a paste of the flour, mustard, and turmeric, adding enough cold vinegar to bind smoothly. Stir this paste into boiling mixture. Cook until thickened, stirring constantly.

● Pour hot relish into jars, and seal immediately. Let stand a few weeks before eating or giving as a gift.

Mary Elizabeth Newland Heisey

Potpourri

Jalapeño Jelly

1 can or jar (10 ounces) jalapeño
    peppers
1 large red or green bell pepper,
    seeded
¼ cup cider vinegar
6 cups sugar
1 cup vinegar
½-1 teaspoon red or green food
    color
1 bottle (6 ounces) pectin

3 pints
● Purée jalapeño peppers, bell pepper, and cider vinegar in blender or food processor.
● Place in a large kettle with sugar and vinegar. Bring to a boil and skim foam. Add food color and pectin.
● Bring to a boil and skim foam again. Remove from heat and cool 10 minutes. Pack in sterilized jars and seal.

Suzanne Rich Beatty

Wine Jelly

1 cup boiling water
2 tablespoons dried marjoram,
    oregano, dill, tarragon, rosemary,
    fennel, sage, or sorrel
Juice of 2 lemons (⅓ cup)
3 cups sugar
½ cup bottled fruit pectin
2-3 drops red, orange, or green food
    coloring

4 cups
● Pour boiling water over herb or herb mixture. Let stand 20 minutes. Strain through very fine cheesecloth and add enough water to make 1 cup.
● Strain lemon juice through fine cheesecloth. Mix with steeped herbs in a heavy saucepan. Bring to a boil. Add sugar and stir well. Return to boiling point and vigorously stir in pectin. Add food coloring and continue to stir until liquid comes to a full, rolling boil.
● Boil hard for 30 seconds. Remove from heat and skim foam from the surface. Pour into hot, sterilized glasses and cover with melted paraffin. Serve as a meat accompaniment.

Anne Ruthrauff Seltzer

Potpourri

Three-Fruit Marmalade

6 cups

1 cantaloupe
1 can (15¼ ounces) crushed
   pineapple, drained
10-12 fresh peaches
2 tablespoons lemon juice
1 package (1¾ ounces) powdered
   pectin
8 cups sugar

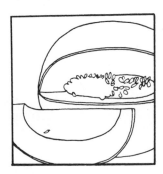

● Peel cantaloupe and force fruit through coarse chopping blade of a food chopper. Drain juices from cantaloupe and crushed pineapple.
● Grind pitted, peeled peaches. Drain and add to the other fruits to make 6 cups. Place in a kettle or dutch oven with lemon juice, pectin, and sugar. Bring to a boil, stirring constantly.
● Boil 8 minutes. Pour into hot sterilized jelly glasses and seal with melted paraffin.

Violet Kozdra Galanek

Mincemeat

12 quarts

7 pounds green tomatoes
3 pounds apples, peeled and ground
½ pound suet, ground
1 cup vinegar
2 pounds brown sugar
1 pound raisins
½ pound currants
½ pound citron
1½ tablespoons cinnamon
1½ tablespoons salt
1 tablespoon cloves
1 tablespoon allspice
½ teaspoon nutmeg

● Chop tomatoes finely and drain. Cover with cold water. Boil 1½ hours, then drain again.
● Boil cooked tomatoes with all other ingredients in a large kettle over low heat. Stir frequently. Cook 2 hours.
● Pour into hot. sterilized jars and seal immediately. Stores at room temperature and keeps for months in the refrigerator. Use in any recipe which calls for mincemeat.

Ruth Patch Barron

301

Potpourri

Freezer Pickles

1 medium onion, thinly sliced
6 cups thinly sliced cucumbers
1 tablespoon salt
1 cup sugar
½ cup white vinegar

4 cups
● Place sliced onions and cucumber in a large bowl. Sprinkle with salt. Refrigerate 2 hours or longer, then squeeze out moisture.
● Mix sugar and vinegar. Pour over well-drained onion and cucumbers.
● Serve now, or freeze so the mixture gets crispy. Defrost frozen pickles in refrigerator before serving.

Paula Kirchmaier Brown

Green Tomato Pickles

4 quarts thinly sliced green tomatoes
4 cups thinly sliced onions
⅓ cup salt
3 cups white vinegar
3 cups packed brown sugar
1 lemon, thinly sliced
1 tablespoon black peppercorns
1 tablespoon mustard seed
1 teaspoon whole allspice
1 teaspoon celery seed
⅛ teaspoon cayenne pepper

5 pints
● Put tomatoes and onions in a large bowl. Sprinkle with salt. Cover and let stand overnight.
● Drain tomatoes and onions well. Bring remaining ingredients to a boil. Add drained tomatoes and onions. Return to boiling point. Simmer for about 10 minutes, stirring gently.
● Pour into hot, sterilized jars, and seal. Store in refrigerator, or process for 5 minutes in canner to preserve.

Madeleine Galanek Egan

Potpourri

Barbecued Pecans

¼ cup worcestershire sauce
2 tablespoons melted butter
1 tablespoon catsup
½ teaspoon minced garlic
⅛ teaspoon tabasco sauce
4 cups pecan halves
Salt

4 cups
● Combine first five ingredients in a mixing bowl. Stir in pecans and mix well. Spread evenly in a shallow baking pan. Bake 30 minutes at 300°, stirring at 10 minute intervals.
● Drain on paper towels. Sprinkle with salt to taste.
● Store in an airtight container in refrigerator. Before serving, warm quickly in oven.

Victoria Eastman Ohlandt

Provincial Herb Sachets

1½ cups dried sweet basil leaves
1½ cups dried thyme leaves
1½ cups dried marjoram leaves
¾ cup dried rosemary leaves
10 calico-print sachet bags, 3″ x 5″
2¼ yards ½″-wide ribbon or yarn, cut in 8″ lengths

10 bags
● Combine herbs in large bowl and mix well. Crush half the herbs at a time to a medium texture in blender or food processor.
● Place about ½ cup of the herb mixture in each calico bag. Tie bags securely with ribbon or yarn.
> Note: This makes a pretty, aromatic stocking-stuffer. Store in an airtight container until gift-giving time.

Nancy Beck Hoggson

restaurants

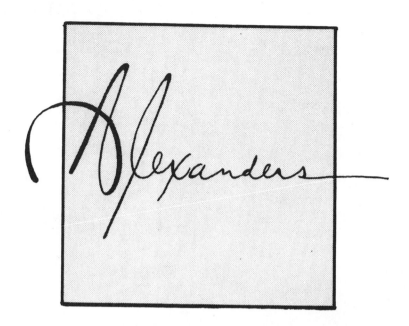

Alexander's, South Salem, New York. Flowers and candlelight add warmth and grace to a wonderfully refurbished old hayloft. Renamed Tatters in 1981.

Russian Eggs

1 cup hollandaise sauce (see Index)
8 large eggs
2 tablespoons butter
2 tablespoons anchovy paste
8 slices toast
2 ounces black caviar
Minced fresh parsley

Serves 4
- Prepare hollandaise sauce.
- Poach eggs in salted water. Drain and keep warm.
- Cream butter with anchovy paste. Spread on warm toast. Place a poached egg on each slice. Divide hollandaise evenly over the eggs.
- Top each egg with caviar. Garnish with parsley.

Appleby's, Mt. Kisco, New York. American food with an imaginative twist. Famous for their popovers, cornbread sticks, and desserts.

Baked Apples

Serves 4

4 large Rome apples
¼ cup raisins
¼ cup almonds, finely chopped
¾ cup brown sugar
Cinnamon
Freshly squeezed juice from 10 large oranges

● Core apples and place in a buttered baking pan. Combine raisins and almonds. Fill apple cavities with this mixture. Top each with *1 tablespoon* brown sugar and a sprinkling of cinnamon.

● Combine orange juice with remaining ½ cup brown sugar. Pour into baking pan to fill halfway.

● Bake at 350° for 30-40 minutes.

AUBERGE ARGENTEUIL

Auberge Argenteuil, Hartsdale, New York. Well-known for its grand cuisine in the French manner. An imposing old house with dining in lovely, small rooms.

La Truite Auberge

½ cup butter
3 tablespoons chopped shallots
2 fresh brook trout
⅓ cup cider vinegar
⅔ cup dry white wine
1 bay leaf
Salt and ground white pepper
⅓ cup heavy cream

Serves 2

● Melt *1 tablespoon* butter in a skillet and sauté the shallots. Add trout, vinegar, wine, bay leaf, and salt and pepper to taste. Cover and bring to a boil. Simmer for about 10 minutes until fish is cooked. Remove trout to a serving platter and keep warm.

● Cook pan juices until almost evaporated. Add cream and cook for 3-4 minutes. Add remaining 7 tablespoons butter. Beat until it is melted and blended to produce a creamy, light sauce. Strain sauce over trout.

Auberge Maxime, North Salem, New York. Sophisticated haute cuisine served in an intimate country inn.

Canard aux Navets et Foie de Volaille (Duck with Glazed Turnips)

1 duck (4-4½ pounds)
2 cups duck stock (if unavailable, substitute chicken broth)
1 tablespoon purée of raw duck liver
2 tablespoons cognac
1 pound white turnips, peeled and quartered
1 tablespoon butter
1 tablespoon sugar

Serves 2

● Truss and roast duck in a hot oven (500°) for 25 minutes. Add duck stock, and cook an additional 25 minutes. Marinate purée of duck liver in cognac while duck is cooking.

● Blanch turnips by pouring boiling water over them. Drain well. Sauté with butter and sugar until caramelized.

● Remove duck from the pan. Add turnips and purée of duck liver. Simmer 5 minutes.

● Quarter duck. Serve with wild rice and pan juices. Garnish with watercress.

THE BRITISH BUTLER

The British Butler, Celia and Victor Wakefield, Chappaqua,
New York. A British husband and wife team. She cooks and he
serves. Their specialties are dishes made from fresh and local
produce. An elegant touch at a reasonable price.

Restaurants

How to Work with Phyllo Pastry

Necessities

1-pound package of phyllo pastry

1 pound sweet butter or a mixture of ½ pound sweet butter and 1 cup olive oil

Have on hand 2 cotton tea towels, wax paper, double boiler, 1" pastry brush, spatula, measuring spoons, baking sheet, and a sharp knife.

Following the filling recipe of your choice. See Index for Duxelles. For a 1-pound package of phyllo, 3 cups of cooled filling will be needed.

Preparation

● Melt butter in top of a double boiler. Use butter-olive oil mixture for savory recipes. Keep butter warm and liquid throughout the entire procedure.

● Clear a counter space at least 4' long. Dampen tea towels and wring them out well. Lay a towel at one end of the work space. Cover it with a sheet of wax paper. Open the phyllo package and carefully unroll pastry. Lay it on the wax paper. Cover with a second sheet of wax paper and the other dampened tea towel. Lay another sheet of wax paper on the counter beside the phyllo.

● Brush a baking sheet with melted butter.

For hors d'oeuvres

● Roll back tea towel and wax paper to uncover phyllo. Lift top sheet carefully. Lay it on the wax paper. Cover remaining phyllo. Using the pastry brush, paint phyllo with melted butter. Cover this with a second sheet and paint it as well. Always cover remaining phyllo with a cloth to prevent drying.

● Spread about ¼ cup filling along bottom edge of buttered phyllo, leaving a 1" border. Lifting wax paper, cover filling with the border and roll the entire sheet. Cut roll diagonally to make 10-12 pieces, and transfer these to the baking sheet. Paint tops with more melted butter.

311

Restaurants

continued

● Continue as above until all pastry sheets are used. Then bake, or wrap hors d'oeuvres and freeze.
● Bake hors d'oeuvres in a preheated 375° oven for 20-25 minutes, until puffed and golden brown. Serve hot.

To prepare a phyllo meat roll for 8
● Place sheets of wax paper on the counter, with long sides parallel to counter edge. Lay 2 sheets of phyllo on the paper, overlapping sheets by 3" in the middle. Butter the two sheets and repeat until there are 6 layers of phyllo. Place prepared filling along the long sides, leaving a 4" border, and roll. Tuck in edges to contain the filling. Use wax paper to roll the completed pastry onto a buttered baking sheet. Brush with butter and bake in a preheated 350° oven for 1 hour until golden.

Chicken Filling for Phyllo

½ cup diced bacon
4 green onions, diced
½ cup diced chicken livers
1 cup diced, cooked chicken
1 cup Duxelles (see Index)
4 tablespoons chopped parsley
1 teaspoon tarragon
Dash worcestershire sauce
Salt and freshly ground pepper to
    taste
2 eggs
½ cup heavy cream

3 cups
● Sauté bacon gently until limp and partially cooked. Add green onions and cook until soft. Add chicken livers and cook for 2 minutes longer. Add cooked chicken. duxelles. and seasonings.
● Combine this mixture with eggs and cream in a food processor. or beat eggs and cream in a bowl and fold in remaining ingredients.

The Box Tree, Purdys and New York City. The epitomy of chic and the ultimate in style. Superb French cuisine in two locations, New York's East Side and an old country inn.

Vacherin Box Tree

5 ounces egg whites
1¼ cups sugar
¼ cup granulated hazelnuts
3 cups heavy cream
2 pints strawberries or raspberries, washed, hulled, and halved
3 tablespoons Grand Marnier
2 teaspoons vanilla extract

Serves 10

● Preheat oven to 200°. Make three circles (9″ each) on parchment paper. Place paper on baking sheets.

● Beat egg whites until stiff. Add *half* the sugar and beat until firm. Combine remaining sugar with hazelnuts and fold gently into egg whites.

● Spread mixture evenly on the three circles with a spatula. Bake 3-5 hours until crisp. Cool.

● Assemble cake an hour before serving. Whip cream and flavor it with Grand Marnier and vanilla. Put strawberries and whipped cream on two of the meringues. Place one on top of another. Lay third meringue carefully on top. Sprinkle with confectioners sugar.

Capriccio's, Brewster, New York. Once a fine, old country estate, now an elegant, continental restaurant with an added bonus of a spectacular lake view.

Mussels Capriccio

2 dozen mussels
1 tablespoon finely chopped shallots
1 teaspoon finely minced garlic
1½ tablespoons butter
¾ cup white wine
1 tablespoon chopped parsley
Dash red pepper

Serves 2

● Scrub mussels well in cold water and let drain.

● In a 4-6 quart pot, sauté shallots and garlic in butter until translucent. Add mussels, wine, parsley, and red pepper to taste. Cover and cook over medium heat for 15 minutes until all mussels are opened.

● Serve in a deep dish or platter. Pour sauce from pan over mussels.

The Cook's Corner, Chappaqua, New York. A well-organized shop, featuring high-quality, professional cookware for home use.

White Chocolate Mousse

Serves 8

10 ounces white chocolate
½ cup butter, at room temperature
8 egg yolks
2 cups heavy cream, whipped
1 package (10 ounces) frozen
    strawberries, defrosted
16 small cream puffs

● Melt white chocolate in top of double boiler over simmering water. Combine with softened butter in bowl or food processor. Mix to blend well.
● Add egg yolks one at a time, beating after each addition. Fold in whipped cream. Cover tightly with plastic wrap. Chill for several hours.
● Purée defrosted berries in food processor or blender. Chill.
● Serve mousse in cream puff shells topped with strawberry sauce.

Fritz's, Somers, New York. A café-style luncheonette during the day that becomes a candlelit restaurant at night. The emphasis is on the homemade. Evening fare is French and Northern Italian.

Green Goddess Dressing

6 garlic cloves, minced
7 anchovies, mashed
1 small onion, finely grated
¼ cup oil
2 cups mayonnaise
2 cups sour cream
2 tablespoons snipped chives
1 tablespoon minced parsley
Dash sugar
Dash lemon juice or vinegar

4 cups
● Combine all ingredients. Refrigerate overnight. Serve with any green salad.

Huckleberry's, Yorktown Heights, New York. A very popular meeting spot for luncheons, cocktails, and informal dinners. The decor is ecletic and the atmosphere is lively.

Spinach Strudel

Serves 4

2 pounds chopped spinach, fresh or
frozen
3 bunches green onions
¼ cup olive oil
1 pound crumbled feta cheese
6 eggs
1 tablespoon fresh dill
½ pound phyllo dough, defrosted
½ cup butter, melted

● Cook spinach partially. Drain well.
● Peel and slice green onions. Sauté in olive oil. Mix with cheese. eggs. dill, and cooked spinach. Set aside to cool.
● Preheat oven to 400°. Place a sheet of phyllo on a buttered baking sheet. (See Index for directions on working with phyllo.) Brush phyllo sheet with melted butter. Top with another phyllo sheet and brush again with butter. Spread 1 cup spinach filling on top of buttered dough. Roll like a jelly roll. Brush with additional melted butter. Bake for 45 minutes.

Mary Ho, Chappaqua, New York. A caterer and teacher who specializes in many varieties of Chinese regional cooking. Classes are given in her home and in the community.

Restaurants

Egg Rolls

6-8 Chinese mushrooms (or
   well-sautéed fresh mushrooms)
2 cups finely shredded pork
4 tablespoons medium-light soy
   sauce
½ teaspoon sugar
4 teaspoons plus 2 tablespoons
   cornstarch
2 cups finely shredded Chinese
   cabbage
½ teaspoon salt
¼ cup oil
½ cup drained bamboo shoots,
   shredded
1 cup bean sprouts, tightly packed to
   measure
4 green onions, sliced
20 egg roll wrappers

20 pieces

- If using Chinese mushrooms, soak them in hot water until soft, about 30 minutes.
- Mix shredded pork with *2 table-spoons* soy sauce, sugar, and *4 tea-spoons* cornstarch. Let soak for 20 minutes.
- Soak shredded Chinese cabbage in the salt for 20 minutes. Squeeze out excess moisture.
- Sauté marinated pork in hot oil for 3 minutes. Add bamboo shoots, mushrooms, and remaining 2 tablespoons soy sauce. Stir for another 2 minutes. Remove from heat. Place this filling in a bowl and cool. Add Chinese cabbage, bean sprouts, and green onions. Mix well.
- Make cornstarch paste by mixing remaining 2 tablespoons cornstarch with 3 tablespoons cold water until smooth.
- Place 1 heaping tablespoon of filling on one corner side of the wrapper. Roll once and tuck in gently to secure. Turn over and fold in the ends. Turn again. and seal the egg roll with the cornstarch paste.
- Repeat until all filling is used. Deep fry in hot oil at medium-high heat until golden brown. Turn once. Serve plain. with duck sauce. or a mixture of soy sauce and vinegar.

The Kitchen Emporium, Pleasantville, New York. Where the gourmet cook turns for advice, demonstrations, equipment, and gifts.

Filet de Boeuf en Croûte

Serves 4

¼ cup butter
1½ pounds filet of beef
1 garlic clove, minced
¼ pound mushrooms, sliced
4-5 tablespoons madeira wine
½ teaspoon salt
⅛ teaspoon freshly ground pepper
4 ounces puff pastry (see Index), or
    7½ ounces frozen puff pastry
Milk for glazing
Sauce Madère (recipe follows)

● Melt butter in a skillet. Add the whole filet and minced garlic. Fry 10-15 minutes for a rare center to the beef or 25 minutes for well done. Turn to cook all sides. Remove beef and chill.

● Add mushrooms to the same skillet. Cook until soft. Add madeira and simmer with mushrooms to reduce liquid by half. Remove pan from heat and add seasonings.

Restaurants

continued

- Roll pastry into a 9″ x 12″ rectangle. Vary shape to size of the filet. Put chilled, cooked filet in center of pastry. Spoon mushrooms and sauce on top and fold pastry over. Moisten edges and seal firmly with the fold on top so the juices won't run out. Chill at least 30 minutes or up to 12 hours before baking.
- Prepare Sauce Madère.
- Preheat oven to 400° 35 minutes before serving time. Place chilled filet en croûte on a baking sheet and brush pastry with milk to glaze. Bake about 25 minutes in preheated oven until pastry is golden. Serve with Sauce Madère.

Sauce Madère

2 tablespoons butter
1 onion, sliced
1 carrot, sliced
1¼ cups water
1¼ tablespoons tomato purée
1 beef bouillon cube
2 parsley sprigs
1 thyme sprig
1 bay leaf
2½ tablespoons cold water
1¼ tablespoons flour
1¼ tablespoons red currant jelly
½ cup madeira wine

1 cup
- Melt butter and sauté vegetables slowly until soft. Add 1¼ cups water, tomato purée. bouillon cube, and herbs. Simmer for 20 minutes.
- Stir cold water with flour and add to sauce. Simmer. stirring until thickened. Stir in jelly and simmer until it dissolves.
- Strain sauce into a clean pan and add madeira. Reheat before serving.

321

Paul Ma's China Kitchen, Pleasantville and Yorktown Heights, New York. A unique Chinese restaurant and cooking school, alternating between a Pleasantville and Yorktown Heights address, depending on the day of the week. Only one dinner party booked per evening.

Agar with Chicken Breast and Cucumber

1½ teaspoons cornstarch
3 tablespoons soy sauce
1 large chicken breast, shredded
1 cup dried agar
3 cups cold water
4 tablespoons vegetable oil
2 large cucumbers, seeded and
    shredded
1 garlic clove, minced
4 tablespoons dark Chinese vinegar
2 tablespoons sugar
2 tablespoons sesame oil (optional)

Serves 2

● Mix cornstarch with *1 tablespoon* soy sauce. Marinate shredded chicken in this mixture for 10 minutes. Soak agar in cold water for 3 minutes. then drain.

● Heat oil in a wok. Add marinated chicken and stir-fry for 2 minutes. Cool on a plate.

● Layer shredded cucumber. agar. and chicken on a serving platter.

● Prepare sauce by stirring together minced garlic. vinegar. sugar. sesame oil. and the remaining 2 tablespoons soy sauce. Pour over chicken and serve.

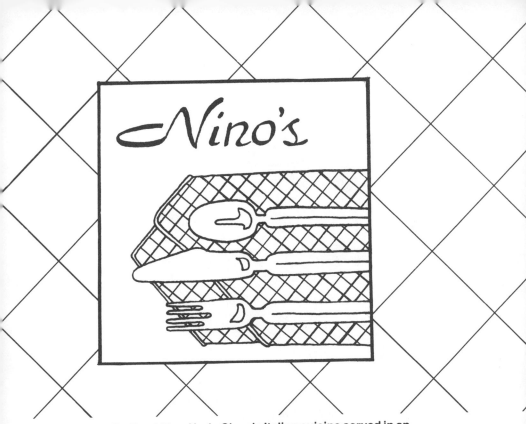

Nino's, Bedford, New York. Classic Italian cuisine served in an elegant country home.

Shrimp Scampi

16 jumbo shrimp
½ cup butter
Paprika
1 tablespoon minced garlic
½ cup brown gravy
1 teaspoon monosodium glutamate
Pinch freshly ground pepper

Serves 4

● Clean and butterfly shrimp, leaving tails on. Arrange in a pan and drizzle with *4 tablespoons* melted butter. Sprinkle with paprika. Broil 5-8 minutes.

● To prepare sauce, sauté garlic in remaining 4 tablespoons butter until golden brown. Add remaining ingredients. Bring to the boiling point, mixing with a whisk. As soon as the sauce boils, remove it from the heat. Pour over broiled scampi.

OLD·DROVER'S·INN DOVER·PLAINS·N.Y.

Old Drover's Inn, Dover Plains, New York. A romantic early American inn dating from 1750. A spectacular bill of fare, carefully prepared and graciously served in the low-beamed, candlelit tap room. Three rooms are available for overnight stays.

Key Lime Pie

5 egg yolks
19 ounces sweetened condensed
   milk
Grated rind of 1 lime
½ cup freshly squeezed lime juice
8″ graham cracker crust, baked and
   cooled

Serves 6
● Beat egg yolks with a wire whisk and blend in sweetened condensed milk. Add grated lime rind and lime juice. Mix well.
● Pour into crust. Chill for 2 hours.

Peter Pratt's Inn, Yorktown Heights, New York. A prerevolutionary inn with three separate dining areas each with its own special atmosphere.

Breast of Chicken Madrilène

1 tablespoon oil
1 tablespoon butter
2 whole chicken breasts, boned and
    trimmed
Flour to dredge
1 egg, beaten
1 garlic clove, minced
½ pound fresh mushrooms
Salt and freshly ground pepper
½ cup chicken or beef stock
Juice of 1 lemon
¼ cup heavy cream

Serves 2-4
● Heat oil. Add butter. Dredge chicken in flour. dip in beaten egg. and drop in the hot oil. Sauté on one side.
● Turn chicken. Add garlic. mushrooms. salt. and pepper. Lower heat and sauté uncovered until almost cooked.
● Add stock and lemon juice. blending all together. Continue to cook uncovered. Be careful not to overcook chicken breasts.
● Remove cooked chicken to serving platter. Add cream to the pan. Blend sauce. and cook to reduce until smooth. Pour over chicken breasts and serve immediately.

Plumbush, Cold Spring, New York. A rambling, Victorian homestead set in the Hudson River town of Cold Spring. Perfectly executed continental dishes served in small, charming rooms.

Restaurants

Plumbush Apple Fritters

4 fresh, unbruised apples
Flour to coat apple slices
1¾ cups flour
1 teaspoon paprika
Pinch salt and pepper
1 bottle (12 ounces) beer, at room
    temperature
½ cup superfine sugar
½ teaspoon cinnamon
Bavarian Cream Sauce (recipe
    follows)

Serves 8
● Peel and core apples. Cut in ½"
slices. Dust with flour on all sides.
● Prepare beer batter: Sift 1¾ cups
flour into bowl. Add paprika, salt, and
pepper. Pour in beer and whisk to mix
all ingredients.
● Immerse apple slices in beer batter.
Remove. Place carefully in a deep
"friteur", or pot filled with oil which has
been heated to 325°. Turn when
browned on first side. Remove when
golden brown, and place on a paper
towel to drain.
● Mix sugar and cinnamon. Dust frit-
ters on all sides with cinnamon sugar.
● To serve, spoon a small amount of
Bavarian Cream Sauce onto a warm
plate. Arrange fritter rings on sauce.

Bavarian Cream Sauce

2 eggs
3 tablespoons sugar
1 tablespoon cornstarch
2 cups milk
½ teaspoon vanilla extract
½ cup heavy cream
½ cup Kirschwässer

2 cups
● Mix eggs, sugar, cornstarch, and ½
cup milk. Bring remaining 1½ cups
milk to a boil. Add egg mixture and
return to a rolling boil. Remove from
heat, add vanilla, and chill completely.
● Whip cream to stiff peaks. Fold into
chilled Bavarian Cream. Stir in kirsch
with a fork or whisk.

327

Rags, Bedford Hills, New York. The perfect mix of a warm and inviting old home, wonderful food, friendly service, and a lively, varied clientele.

Filet Slices Dijonnaise

1 pound beef filet
2 tablespoons butter
1 tablespoon chopped shallots
1 tablespoon Moutarde de Meaux
¾ cup heavy cream
Salt and freshly ground pepper
1 tablespoon finely minced mixed
    green herbs (fresh, if possible)

Serves 4
● Slice filet across the grain in ¼″ slices. Sauté briefly in butter. Remove from pan and keep warm.
● Sauté shallots in pan drippings until soft but not brown. Stir in mustard and cream. Cook to reduce liquid by half. Season to taste with salt and pepper.
● Pour sauce over filet. Garnish with minced green herbs. Serve at once.

THE WOODLANDS

The Woodlands-Stouffer's Inn of Westchester, Harrison, New York. The intimacy of a formal dining room in a private home enhanced by views of the woodland setting outside.

Sicilian Pea Soup

¼ pound green split peas
1 onion, chopped
1 celery rib, chopped
1 leek, washed, peeled, and
    chopped
1 garlic clove, minced
6 bacon strips
10 crushed black peppercorns
2 bay leaves
1 teaspoon rosemary
1 teaspoon marjoram
1 cup tomato purée
8 cups beef stock
Salt
1 cup half-and-half

Serves 6

● Soak split peas overnight in cold water. Drain.

● Place all vegetables and garlic in a large kettle. Cut bacon in small pieces and add to the kettle. Cook to braise vegetables. stirring. Add pepper, herbs. tomato purée. stock. and split peas. Season to taste with salt.

● Cook 1 hour and 15 minutes. Strain and return to the pan. Add warm half-and-half and blend well. Garnish with small croutons.

Index

Index

Index

Index

Index

Index

Index

337

Index

Index

Index

Index

Index

THE EVERYDAY GOURMET
Box 214
Chappaqua, NY 10514

Please send me _____ copies of *The Everyday Gourmet* at $10.00 per copy. I am enclosing $1.50 per book to cover postage.

Name_____

Address_____

City_____State_____Zip Code_____

The proceeds from the sale of this book will be used for community projects and programs.

 THE EVERYDAY GOURMET
Box 214
Chappaqua, NY 10514

Please send me _____ copies of *The Everyday Gourmet* at $10.00 per copy. I am enclosing $1.50 per book to cover postage.

Name_____

Address_____

City_____State_____Zip Code_____

The proceeds from the sale of this book will be used for community projects and programs.

 THE EVERYDAY GOURMET
Box 214
Chappaqua, NY 10514

Please send me _____ copies of *The Everyday Gourmet* at $10.00 per copy. I am enclosing $1.50 per book to cover postage.

Name_____

Address_____

City_____State_____Zip Code_____

The proceeds from the sale of this book will be used for community projects and programs.